Danish Yearbook of Musicology
35 · 2007

Danish Yearbook of Musicology
Volume 35 · 2007

PUBLISHED BY

Danish Musicological Society

EDITED BY

Michael Fjeldsøe
and
Thomas Holme Hansen

Distributed by Aarhus University Press
Århus 2008

Danish Yearbook of Musicology • Volume 35 • 2007
Dansk Årbog for Musikforskning

EDITORS
Michael Fjeldsøe • fjeldsoe@hum.ku.dk
Thomas Holme Hansen • musthh@hum.au.dk

EDITORIAL BOARD 2007
Lars Ole Bonde, *University of Aalborg*
Peter Woetmann Christoffersen, *University of Copenhagen*
Bengt Edlund, *Lund University*
Daniel Grimley, *University of Nottingham*
Peter Hauge, *The Royal Library, Copenhagen*
Lars Lilliestam, *Göteborg University*
Morten Michelsen, *University of Copenhagen*
Steen Kaargaard Nielsen, *University of Aarhus*
Nils Holger Petersen, *University of Copenhagen*
Søren Møller Sørensen, *University of Copenhagen*
Ståle Wikshåland, *University of Oslo*

PRODUCTION
Layout by Hans Mathiasen
Printed by Werks Offset A/S

Danish Yearbook of Musicology is published with support from
the Danish Research Council for the Humanities.

ADDRESS
Danish Yearbook of Musicology
c/o Section of Musicology
University of Copenhagen
Klerkegade 2, DK-1308 København K
E-mail: editors e-mail-addresses
Website: http://www.hum.au.dk/musik/dsfm

Distributed by Aarhus University Press, www.unipress.dk

ISBN 978-87-88328-26-4
ISSN 0416-6884

Printed in Denmark 2008

Contents

REVIEWS

BIBLIOGRAPHY 2007

INFORMATION

With the present issue *Danish Yearbook of Musicology* continues its ongoing development towards status as a journal of international standards. Following the improvements of the preceding years, including peer review and the choice of English as the prevailing language of the journal, the journal will as of now be distributed by *Aarhus University Press*. As an academic publishing house, *Aarhus University Press* can provide new opportunities for future developments, including an e-book version of the yearbook. The editors hope and expect that this new cooperation will improve the accessibility and visibility of the yearbook.

Volume 35 presents three articles, an introductory viewpoint and a number of reports and reviews of books and music. Furthermore, the bibliography listing publications of 2007 related to Danish musicology is included as well as various information. In the viewpoint, Axel Teich Geertinger and Bjarke Moe challenge the community of musicologists to consider the scope of possibilities provided by means of digital editing. The article by Andrea F. and Philip V. Bohlman discusses Hanns Eisler's *Hollywood Liederbuch* as a body of songs in which intertextuality transforms musical and textual meanings. They propose a theory of covering that extends its application from popular music to art and composed song. René Michaelsen reflects upon modes of musical and textual self-reflexivity, comparing textual procedures in H.C. Andersen's fairytales and poems with musical procedures used by Robert Schumann. In the third article, Steen Kaargaard Nielsen gives consideration to strategies employed to transform film music scores into soundtrack albums, using Max Steiner's music for *Gone with the Wind* as a case study.

The editors would like to thank all the contributors to the present volume. A special thank goes to Peter Hauge who once again has proved himself indispensable when it comes to proof reading the ever expanding percentage of texts in English in the yearbook. Axel Teich Geertinger, too, needs to be thanked for proof reading the German texts. The Danish Research Council for the Humanities is once again thanked for providing the funding for the publication.

Copenhagen and Århus, April 2008
Michael Fjeldsøe & Thomas Holme Hansen

Viewpoint

Digital Editing of Music – Time to Take a Stand

AXEL TEICH GEERTINGER and BJARKE MOE

In the course of the past decades, digital media have increasingly influenced the methods of musicological research. A look around reveals that developments are taking place also in the international field of music editing, which in some ways may fundamentally change our conception of modern editions and editorial practices. But whereas the publishing industry has long been forced to face digital media as an inevitable fact to be handled somehow, not least for economical reasons, it seems that musicology is largely unaware of the perspectives. Digital music editing is generally regarded as just an option among others, at best as a promising possibility. We, however, would like to argue that it might be useful to put the worries of the publishing industry into perspective and to demand musicology to take a position on the challenges.

The reluctance among musicologists, editors, and publishers to engage in digital music editing may to some extent be simply due to a feeling of uncertainty about what digital media can and cannot do, or due to a scepticism rooted in the incredibility or low status still generally associated with online publications. Some scepticism is of course appropriate, also when assessing digital editions, but our scepticism should as always be a constructive one, aiming not at rejecting the media in general, but at optimizing its benefits. Current projects, some of which were presented at the symposium *Digital Editions of Music – Perspectives for Editors and Users* held at the University of Copenhagen 19 January 2008,[1] appear to us as having the potential to silence discussions on whether digital media are relevant to music edition at all, and instead turn our focus to questions as for instance *how* to use digital media and under which premises.

Basic methods for the preparation, storage, and dissemination of texts in digital media have been in use for many years now. Also, theoretical frameworks for scholarly working with digital representations of texts and objects have been developed.[2] Digital media may actually prove to be even more promising for the future of music editing than for textual editing due to the complex ontology of the musical work. But before looking at some of the perspectives, we may need to ask what a digital edition is. A traditionally conceived paper edition, converted to the PDF file format

---

1 See the conference report elsewhere in this issue.
2 For an introduction, see Dino Buzzetti and Jerome McGann, 'Critical Editing in a Digital Horizon', in Katherine O'Brien O'Keeffe et al. (eds.), *Electronic Textual Editing* (New York, 2006), 53–73, http://www.tei-c.org/About/Archive_new/ETE/Preview/mcgann.xml; Jerome McGann, 'The Rationale of HyperText' (1995), http://www.iath.virginia.edu/public/jjm2f/rationale.html.

and published on the Internet certainly is a digital edition, though only in a very limited sense. At best, a PDF edition may overcome some limitations of printed editions as to the production costs and distribution. But valuable information has been lost – or at least made inaccessible – during the process of creating the files. PDF is a file format describing the graphical appearance of text and images, producing a visual output intended to be read and decoded by the human eye and mind. Data structures representing the music in a computable way have no place in it. By choosing the PDF or any other graphic format, users are effectively precluded from further processing the data, thus loosing some of the most powerful advantages of digital media.

Various strategies for translating music into structural, computable data have been designed, and certain standards have emerged, some also discarded. Structural representations (encodings) provide a very different approach to digital editions than the one inherent to PDF publications, for instance. They not only make the music computable (i.e. editable, searchable etc.), they may also contain annotations or any other related information about the work or specific parts of the music. Graphical representations like PDF can easily be generated from structural data – even on the fly, i.e. at the moment the user hits the download button. By contrast, the reverse process – converting graphical representations into structural ones – is at best problematic.

Though digital technology may also encourage and facilitate the trend towards purely image-based editions, interesting perspectives are opened by the combination of image-based representations and structural encodings of the same sources: as the encoding can relate each part of the text to its location on digital images of the source, graphical and structural domains can be tied together. In this way, facsimile editions may be turned into critical editions by overlaying editorial and contextual information onto photographic reproductions. In the future, the traditional distinction between facsimile and critical edition thus may blur or even disappear as features from both sides are combined: the greatest possible amount of information on the physical appearance of the source on the one hand and the highest standards of scholarly editing on the other. Some easy switching between or parallel views of the facsimile and a transcription or edition may even help overcome the usual trade-off made in printed facsimiles, where the legibility of modern printed editions is traded for a detailed reproduction of the source.

A highly versatile basis for future scholarly editing is achieved with the concept of hypermedia archives storing various kinds of data on a particular work, including facsimiles, their digitally encoded representations, audio and video recordings, the editor's annotations, contextual information, internal links between sources and external links to related works.[3] An edition in printable, modernized notation is just one of many possible outputs that may be generated by a certain combination of the data stored in such a digital archive, others being analytical and statistical studies or searchable music

---

3   Frans Wiering, Tim Crawford, and David Lewis, 'Digital Critical Editions of Music: A Multidimensional Model' (2006), http://www.methodsnetwork.ac.uk/redist/pdf/wiering.pdf. Whether the hypermedia archive itself may be called an edition depends on the definition of the term. In this article, the word edition is reserved for outputs involving a certain degree of critical editorial engagement in the musical matter.

databases. One of the great strengths of a truly digital edition is its dynamic nature, as may be illustrated by the situation where an important source – previously unknown or believed to be lost – turns up too late to be included in the printed edition. In a digital edition based on an archive of encodings of the sources, a situation like this would pose no serious problem. An encoding of the newly discovered source could be added to the archive along with the editor's annotations and decisions on the changes to be made in the edition, resulting in a new, updated edition immediately available.

An argument often held against digital editions is their transient nature. Printed editions or any other representations of a work of course also have a limited life-span, but the life expectancy of a digital edition appears to be considerably shorter, or at least uncertain due to ever changing technologies and the inescapable need of electronic devices to translate digital data into representations comprehensible by humans. The preservation of digital media is indeed a serious issue still calling for long-term technical solutions. On the other hand, the apparent volatility emphasizes that digital editions are renewable. They allow for changes and improvements. Editorial practice may be changed over time, yielding updated editions without having to start all over each time. A change in an edition's guidelines may in principle be reflected instantly in an online edition, keeping the works published updated in accordance with the guidelines and ensuring a homogeneous editorial practice across all the works presented at all times, something that could be difficult in long-term edition projects like the *Neue Mozart Ausgabe*, spanning more than half a century. From this point of view, the digital edition's volatility is also its strength.

Perspectives for the use of digital archives go far beyond producing editions. The potential range of applications and analytical tasks is overwhelming, provided the data are freely accessible. The encoding of the sources certainly requires a great amount of time, but once done, the data may be used to perform countless analytical tasks with a minimum of additional effort – or to generate editions, whether printed or digital, now and in the future. Thus, archives of digitized sources of music could be just as valuable to the public – or to scholars at least – as the edition produced from them. Under no circumstances should they be regarded as just an internal working database for a board of editors.

As digital editions can be generated at runtime – that is, at the user's request – the user may be given authority over certain aspects of the edition. By giving the user the opportunity to choose from a range of notational standards, levels of modernization or different page layouts, the edition may be customized to meet the user's requirements without compromising the edition's scholarly quality. In a model less restricted, the user may in principle also be allowed to choose the 'reading path' through the material, thus deciding not only on certain preferences of presentation, but also on the sources to be used and by which criteria. The user may ultimately create his own edition without any restrictions. But the user's freedom, or the empowerment of the user – which of course also may have ideological undertones – seems to have its price: with unlimited control given to the user, the scholarly standard of the edition generated can no longer be guaranteed. Yet such non-scholarly activity is not fundamentally different from the unlearned copying by hand that has always been an option in the era of written music. Nevertheless, it is a matter to be taken into consideration in a digital edition's design.

Even though the editor's working processes do change in order to integrate new media, scholarly standards can be maintained. With appropriate technical set-ups and editorial principles, neither the transient nature nor the apparently low status of digital editions threatens the quality of the editions produced. What needs to change most is therefore perhaps the attitude towards digital editing as a potential scholarly tool. For instance, digital media allow the editor to present primary sources, transcriptions or editions as well as editorial remarks in an interactive device and may thus encourage a more open-minded, cooperative attitude towards editing music than has been prevalent; an attitude that may very well improve the final edition. By making available online preliminary editions and inviting comments from the public during the process of editing, one may potentially have the entire community of scholars reviewing and proof-reading one's work (for free!).

The perspectives for such work-in-progress editions involving user discussions are auspicious, albeit they require the editors' readiness to change their working habits and methods. Some editing processes seem to be dependent on the edition's mediation: as the media changes from printed to digital, the editor needs to rethink his own position. The challenge for the editor is to keep focus on the scholarly standards when adapting his work to new technologies. A worst-case scenario would be the agenda of technological development replacing the one of the editor. For present-day editors at the edge of digital development such scenarios are fortunately long gone and replaced by fruitful exchanges between the disciplines of computing and humanities, but this is not a matter-of-course. Humanities, or musicology in our case, needs an agenda of its own to make the standards of digital edition in compliance with the object to be edited. By realizing that digital editing is not emerging because of new technology, but by means of it, we are able to put music in focus of the development. Waiting for computer experts to develop music editing or publishing software first just to realize that it was made without the sufficient expertise in music editing would be an unsatisfactory position. Success or failure in software development is highly dependent on the dialogue between users (i.e. editors in this case) and developers. Editors are the ones in the position to judge what is or is not helpful. Why not turn things around, challenging software engineers with ideas for future music editing?

Numerous questions are raised by the issues addressed here, the answers to which cannot be provided by editors alone, but only by an interdisciplinary network of professionals, cooperating on establishing models and standards for digital editing tools. This network should – like networks involved in publishing books – also consider the supporting foundations which often provide the financial basis of music editions. These foundations do not always seem to favour projects involving open-access publication or similar approaches, making the development of public, large-scale, high-impact digital publishing projects difficult. To change this, musicologists in the first place need to put forward a re-evaluated agenda that brings digital editing into the light of scholarly awareness.

(Un)Covering Hanns Eisler's
Hollywood Songbook

ANDREA F. BOHLMAN and PHILIP V. BOHLMAN[1]

RECOVERING HANNS EISLER

The music of Hanns Eisler (1898–1962) has never enjoyed greater popularity, and it has never been performed in so many different genres and contexts than in recent history. In this article, we ask why that is. We are particularly concerned with the resurgence of Eisler's music and the re-evaluation of Eisler as a twentieth-century composer in the almost two decades since the end of the German Democratic Republic (GDR), in other words, the end of the great socialist project of East Germany, to which Eisler devoted his musical energies in the closing years of his life. Why, in other words, does Eisler's music thrive in a post-GDR, post-socialist, and post-modern world?

Though we consider the historical contexts of Eisler reception, our primary concern here is with the musical texts and their transmission, particularly in the ways Eisler's music lends itself to covers and covering, being a composer who covers music of his own and from others in the course of his compositional process as well as a composer, whose music was extensively covered by others. More commonly focused on the adaptation and transmission of popular music, theories of covering might, we argue, be extended to art music and composed traditions, in which authority and authenticity seemingly rest in the privileged object of a score. Covering, nonetheless, also results from the fluid movement between written and oral tradition, in other words, the transformation of the score through performance. Boundaries between genre and performance, between original versions and covers, therefore, become increasingly blurred. The different musical texts in a network formed of intertextuality enter different contexts, in the case of Hanns Eisler, those formed of a world very different from one he imagined for the socialist project of East Germany.

---

1 Throughout this essay we employ the collective personal pronoun 'we', which we consciously cover with multiple meanings. In the first order, it refers to the authors, whose engagement with Hanns Eisler began in different ways but has insistently converged over the past few years. Together, they presented an earlier version of this essay as a lecture at the Department of Musicology of the University of Copenhagen on 6 June 2005. The response and engagement of colleagues there lent new dimensions to 'we', for the authors found themselves indebted to the stimulating discussion and critical remarks of our Copenhagen colleagues, whom we now thank: Michael Fjeldsøe, Jette Barnholdt Hansen, Fabian Holt, Diddan Degn Karstensen, Annemette Kirkegaard, Tore Tvarnø Lind, Morten Michelsen, Nils Holger Petersen, Jane Mink Rossen, and Heinrich W. Schwab. We should like to thank the Deutscher Akademischer Austauschdienst (DAAD) and the Alexander von Humboldt-Stiftung, which brought us as student and professor, daughter and father, to the Humboldt-Universität zu Berlin in 2005.

Hanns Eisler did, however, recognize and shape the potential for covers and covering in many of his compositional projects, not least among them the *Hollywood Songbook,* composed during his American exile during 1942–43. It is only with difficulty that the *Hollywood Songbook* allows itself to be pinned down as, say, a song cycle, mass songs, or newly-composed folk songs. Instead, it reveals a striking affinity to repertories of popular song, such as the so-called 'Great American Songbook', which exists primarily as an intertextual network lending itself to covering. As performative transmission, even of printed and recorded texts, the theory of covering that we develop from examination of the *Hollywood Songbook* offers new possibilities for understanding the music history of the present.

There seems to be no end to the obituaries for the GDR. Almost two decades after the Fall of the Berlin Wall and the dissolution of the East German state, the counterpoint of ideological and political pronouncements that nervously project the life-after-death of the GDR shows few signs of reaching a final stretto. Recovering the past has a name, *Ostalgie,* coined to convey a shared sense of 'nostalgia for the East'. Song intones meaning for a past that will not go away, finally or irrevocably. Anthologies of GDR composers and compilations of GDR youth groups appear frequently, recovering the official and the unofficial music from the past, celebrating the sense of solidarity that died with the state.[2]

The quality of a cover song to transform ownership and to sustain the past could not be clearer than in the vocal repertory of Hanns Eisler.[3] Eisler's songs live in the present, providing historical meaning and memory for the GDR. It is hardly surprising that they contribute to an aesthetic and ideology of covering *Ostalgie* itself, not infrequently under the banner, 'Hanns Eisler heute!'[4] Covering Eisler, it seems all too obvious, must establish the ethnographic present so trenchantly vibrant in proclamations of 'Hanns Eisler today'.

---

2 See, e.g., Michael Berg, Albrecht von Massow, and Nina Noeske (eds.), *Zwischen Macht und Freiheit: Neue Musik in der DDR* (KlangZeiten – Musik, Politik und Gesellschaft, 1; Cologne/Weimar/Vienna: Böhlau Verlag, 2004); *Unser Zeichen ist die Sonne: Die schönsten Lieder der FDJ* (BMG 74321 69977 2), 1999.

3 His songs for piano and voice were collected in the GDR as Hanns Eisler, *Lieder für eine Singstimme und Klavier,* ed. Stephanie Eisler and Manfred Grabs (Leipzig: VEB Deutscher Verlag, 1976). They will appear again in a new volume in the Eisler complete edition as Hanns Eisler, *Musik für Singstimme und Klavier* (Wiesbaden: Breitkopf und Härtel, forthcoming). Eisler's songs constitute a large percentage of other collections, for example, in Fritz Henneberg, *Brecht Liederbuch* (Frankfurt am Main: Suhrkamp Verlag, 1984). The North American folk-music revival, with its socialist underpinnings, also created its own Eisler compilations, crucially with 'singable' English translations; see, e.g., *Songs of Bertolt Brecht and Hanns Eisler: Forty-Two Songs in German and English,* music edited by Earl Robinson, with piano arrangements and guitar chords (New York: Oak Publications, 1967).

4 'Hanns Eisler today!' See Heiner Goebbels, compiler, *Eislermaterial* (Munich: ECM Records, 2002). The calls for an Eisler of today to seize the mantle of an earlier rhetoric; see, e.g., Manfred Grabs (ed.), *Hanns Eisler heute: Berichte, Probleme, Beobachtungen* (Berlin: Akademie der Künste der Deutschen Demokratischen Republik, Henschelverlag Kunst und Gesellschaft, 1974).

THE GENEALOGY OF COVER SONGS

Covers spawn multiple offspring and span multiple generations. Covers bridge the gaps between oral and written transmission, and they repopulate the border areas between genres.[5] Covers become meaningful through their mobility and their migration from one musical medium to another. On the move, covers are claimed by new singers wanting to make old songs their own. The use-value of covers increases as versions enter the everyday, where they are revoiced as a people's music. Thus, for a committed creator of people's music such as Hanns Eisler, covers spread the aesthetic and political cause across a vast genealogy.

The proliferation of cover songs also generates paradox, for it lays bare the distinctions between an original and a covered version. If covers are everywhere and if ownership is universalized, who can claim authority and authorship? Does the authenticity of a song – the song itself in any authentic, composed form – diminish or disappear? Ironically, the modern conditions of covering songs render these questions more paradoxical. With modernity, the media that disseminate songs proliferate themselves.[6] Each generation of recording technology makes covering easier, but complicates the problem of ownership. The musical culture of modernity may well be awash in covers, and it may be that the very superabundance of covered music has emerged as an abiding symbol of postmodernism.[7] Hanns Eisler's genealogy of covering emerged during the transition from modernism to postmodernism and was steeped in the paradox of covering that came to characterize this age. Eisler inhabited an age of in-betweenness, and the question we must consider is whether Eisler's propensity to cover was symptomatic of this age of in-betweenness or whether Eisler seized the violent change of the era and the crisis of modernity to stake new claims on the practice of covering itself.[8]

At each stage in his biography, Hanns Eisler assumed not just numerous roles but different and contradictory roles. As a composition student of Arnold Schoenberg, organizer of workers' choruses, composer of serial chamber music, Brecht collaborator, Austrian in the Hollywood exile community of artists, co-author with Theodor W. Adorno of *Composing for the Films,* composer of the national anthem of the GDR, and more, Hanns Eisler participated in many and varied musical communities.[9] In the

---

5　The question of genre in-betweenness receives especially incisive treatment in Fabian Holt, *Genre in Popular Music* (Chicago: University of Chicago Press, 2007), passim but esp. 31–49.

6　The mediation of modernity is the fundamental argument in the now-classic Friedrich A. Kittler, *Aufschreibesysteme 1800/1900,* 3rd edn. (Munich: Wilhelm Fink Verlag, 1995).

7　George Plasketes suggests that the plenitude of covers in music has led to a generation he calls the 'Cover Age'. See his 'Re-Flections on the Cover Age: A Collage of Continuous Coverage in Popular Music', *Popular Music and Society,* 28/2 (2005), 137–61.

8　Eisler himself insisted that music and musical performance were never separable from the age in which music was created and performed. His abundant writings insist upon a consideration of the historical and political contexts of the work of art. See, e.g., Hanns Eisler, *A Rebel in Music: Selected Writings,* ed. Manfred Grabs, transl. Marjorie Meyer (London: Kahn & Averill, 1999).

9　Theodor W. Adorno and Hanns Eisler, *Komposition für den Film,* ed. Johannes C. Gall (Frankfurt: Suhrkamp, 2006).

years since his death, performers and musicologists have in turn identified with and focused on specific languages of this musical 'polyglot'.[10]

In order to locate Hanns Eisler in this world of covers, we turn to a few theoretical considerations about covering music. As we do so, we want to make it clear from the outset that we are thinking about covering and uncovering Hanns Eisler from two perspectives. First of all, we want to think about Eisler as a composer who covers music in the course of his compositional process. Second, we examine the extraordinary degree to which Eisler's music was itself covered. Eisler was an inveterate self-borrower, and part of the enigma of his identity is due to the diverse ways in which he reused the same music in different ways. The question, nonetheless, is whether self-covering and other-covering are mutually dependent. These may well be two separate topics, but in fact we prefer to think of them as related, even dialectically so.

The two perspectives we employ here rely on the grammatical flexibility of the word 'cover' itself, both as a noun and as a verb. As a noun, a cover is an object, which derives its initial meaning from the surface of a musical piece, usually a song. The objective attributes of the surface necessarily establish a particular relation to what is covered, to the objective attributes below the surface. As a verb, to cover results from an act and therefore specifies an agent and agency. Covering music transforms it into a subject, and it establishes the conditions of subjectivity. A covered song – as subject – might do cultural work different from that of the original version of a song – as object. The subject positions of the creator/performer/coverer change in the course of the song's transformation from its original form to its covered version.

We also wish to use the concept of cover in both general and specific ways. Specifically, we really do mean to address the use of covers in popular musics of the twentieth and twenty-first centuries. One musician performs a song created by another, transforming and personalizing it through performance. In popular music, a cover refers both to songs and to recordings. Although there is slippage between the two, the distinctions are relevant in this essay. A *cover song* is one that has been previously recorded, but then is performed by musicians. A *cover record* refers to a recording that is exactly like an original, previously recorded song, but now with different musicians. The cover record provides an attempted objective reproduction to the original; the cover song serves as a subjective response.[11]

In the broader historical sense, it is important to remember that covers have been around for a long time, and that they assume many forms and genres. In folk and popular music, covers go by all sorts of names: contrafact and broadside ballad in English; *Flugblattlied, Moritat,* and *Bänkelsang* in German; *skillingsblad* and *skillings-vise* in Danish, to list just a few. In sacred music, covers proliferate during periods when popular religion is on the rise: the explosion of Marian songs during the Counter-Reformation, shape-note hymnody during the American Great Awakenings

10 Joy Haslam Calico, 'Hanns Eisler, Marxist Polyglot' (*Perfect Sound Forever*: Sept. 2002, http://www.furious.com/perfect/hannseisler.html, accessed 16 Sept. 2007).

11 For more on this distinction see Don Cusic, 'In Defense of Cover Songs', *Popular Music and Society*, 28/2 (2005), 174.

in the eighteenth and nineteenth centuries, or hymnody as a national historical narrative in the United States.[12] Covers are crucial to the spread of ideological movements, for example, in the Grundtvigian *Folkehøjskole* movement in Denmark. Because of their constant transformation of meaning through processes such as parody, covers may become the canonical repertory in some genres, say, cabaret.

As we seek to expand a theory of covers and covering, we recognize that we confront paradox and contradiction. We necessarily untether covering from its application to popular music, with the implicit teleology leading from oral performance to written transmission. There is a danger of broadening the theory to the extent that it might seem as if all music, once a performance moves beyond some initial version, even the composer's intent, is a cover in one form or another. How, we ask in this article, can we expand the metaphysical borders of covers and covering without, at the same time, eliminating them?

First of all, it is crucial to recognize that certain borders are more fluid, so much so that they may not *separate* a cover from an original. This is the case when we consider orality and literacy. We are hardly the first to claim that all musics are both oral and literate. Critically, then, art song might not be, *ipso facto,* different from popular song because the former is literate and the latter oral. This is surely the case in Hanns Eisler's aesthetic of mass song. It is also one of the reasons that he deliberately leaves the traces of folk, popular, and vernacular song in art songs, such as those in the *Hollywood Songbook*.

Second, just as we draw a distinction between a *cover* and *covering,* so too do we recognize a distinction between a *performance* and the *performative*. We should go so far as to represent these related distinctions with the algorithm, a cover is to covering what a performance is to the performative, or:

$$\text{cover : covering :: performance : performative}$$

The two pairs in the algorithm each embody the relation of object to subject, or product to process. We represent them in this way to emphasize aspects of each pair that might otherwise be overlooked, or rather oversimplified, in other words the dynamic subjectivity of covering and the objective limitations of performance.

Third, as interested as we are in pushing the theoretical boundaries of covers and covering, we do not wish to remove them or even to suggest they can conceptually be removed. We do not believe that all covers are the same, or that all performative acts of covering are the same. Here is where distinctions between text and context do enter into the algorithm. Eisler–Brecht songs in the American folk-song revival of the early Cold War have a very different historical context than do Eisler–Brecht songs in the GDR in the post-Cold War. In the former, Eisler songs almost statically slipped into fixed covers, which we felt and feel compelled to perform in a frozen,

---

12 See, e.g., the essays on American hymns and hymnody in Philip V. Bohlman, Edith L. Blumhofer, and Maria M. Chow (eds.), *Music in American Religious Experience* (New York and Oxford: Oxford University Press, 2006).

1950s, authentic version.[13] In the latter, Eisler songs have entered a fluid oral tradition, moving into and out of popular genres. In this article, we call for the necessity of examining these two historical contexts comparatively, not to explain the ways in which covers and covering were the same, but rather why they are different.

The various historical and cultural roles of the cover, therefore, pose metaphysical questions to musicology, asking us to rethink questions about sameness and difference in music. First, all these covers appear at the boundaries between orality and literacy, and they create a process of movement between them. The mobility of covers generates both intertextual and intergeneric signification. There is constant and necessary slippage between the objective and subjective attributes of covers.[14] Second, covers become possible through the intervention of technologies of one kind or another – the printing press in early modern Europe or digital sampling at the beginning of the twenty-first century. Third, covers are inherently performative through the ways they create a new musical object that is meant to be performed with as much ease as possible.[15] Finally, covers connect the popular and the political because, musically, they create a public space in which the popular and the political overlap.[16]

It is because of all these characteristics that covers have a bad name in the Modern Era and in the music of twentieth-century modernism, which implicitly and explicitly privileges art music over popular music. Wrenched from its objective status as a musical work, the cover loses its privileged status in the post-Enlightenment museum of musical works.[17] Covered music, moreover, lacks the attributes of Modern music, for its reference and identity come from the past, reviving it and musically retrofitting it. Anchored partly in the past, covered music falls short of fully joining the present, for it does not possess the sense of moving forward or of telos. Speaking of cover songs in popular music, Don Cusic goes so far as to suggest that they express 'the songwriter's soul and not the artist's' and 'this denies the timelessness of great works'.[18] Ultimately, the autonomy of music and the capacity of music to be self-referential, so crucial to modernity and aesthetic modernism, are sacrificed through the processes of covering.

Situated in a modernist aesthetic, covering would not only be anti-modernist, but also anti-art music; it would undermine the work of art, and return it to the people.

---

13 Cf. *Songs of Bertolt Brecht and Hanns Eisler.*

14 Among these are the attributes of in-betweenness that Fabian Holt describes in Holt, *Genre in Popular Music*. Intertextuality itself maps the movement between versions in different ways, not least in the different media of reproduction and performance; see Serge Lacasse, 'Intertextuality and Hypertextuality in Recorded Popular Music', in Michael Talbot (ed.), *The Musical Work: Reality or Invention?* (Liverpool: Liverpool University Press, 2000).

15 Eisler, for example, meant that his songs should be singable; see the essays on workers' music in Eisler, *A Rebel in Music.*

16 Because of its public performativity, particularly through improvisation, jazz persistently, one might say, insistently, politicizes the standards on which it is based. See also Middleton's discussion of popular song and 'the subjects of repetition' in Richard Middleton, *Voicing the Popular: On the Subjects of Popular Music* (New York: Routledge, 2006), 137–97.

17 See Lydia Goehr, *The Imaginary Museum of Musical Works: An Essay in the Philosophy of Music* (Oxford: Clarendon Press, 1992).

18 Cusic, 'In Defense of Cover Songs', 176.

In the aesthetic vocabulary of marxist folk- and popular-music scholarship, covering would affirm songs as 'democratic' and 'oppositional' (*demokratisch-oppositionell*), transforming art song so that it would become 'functional' (*werktätig*).[19] It was to do precisely this – to complicate art song and unravel its intertextuality – that attracted Hanns Eisler to the potential for covering in the *Hollywood Songbook* and in his other vocal compositions. Covering for Eisler politicized art song.

It should come as no surprise that one of the reasons Hanns Eisler comes under attack is that he frequently borrows from the past and uses it to cover in the present. Listening to Hanns Eisler's songs, we often have the feeling that we have heard them before – and, of course, we have, often as fragments, but sometimes relatively intact.[20] His *Neue deutsche Volkslieder* are a return to, not a departure from, German folk song in the GDR. Clearly, Eisler turns to previously existing material consciously, and no less clearly, he uses that material to realize connections between the past and the present. In a word, he approaches composing itself from an awareness of the creative processes set in motion by the performativity of covering, the *Vortragsweise* (both 'melody' and 'means' of performance) that connects a song to its covers.[21] In the composer's hands, the cover is more, rather than less, creative. In a performer's hands (or voice), such as that of the great Eisler interpreter, Ernst Busch, covering is more, rather than less, performative. In his own compositions, therefore, Eisler draws attention to the cover rather than obscuring it.

Recovering the *Hollywood Songbook*

Sixty-five years after it came into being, questions of identity still surround the *Hollywood Songbook*. Just what is the *Hollywood Songbook*? Is it a song cycle? What relation does it have to the poetry of Bertolt Brecht's poems of the same name, *Hollywood Liederbuch,* which were themselves written as a response to the rise of fascism in Germany and exile from Germany, not only in Hollywood but in Denmark, Sweden, and Finland *en route* to the United States? Did these poems of Brecht's exile resonate with Eisler's exile, which in some ways paralleled that of Brecht, passing through Denmark before reaching Los Angeles? If there is an indebtedness to Brecht, his collaborator for song and stage for many years, what does it mean that the closing songs in the *Hollywood Songbook* detour toward other poets and other forms of literature? We might understand that Eisler would generate some of his own texts for his own exile (e.g., 'Nightmare'), but how does this explain a turn toward earlier

---

19 For the crucial role of these concepts in East German musicology and ethnomusicology, see Wolfgang Steinitz, *Deutsche Volkslieder demokratischen Charakters aus sechs Jahrhunderten* (Berlin: Akademie-Verlag, 1978); cf. the original use of such concepts in Karl Marx and Friedrich Engels, *Über Literatur und Kunst,* vol. 2 (Berlin: Dietz Verlag, 1968), 218–29. Ethnomusicologist Jürgen Elsner redeploys the concepts from folk song to Eisler's composed songs in Jürgen Elsner, *Zur vokalsolistischen Vortragsweise der Kampfmusik Hanns Eislers* (Leipzig: VEB Deutscher Verlag für Musik, 1971).

20 See Elsner, *Zur vokalsolistischen Vortragsweise,* 77–79 and 134–36, for comparative transcriptions of songs taken by Eisler from oral tradition and composed for piano and voice.

21 Ibid.

poetry, to Goethe ('Der Schatzgräber'), Eichendorff ('Erinnerung an Eichendorff und Schumann'), Hölderlin ('Hölderlin-Fragmente'), and even the Bible ('Der Mensch')? What forms of narrative unity and continuity do the songs have in common with each other? With other Brecht poems and Eisler songs that bear similar names, such as the *Hollywood Elegien*? For that matter, what does 'Hollywood' have to do with the songs?

The simple answer to all these questions is that there is no simple answer to them. Composed in 1942–43, the songs of the *Hollywood Songbook* seemingly resisted unity and completion. We can speculate that he meant the songs to appear as a single volume, for he sketched a preface for that volume, stating 'in a society that understands and loves such a songbook, life will be lived well and without danger. These pieces have been written with such a society in mind'.[22] The potential wholeness of Eisler's projection notwithstanding, he was never to hear a complete performance of the *Hollywood Songbook* during the remaining two decades of his life, in exile or after his return to the GDR.

Whatever the *Hollywood Songbook* might be – a song cycle, an autobiographical conversation between artists in exile, a metaphorical journey, or diaspora and return – it resists being bounded by any single category of repertory, style, or genre. Many of the songs explicitly announce themselves as art songs, using allusions to the great Lieder repertories of the nineteenth century. Others are explicitly folk-like. The small range of most melodies suggests ease of singing but belies the underlying difficulty with which other songs challenge performers. There is modernist, non-tonal writing, no less than there are songs bearing witness to the Jazz Age in Germany and America, at once distant and close. It is with great difficulty that one identifies which Eisler songs are or are not in the *Hollywood Songbook*. Only perhaps one third of the songs actually come from Bertolt Brecht's poems gathered under the same name. Others enter the songbook from other Brecht sources, for example, 'Über den Selbstmord' from *Der gute Mensch von Sezuan* and 'Winterspruch' from *Die heilige Johanna der Schlachthöfe*. At least another third has no claim to the name beyond common textual themes and the consciously similar musical style with which Eisler treats them. Finally, there is the third that does not fit, seemingly flaunting any distinctive style and the violent shifts between mood and texture. At one moment, we imagine we have unraveled the *Hollywood Songbook*; at the next, Eisler calls us to task for our presumptiveness.

If contrast and contradiction abound, one way to account for their presence in a work with fluid boundaries is to concentrate on the autonomy of individual motifs, songs, and meanings. If priority is given to what Claudia Albert, following Adorno, calls the 'autonomization of aesthetics', the 'materials' employed by Eisler acquire meaning because they are indices of negativity.[23] Their very materiality – in other words,

---

22 Quote in Albrecht Dümling, 'Expelled into Paradise – On the *Hollywood Songbook* of Hanns Eisler,' liner notes for *Eisler: The Hollywood Songbook* (London: Decca 289 460 582-2, 1998), 9.

23 Claudia Albert, *'Das schwierige Handwerk des Hoffens': Hanns Eislers 'Hollywooder Liederbuch'* (Stuttgart: J.B. Metzlersche Verlagsbuchhandlung, 1991), 12–14.

the performativity that arises from materiality – resists the unified wholeness that would lead to an understanding of the *Hollywood Songbook* as a song cycle. The musical setting of a poem, therefore, creates an interpretive subjectivity, which, according to Albert, sets various processes of exchange between music and language in motion. Hollywood is both a theme, or *topos,* in the songbook and a reality in Eisler's life in exile.[24]

Performances, recorded and from the stage, must also presume if they are to suture the parts into a whole, but there is simply no single version that scholars or musicians could claim as authentic. In the complete editions of Eisler's songs or of the musical settings of Brecht's poetry, the identity is no less confused, beyond a sort of vague realization of common ground, the world of exile and its complex intersections of historical narrative, shared by Eisler, Brecht, and other exiled artists in wartime Los Angeles.[25] In the 1985 GDR edition of Eisler songs, the songs begin with 'Der Sohn' and conclude with 'Die Landschaft des Exils', but there is otherwise no differentiation of the songs from other songs by Brecht and the poets to whom Eisler commonly turned.[26] This grouping approximates the dates of composition that we can determine for the songs, the two parts of 'Der Sohn' dated on 30 May 1942 and 'Die Landschaft des Exils' dated on 2 September 1943.[27] The generally accepted order of the songs, as well as the contents of the songbook, follow what we know of Eisler's work on them over the course of approximately fifteen months.

Perhaps the boundaries of identity are clearest in their fuzziness if one compares modern recordings of the *Hollywood Songbook.* The most extensive recording project solely committed to the *Hollywood Songbook,* Matthias Goerne (baritone) and Eric Schneider's (piano) recording for the 'Entartete Musik' series of 'Music Suppressed by the Third Reich', contains 46 tracks and unfailingly follows the GDR complete edition, affording it the authority of an *Urtext* that stands as a simulacrum for Eisler's life in exile.[28] On the Dietrich Fischer-Dieskau recording entitled *Hollywood Songbook,* which contains other Eisler songs, there are 32 tracks. Eisler songs in general and the *Hollywood Songbook* in particular, have become staples in the revival of twentieth-century cabaret. Recordings that revive Weimar German and Jewish exile cabaret commonly draw extensively from the *Hollywood Songbook.*[29]

Musically and stylistically, the common turf of the *Hollywood Songbook* grows from the extreme degree of intertextuality. In this essay we claim that this intertextuality is

24 Ibid. 36–54.
25 Writing as a German scholar of exile, Albrecht Dümling equates virtually every piece of evidence associated with Eisler's North America years to be a chronicle of the tragic dimensions of exile; see Dümling, 'Expelled into Paradise', 7–9. Exile in the songs themselves of the *Hollywood Songbook* provides the analytical framework in Markus Roth, *Der Gesang als Asyl: Analytische Studien zu Hanns Eislers 'Hollywood Liederbook'* (Hofheim: Wolke Verlag, 2007).
26 Eisler, *Lieder für eine Singstimme und Klavier,* 73–155.
27 Albert, *'Das schwierige Handwerk des Hoffens',* 59–60.
28 *Eisler: The Hollywood Songbook.*
29 See, e.g., Geoffrey Burleson and Maria Tegzes, *Urban Cabaret* (Acton, Mass.: Neuma 450-83, 1993); see also the CD accompanying Philip V. Bohlman (ed.), *Jewish Musical Modernism, Old and New* (Chicago: University of Chicago Press, 2008).

dependent on Eisler's understanding of covering songs in order to transform them into a corpus of self-referential works with specific historical narratives.[30] Common to these topical songs sold and sung on the streets of the metropole are the specific references to time, place, and event. Eisler and Brecht, too, specify dates and places in the songs, for example, 'Hotelzimmer 1942' or 'Speisekammer 1942'. Eisler, however, tends to appropriate these specific references as his own. Brecht's title for 'Speisekammer 1942' is, in fact, 'Finnische Gutsspeisekammer 1940', thereby using the song to locate him in the time and place of his Finnish exile on the eve of his 1941 travel to Los Angeles. In the most literal sense, Eisler uses the narrative specificity of the broadside to craft a new broadside. His song covers Brecht's poem. The literal appropriation of covering in popular music also appears in other songs. Tragic events are memorialized in 'Gedenktafel für 4000 Soldaten, die im Krieg gegen Norwegen versenkt wurden' (Memorial Plaque for the 4000 Soldiers Drowned in the War against Norway). Here, again, Eisler covers Brecht's meaning by removing the phrase, 'des Hitler', from its qualifying position before the war, in other words 'Hitler's war'. It is hard to know why, or even if, this is an act of depoliticizing, or simply personalizing. Subtle shifts in ownership are sometimes very significant in the covers, for example, in the penultimate song of the complete edition, which Brecht called 'Rückkehr' (Return), but Eisler renamed as 'Heimkehr' (Homecoming).

The songs of the *Hollywood Songbook* also rely on parody, particularly on a type of parody resulting from the juxtaposition of the real and the unreal, history and fantasy, the absence of *Heimat* through exile and the ironic playfulness of the *unheimlich*, or uncanny. We witness this in songs such as 'Der Kirschdieb' (The Cherry Thief), in which the narrator awakens to a boy outside his window, who is stealing cherries from a tree in the garden. There seems to be nothing consequential about this youthful playfulness. It is followed, however, by one of the most consequential and specific of all songs in the *Hollywood Songbook*, 'Hotelzimmer 1942', written in fact when Eisler was living during 1942 in a Los Angeles hotel room. Pairing two songs set in what amount to bedrooms in this way, Eisler renders the local at once real and eerie (see Figure 1).

Finally, we want to suggest as part of our thesis about covering in Hanns Eisler that it depends on the ways in which there is constant referentiality to the machines and the machinery of modernity. In the songs explicitly about war and exile, history – in other words, war and its victims, exile and death – is accomplished through machines, the ships and trains, the vehicles that take men into battle and those allowing them to flee to the farthest parts of the earth. The counterpoint of narrative and musical voice, too, is possible because of machines, radios and loudspeakers. Narration turns to agency, the mediation of the radio performs exile (see Example 1).

The personal nature of songs becomes more and more intense through the impersonality of machines. There are the machines that represent reality by transforming it

---

30 See Lacasse, 'Intertextuality and Hypertextuality'.

An der weißgetünchten Wand steht der schwarze Koffer mit den Manuskripten.
Drüben steht das Rauchzeug mit dem kupf'rnen Aschenbecher.
Die chinesische Leinwand, zeigend den Zweifler, hängt darüber.
Auch die Masken sind da.
Und neben der Bettstelle steht der kleine sechslampige Lautsprecher.
In der Frühe drehe ich den Schalter um
Und höre die Siegesmeldungen meiner Feinde.

Against the white-washed wall stands the black suitcase, filled with manuscripts.
Beyond it rests the smoking materials, next to the copper ashtray.
Above it hangs the Chinese canvas, showing the doubter.
Also, that's where the masks are.
And next to the bed stands the little speaker, with its six radio tubes.
In the morning I turn it on,
Only to hear the reports of my enemies' victories.

Figure 1. 'Hotelzimmer 1942' – 'Hotel Room 1942', from the *Hollywood Songbook*.

into fantasy. In a word, we witness in these songs Hollywood itself, which draws Brecht and Eisler toward it, texts and scores in the suitcases standing in their 'Hotel Room 1942'. For Hanns Eisler, Hollywood's machines of modernity will accelerate his aesthetic rethinking of modernity, not only the *Composing for the Films,* which he co-authored with Theodor W. Adorno,[31] but also his later film projects, such as his 1956 collaboration with Jean Resnais on the first documentary on the concentration camp at Auschwitz, *Nuit et brouillard* (Night and Fog). With the machines of modernity and modernism at his disposal, Hanns Eisler would take the techniques of covering to their extreme, truly exposing and unleashing the political power of music.[32]

DISCOVERING AMERICA

Hanns Eisler's Hollywood was already distinct from that of his friend and collaborator, Bertolt Brecht. We have already pointed out the ways in which he personalized it, locating it on the landscape of his own experiences in America. Eisler's Hollywood was also different from that of other German and Austrian immigrants – Arnold Schoenberg, Ernst Toch, Thomas and Heinrich Mann, Alfred Döblin, Friedrich Hollaender, Bruno Walter, to name only a few – who had traveled to the Los Angeles of the 1940s, with its explosive culture of popular music and film. The literature on exile

31 Adorno and Eisler, *Komposition für den Film.*
32 The mediating intertextuality of modern machines provides the central theoretical metaphor in Friedrich A. Kittler, *Gramophone, Film, Typewriter,* transl. Geoffrey Winthrop-Young and Michael Wutz (Stanford: Stanford University Press, 1999).

Example 1. Score of 'An den kleinen Radioapparat' from the *Hollywood Liederbuch* (Copyright by Deutscher Verlag für Musik, Leipzig).

often portrays this generation of intellectuals and musicians with a collective biography of exile. The overwhelming emphasis on exile as expulsion denies the influence of America, and it belies the possibility of American music as a context for hermeneutic interpretation. The question must therefore be posed: Are there other meanings of America – of Hollywood – in the creation and reception of the *Hollywood Songbook*?

We believe that the answers to that question lie in the role played by covers and covering. The *Hollywood Songbook* does, after all, announce itself as an American songbook, and in so doing, we wish to argue, it bears comparison with the 'Great American Songbook', a comparison it has heretofore never received. If one asks any performer or arranger of popular song in the United States about the existence of the 'Great American Songbook', the responses are unequivocal: Of course there is, because we all (and here the authors mean to include themselves) draw upon it constantly for everything from jazz standards to musicals to revival cabaret. The scholarship on American popular song presumes the existence of the 'Great American Songbook' and has never failed to designate canonic songwriters and repertories.[33] The songbook's composers are well known: Harold Arlen, Irving Berlin, Duke Ellington, George and Ira Gershwin, Cole Porter, Rodgers and Hammerstein, and Kurt Weill, to name only a few.

There is, however, no such 'thing' as the 'Great American Songbook'. It lacks the physicality of a publication, possessing only the materiality of the performative; it resists concrete form; recordings acknowledge it as a source, but they don't reproduce it. The 'Great American Songbook' is no more nor less than a vast source for covering. The songs that enter the source come from every possible genre: musicals and films, vaudeville and stage revues, sheet music and big-band jazz. A song finds its place in the 'Great American Songbook' through displacement, in other words, from the mobility that allows it to determine new residence and spawn new versions. American identity, too, is fluid and hybrid, and the songwriters and lyricists whose works have migrated into the 'Great American Songbook' are overwhelmingly first- or second-generation immigrants or ethnic and racial minorities.

The *Hollywood Songbook* is no more a material object than is the 'Great American Songbook'. Their identities lie in a much more complex and collective subjectivity. By gathering songs in a songbook, Eisler localized them and translated them for a global moment inhabited by immigrants and exiles alike, the American and the European. The songs, however, loosen and destabilize these identities. They represent the ways in which Eisler charted his journey to America by embracing the recording and film industries of Los Angeles. Like the 'Great American Songbook', therefore, the *Hollywood Songbook* is American, with all the mobility, hybridity, and uncanny familiarity that Americanness entails.

---

33 See, e.g., the classic work, Alec Wilder, *American Popular Song: The Great Innovators 1900–1950* (New York and Oxford: Oxford University Press, 1990); for a concise introduction to the canonical practices of American popular song see Stephen Banfield, 'Popular Song and Popular Music on Stage and Film', in David Nicholls (ed.), *The Cambridge History of American Music* (Cambridge: Cambridge University Press, 1999), 309–44; cf. Geoffrey Block, 'The Broadway Canon from "Show Boat" to "West Side Story" and the European Operatic Ideal', *The Journal of Musicology*, 11/4 (1993), 525–44.

COVERING AND UNCOVERING THE *Hollywood Songbook*

The *Hollywood Songbook* lives today through the dissemination of covers that retain the performativity of Eisler's vocal *Vortragsweise*. To evoke the breadth of those covers, we present a representative sample of some of the most recent (see Table 1). Albums by Dietrich Fischer-Dieskau and Matthias Goerne, classical recordings, are one principal cause for interest in the *Hollywood Songbook* outside of the former East Germany. *Lieder* specialists draw attention to the lyricism of Eisler's melodies, and it is this attention to voice that unites a first set of covers. Artists moving in the popular mainstream and in the vocal jazz scenes, such as Sting and Theo Bleckmann, speak openly about the beautiful melodies. Sting's cover of 'An den kleinen Radioapparat', when heard in the context of this article, foregrounds the melody in its abandonment of Brecht's text and renaming, 'The Secret Marriage'. Describing 'The Secret Marriage', Sting embraces the contemporaneity of covering:

> [Hanns Eisler and Kurt Weill] were classically trained musicians, students of Schoenberg, who crossed a bridge to Broadway shows, to popular music. That bridge still exists. So I'm going from pop music, finding out about them and how they wrote chromatically, and hopefully bringing it back.[34]

Another set of CDs, this time recordings of Eisler in radio interviews and singing his own music, in part inspired the avant-garde German composer Heiner Goebbels to 'cover' Eisler by turning attention to these sound documents and, more significantly, the sound and melody of Eisler's voice. For his album *Eislermaterial,* which is based on a music theater project, he sought out an untrained singer, Josef Bierbichler, to sing in a seemingly strained tenor quite similar to the thin, hesitant timbre of Eisler's own voice. The links between Bierbichler's covers of *Hollywood* songs and the composer are even clearer when the songs are juxtaposed with Goebbels's splicing of Eisler's interviews, set against a backdrop of free improvisation. The composer's presence is invoked through the voice of covering, juxtaposition, and translation to the machinery of mass production, presented visually as a diagram in the liner notes of the mixing board used for the CD. Heiner Goebbels belongs to a group of musicians from 'generation 68' (*die 68er*), for whom Eisler is a model for their own musical politics. Assorted albums emerged from this scene and the *Hollywood Songbook's* capacity to serve as anti-war music through revival.

A final example from 2003, in which Brecht and Eisler's music-political aims play a large role in informing the artistic presentation, is Ana Torfs's art installation that consists of a series of videos accessible on the internet. In these films, actors are filmed for songs of the *Hollywood Songbook* in three stages. In the first, they listen to the song's accompaniment and act out the emotional content without singing. Then, still dressed in all white, they repeat this process, but vocalize the text and

---

34 Sting, liner notes to ' ... *nothing like the Sun*' (London: A&M, 1987).

ART BEARS
Hopes and Fears, Rerelease. Recommended Records, 1992 (Random Records, 1978).

THEO BLECKMANN
Ori-ga-mi. Vancouver, Songlines, 2001. SGL 1534-2.
Berlin: Songs of Love and War, Peace and Exile. Winter & Winter 910 138-2, 2007.

DIETRICH FISCHER-DIESKAU
Hollywood Song-Book. Hamburg: Teldec, 1994. Teldec 97459.

HEINER GOEBBELS
Eislermaterial. Munich: ECM Records, 2002. 461 648-2 ECM.
    With the Linksradikales Blasorchester.

MATTHIAS GOERNE
The Hollywood Songbook. New York: London Records, 1998. 289 460 582-2 London.

CHARLIE HADEN AND THE LIBERATION MUSIC ORCHESTRA
Liberation Music Orchestra. New York: Impulse, 1969. AS-9183 Impulse.

Keiner oder Alle: Kampfmusik von Hanns Eisler. Berlin: Barbarossa, 2005.

DAGMAR KRAUSE
Angebot und Nachfrage. Hannibal Records, 1986.
Panzerschlacht: Die Lieder von Hanns Eisler. Island Records, 1986.

GISELA MAY AND ERNST BUSCH
Hanns Eisler Dokumente. Berlin: Berlin Classics, 1995. BC 9058.

NEW BUDAPEST ORPHEUM SOCIETY
Dancing on the Edge of a Volcano. Chicago: Cedille Records, 2002. CDR 90000 065.
Moments musicaux of Jewish Musical Modernism. CD accompanying Philip V. Bohlman (ed.),
    Jewish Musical Modernism, Old and New (Chicago: University of Chicago Press, 2008).

STING
'*... nothing like the Sun*'. London: A&M, 1987.

ANA TORFS
Performance art installation. http://www.diacenter.org/torfs/, 2003.

HANS-ECKHARDT WENZEL
Hanswurst und andere arme Würste: Hanns-Eisler Collage. Conträr Musik, CD9835, 2001.

Table 1. Selected covers of the *Hollywood Songbook*.

Eisler's melody. Finally, they are to perform 'as if for a musical', according to their instructions in full costume, they stare straight at the camera, declaiming Brecht's text, the song now extending beyond even the sum of its parts.[35]

35 Internet access to these installation covers of Hanns Eisler songs is available at: http://www.diacenter.org/torfs/.

In Lieu of a Definitive Version – Recovery and Reconstruction

It has been clear from the outset of this article that its authors are implicated themselves in the covering of Hanns Eisler. We gather our own experiences here, convey-
ing them as ethnographic moments and performance acts. In our own lives, as musicians and scholars, Eisler covers accumulate, making the interpretive processes of
covering more pleasurable and more vexing. The metaphorical songbooks that form
the bodies of our own collections necessarily respond to the intervention of the
politics and history in our own present no less than they did in Hanns Eisler's past.
Even as we search for the incomplete cadence in this essay that, like an Eisler song,
leaves the questions open at the end of song, the New Budapest Orpheum Society
passes from one Eisler project to the next.[36] The ensemble's most recent recording
and the one it is currently producing both locate Eisler songs from the *Hollywood
Songbook* and other parts of Eisler's song œuvre at the symbolic core of the project;
everything else covers and uncovers that core.[37] Since its founding in 2000, the
ensemble has come to thrive on its own mobility, not just its juxtaposition of different genres to create 'Jewish cabaret', but to perform on every imaginable stage: syna-
gogues, Jewish community centers, universities, Holocaust museums, night clubs,
and Broadway. We do not shy away from the political dimensions of a repertory
formed from the tragedy of the twentieth century.

As we now cover Eisler and other songs through the performances of the New
Budapest Orpheum Society, we increasingly witness the ways in which our audiences
in an America no less troubled than that of Hanns Eisler in the 1940s interpret the
everyday in a fascist and racist world of the 1930s and 1940s as if it were an earlier
version of their own world – our own world, that is, during the era of American
imperialism against Islam, the Iraq War, and renewed genocide of global proportions.
Covering these Eisler songs has proved not only to be historical, but historicizing
and politicizing. We claim it as ours and offer it to those keen to listen, learn, and
act. Through Eisler's covers and our covering, the political past has been uncovered
to reveal a present that is our own and that the music does not allow us to deny.

In conclusion, we return to the two different perspectives that we introduced at the
beginning of the essay, the active and passive voices, or the distinction between the
'cover itself' and 'being covered'. It is no longer possible to think about these perspectives as representing objects that could be reified, but rather as subject positions that
Eisler brings to music and politics. Our ultimate focus has been the dynamic movement between covers and being covered, indeed, the tension between the active and

36 Philip Bohlman is Artistic Director of the New Budapest Orpheum Society, a cabaret and Ensemble-
    in-Residence at the University of Chicago; research by Andrea Bohlman guides repertory choice
    and interpretation of the ensemble.
37 The first CD accompanies the book, Bohlman (ed.), *Jewish Musical Modernism*; the second is a CD
    of Jewish cabaret in exile, the title of which covers Eisler's 'An den kleinen Radioapparat': New
    Budapest Orpheum Society, *So That Their Voices Will Not Fall Silent – Jewish Cabaret in Exile*
    (Chicago: Cedille Records, forthcoming).

passive voices. Ultimately, it is this dynamic movement that allows contemporary listeners to hear the new voices that sing Eisler – Hanns Eisler heute! – and that allow his covers to address our own world. By covering and being covered, Eisler gives voice to the political concerns of generations that followed him – and that will also follow us. Uncovering Hanns Eisler, rather, is an act born of responsibility, political and musical, and of the realization that music is always more than itself.

SUMMARY

Composed during 1942–43, years of Hanns Eisler's exile from Nazi Germany in Los Angeles, the *Hollywood Liederbuch* contains 46 settings of poems, largely by fellow exile Bertolt Brecht, but also by other writers, including in two instances by Eisler himself. This article examines the ways in which the intertextuality of the songs, through the multiple sources and changing performances, between the materiality of the song as object and its performativity as subject, transform musical and textual meanings. Hanns Eisler made extensive use of borrowing and covering as a composer, and in the reception history of his work – and of the *Hollywood Songbook* perhaps more than any other body of works created by Eisler – covers have proliferated in the hands of many performers, in art-song traditions no less than popular music. The authors propose a theory of covering, therefore, that extends its application from popular music to art and composed songs, that is, to the fluid spaces of transmission between oral and written tradition, hence between the 'active' and 'passive voice' qualities of the 'cover itself' and 'being covered'. The identities generated for the *Hollywood Songbook* open it to comparison with the fluid canon of American popular song, the 'Great American Songbook', and accordingly to the Americanness of Eisler's compositional work in exile. In conclusion, the authors examine the remarkable vitality of Hanns Eisler in post-Cold War Europe and attribute aspects of reviving the *Hollywood Songbook* to the renewal that covering its songs inspires.

"Wer heisst euch mit Fingern zeigen auf mich?"

Selbstreflexive Illusionsbrüche bei Hans Christian Andersen und Robert Schumann

René Michaelsen

Es ist nicht ganz von der Hand zu weisen: sieht man sich einem Aufsatz gegenüber, in dessen Titel der Name eines Schriftstellers mit demjenigen eines Komponisten kombiniert wird, befürchtet man zunächst methodisch Fragwürdiges. Will man – und das ist in diesem Fall durchaus intendiert – über die Feststellung und Vertiefung biographischer Berührungspunkte hinausgehen, begibt man sich schnell in problematisches Fahrwasser. Schriftlich fixierter Text und klanglich organisierte Musik – ist es wirklich eine gute Idee, diese beiden grundverschiedenen Äußerungsformen in Analogie zu setzen?

Insbesondere in der amerikanischen Musikforschung der späten 1980er Jahre ist dies kontrovers diskutiert worden, wobei sich die Gemüter vor allem an der spezifischen Frage nach narrativen Strukturen in der Instrumentalmusik erhitzten.[1] Kann absolute Musik ohne programmatisches Beiwerk einem literarischen Erzähltext analoge Prozesse ausprägen, so dass es sinnvoll ist, ihr mit der Frage nach ihrer narrativen Gestaltung zu Leibe zu rücken? Zweifel an dieser Idee sind vielfach laut geworden, geht absoluter Musik doch vor allem das für Narrativität geradezu unabdingbare Charakteristikum der klar festzumachenden Referentialität ab.[2] Zudem mangelt es ihr an der Möglichkeit, Unterscheidungen zwischen Fiktionalität und Realität oder verschiedenen Zeitebenen zu artikulieren – kurz: ihr fehlt die Kapazität zur *ästhetischen Illusion*.[3]

Andererseits jedoch rückt ein Merkmal absolute Musik und Erzählung wieder in unmittelbare Nähe zueinander, nämlich die Erzeugung eines linearen Zeitkontinuums. Durch die Ausbreitung in einem begrenzten Zeitraum sind der Instrumentalmusik Mittel eigen, kraft derer sie eine gewisse strukturelle Ähnlichkeit zu narrativen Texten ausprägen kann: Vorbereitung, Spannungsaufbau, Auflösung, Überraschung, Vortäuschung – die Erzeugung einer klanglichen Dramaturgie. Um aber diese Merk-

---

1 Vgl. zur Zusammenfassung dieser Debatte: Janina Klassen, 'Was die Musik erzählt', in Eberhard Lämmert (Hg.), *Die erzählerische Dimension. Eine Gemeinsamkeit der Künste* (Berlin, 1999), 89–107.

2 Vgl. zur aktuellen Diskussion dieses Problems: Alexander Becker und Matthias Vogel, 'Einleitung der Herausgeber', in dies. (Hg.), *Musikalischer Sinn. Beiträge zu einer Philosophie der Musik* (Frankfurt am Main, 2007), 7–24; Christoph Asmuth: 'Was bedeutet Musik? Eine kritische Untersuchung musikalischer Referenz', in Ulrich Tadday (Hg.): *Musik-Konzepte. Sonderband XI: Musikphilosophie* (München, 2007), 70–86.

3 Vgl. zu diesem Begriff: Werner Wolf, *Ästhetische Illusion und Illusionsdurchbrechung in der Erzählkunst. Theorie und Geschichte mit Schwerpunkt auf englischem illusionsstörenden Erzählen* (Tübingen, 1993).

male als Nachbildung einer (nicht unbedingt referentiell festgelegten) Narration zu verstehen, bedarf es vor allem einer unberechenbaren Größe, nämlich der Kooperationsbereitschaft des Rezipienten, die klanglichen Ereignisse im Sinne einer sich entfaltenden Erzählung wahrzunehmen. Dies soll keineswegs als allzu salomonisches "Narrativität ist, was Du draus machst" begriffen werden, vielmehr gilt es meiner Ansicht nach, die unterschiedlichen Deutungsangebote, die ein musikalisches Ereignis offeriert, möglichst ohne hierarchische Abstufung anzunehmen und aufzuzeigen. Wenn ich also im späteren Verlauf dieser Untersuchung Analogien zwischen textlichen und musikalischen Ereignissen feststelle, so geschieht dies im vollen Bewusstsein der Tatsache, dass ich die Bereitschaft zu einem Verständnis, das solche Parallelitäten zulässt, einem bestimmten kulturellen Kontext verdanke, der eine derartige Hörstrategie konditioniert – den Wunsch, "durch Worte zu vervollständigen, was die Musik nicht sagt, weil es nicht in ihrer semiologischen Natur liegt".[4]

"An Ihnen liegt die Schuld allein!"

Freilich tätigt man Analogien zwischen Musik und Text leichteren Gewissens, wenn sich nachweisen lässt, dass sich der betreffende Schriftsteller und der in Frage stehende Komponist der gegenseitigen Anerkennung, ja womöglich sogar der Relevanz der Erzeugnisse des jeweils anderen für das eigene Werk versichert haben – was glücklicherweise bei Robert Schumann und Hans Christian Andersen der Fall ist.

Schumanns erste Beschäftigung mit Texten Andersens geht zurück in das "Liederjahr" 1840. Zu den Dichtern, deren Lektüre Schumanns immense Liedproduktion dieses Jahres vorantrieb, zählt auch Adelbert von Chamisso. Unter den insgesamt 17 Gedichten Chamissos, die Schumann in diesem Jahr der zweiten Auflage seiner *Gesammelten Gedichte* entnahm und vertonte, waren auch vier Andersen-Übertragungen: *Märzveilchen*, *Muttertraum*, *Der Soldat* und *Der Spielmann*. Zusammen mit *Verrathene Liebe*, einer Übertragung aus dem Neugriechischen, formierte Schumann die Andersen/Chamisso-Vertonungen zu der Sammlung *Fünf Lieder* op. 40, für die er ab dem Juli 1840 nach Verlegern suchte.[5] Nach der Ablehnung durch Breitkopf und Härtel versprach Schumann dem norddeutschen Verleger Cranz eine zweisprachige Ausgabe der Lieder – ohne jedoch ein Exemplar des dänischen Originals zu besitzen! So ließ Schumann Andersen durch die mit beiden befreundete Pianistin Amalie Rieffel um eine Ausgabe seiner Gedichte auf Dänisch bitten. Andersen wollte dann offensichtlich bei einem Aufenthalt in Leipzig im Juli 1841 den Schumanns einen Besuch abstatten, traf diese allerdings nicht zu Hause an.[6] Bevor op. 40 im Septem-

---

4 Jean-Jacques Nattiez, 'Can One Speak of Narrativity in Music?', *Journal of the Royal Musicological Association*, 115 (1990), 240–57, hier 245 (Übersetzung RM).

5 Zur Publikationsgeschichte von op. 40 vgl. Irmgard Knechtges-Obrecht, 'Die doppelte Wort-Text-Unterlegung bei vier Liedern aus Robert Schumanns Sammlung *Fünf Lieder für eine Singstimme und Pianoforte* op. 40 nach Texten von Hans Christian Andersen übersetzt durch Adelbert von Chamisso', *editio. Internationales Jahrbuch für Editionswissenschaft*, 16 (2002), 182–95.

6 Vgl. Robert Schumann, *Tagebücher Band II: 1836–1854*, hg. von Gerd Nauhaus (Leipzig, 1987), 176: "Am 9ten Juli trafen wir wieder in Leipzig ein und begrüßten unsere trauliche Wohnung mit

ber 1842 beim Kopenhagener Musikverlag Lose & Olsen erscheinen konnte, gab es jedoch noch etwas anderes zu klären: die Widmung. In dieser Sache kamen sich Schumann und Andersen nun bedeutend näher, wenn auch zunächst nur über die vermittelnde Tätigkeit Clara Schumanns, die Andersen im März 1842 auf einer Konzertreise in Kopenhagen traf.

Zwei Tage nachdem Clara Schumann ihrem Mann am 22. März 1842 in einem Brief von der Bekanntschaft mit Andersen berichtete – allerdings mit durchaus zwiespältigen Worten, bezeichnete sie ihn doch als den "hässlichste[n] Mann, den es nur geben kann", an dessen Wesen "man sich nur nach und nach gewöhnen"[7] könne – kam Schumann im ehelichen Briefwechsel der Widmungsfrage wegen selbst auf ihn zu sprechen: "Hast du Andersen kennen gelernt? Ich lese jetzt von ihm nur weil Du jetzt in Copenhagen bist. Er ist aber ein ganz vorzügliches Dichtertalent, so naiv, so klug, so kindisch".[8] An den im Deutschland der 1830er Jahre äußerst populären Dichter, der jedoch mit seinen heute vornehmlich einem Spezialistenpublikum bekannten Romanen (*Der Improvisator* 1835, *Nur ein Geiger* 1837) und Reiseberichten (*Schattenbilder von einer Reise in den Harz, die Sächsische Schweiz etc. etc. im Sommer 1831*) weitaus größere Erfolge feierte als mit den noch immer breit rezipierten *Märchen und Geschichten*,[9] trat Schumann schließlich am 1. Oktober 1842 im Zuge der Übersendung eines Widmungsexemplars von op. 40 schriftlich heran (siehe Abb. 1: Andersens Exemplar mit handschriftlicher Widmung Schumanns) – und zwar mit größter Empathie:

> Meine Frau hat mir so viel von Ihnen erzählt und ich habe mir Alles so haarklein berichten lassen, daß ich glaube, ich erkenne Sie, wenn ich Ihnen von ungefähr einmal begegne. Waren Sie mir doch schon aus Ihren Dichtungen bekannt, aus dem Improvisator, aus Ihren Mondscheingeschichten und aus Ihrem köstlichen Geiger ... Habe ich nun auch eine vollständige Uebersetzung Ihrer kleineren Gedichte. Da finden sich gewiß noch manche Perlen für den Musiker. Erhalte Sie der Himmel noch lange Ihren Freunden und Verehrern und erlauben Sie, daß ich mich diesen beizählen darf.[10]

Freuden. ... Sehr leid that es mir, den dänischen Dichter Andersen, der hier war u. an mich adressirt war, versäumt zu haben."

7 Brief vom 22.3.1842, zit. nach Clara Schumann und Robert Schumann, *Briefwechsel Band III: 1840–1851*, hg. von Eva Weissweiler (Basel, 2001), 1137. Ähnliche Worte findet Clara Schumann im gemeinsam mit ihrem Mann geführten Tagebuch: "Andersen besitzt ein poetisches, kindliches Gemüth, ist noch ziemlich jung, sehr hässlich aber, dabei furchtbar eitel und egoistisch – trotzdem mochte ich ihn gern, und war mir seine Bekanntschaft interessant und werth. Jedenfalls überwiegen seine Tugenden bei weitem seine Schwächen"; Schumann, *Tagebücher II*, 216.

8 Brief vom 24.3.1842, zit. nach Clara Schumann und Robert Schumann, *Briefwechsel III*, 1140f.

9 Dass Schumann Andersens Romane las, geht nicht nur aus seinem Brief an Andersen, sondern auch aus Eintragungen im Ehetagebuch hervor: "'Nur ein Geiger' v. Andersen mit großer Freude gelesen u. viel an Clara gedacht"; Schumann, *Tagebücher II*, 84.

10 Brief vom 1.10.1842, Original in der Königlichen Bibliothek Kopenhagen, zugänglich auf http://www2.kb.dk/elib/noder/hcamusik//martsviolerne/schumann_hca/. Publiziert in Hermann Erler, *Robert Schumanns Leben. Aus seinen Briefen geschildert* (Berlin, 1887), Bd. 1, 287f. Der gleiche Brief findet sich, im Wortlaut allerdings geringfügig abweichend, bei F. Gustav Jansen (Hg.), *Robert Schumann's Briefe. Neue Folge* (Leipzig, 1904), 221. Mit den "Mondscheingeschichten" ist höchstwahrscheinlich Andersens Miniaturensammlung *Bilderbuch ohne Bilder* (1839) gemeint, in welcher der Mond als Erzählfigur auftritt.

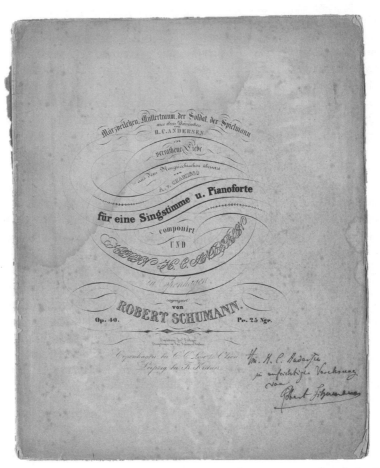

Abb. 1. Andersens Exemplar von Schumanns Lieder op. 40 mit handschriftlicher Widmung Schumanns (Det Kongelige Bibliotek, Kopenhagen).

Zu einem Zusammentreffen zwischen Schumann und Andersen kam es dann jedoch erst am 22. Juli 1844, als Andersen auf einer seiner zahlreichen Deutschlandreisen Leipzig besuchte und bei den Schumanns zu Gast an einem, wie er in seiner Autobiographie *Das Märchen meines Lebens* schrieb, "echt poetische[n] Abend"[11] war, bei dem Livia Frege begleitet von Clara Schumann die Andersen-Vertonungen vortrug. Bei dieser Gelegenheit muss Andersen auch von seinen Plänen für das Märchendrama *Die Glücksblume* berichtet haben, für dessen Komposition Schumann sich in einem Brief vom 25. Juli 1844 interessierte: "Ihre 'Glücksblume' verfolgt mich; es könnte eine schöne Zauberoper werden: ich wollte alle meine Kraft daran setzen".[12] Da Andersen Schumanns Bitte nach einer schriftlichen Handlungsskizze offensichtlich nicht

11 Hans Christian Andersen, *Das Märchen meines Lebens*, übers. von Thyra Dohrenburg (München, 1961), 314.
12 Brief vom 25.7.1844, zit. nach Erler, *Schumanns Leben*, Bd. 1, 313; Jansen, *Schumann's Briefe*, 242.

nachkam, wendete sich Schumann noch einmal im April 1845 in der Sache *Glücksblume* an ihn. Auch in diesem Brief fällt erneut der nahezu überschwängliche Sprachduktus auf: "Könnte ich Ihnen sonst etwas thun in Deutschland, so machen Sie mich zu Ihrem Secretair; mit Freuden wär ich's. Ihr Sie hochverehrender Robert Schumann".[13]

Selbst eingedenk aller üblichen Aufbietung von Höflichkeitsfloskeln in womöglich nicht ohne ökonomische Hinterinteressen zu verstehendem Schriftverkehr – schließlich war Andersen zur Zeit der Publikation von op. 40 ein populärer Name – fallen an Schumanns Briefen doch ihre rhetorisch nicht gerade tiefstaplerischen Wertschätzungs-bekundungen besonders auf. Bemerkenswert in diesem Zusammenhang ist vor allem, dass Schumann Andersens Texte (oder genauer gesagt: die Chamissoschen Übertragun-gen) im bereits erwähnten Brief vom Oktober 1842 konkret als Gegenstände versteht, die im Komponisten eine Form kreativer Reaktion evozieren – "Perlen für den Musi-ker" eben. Und auch sonst lässt Schumanns Wortwahl aufmerken (siehe Abb. 2):

Nehmen Sie denn meine Musik zu Ihren Gedichten freundlich auf. Sie wird Ihnen vielleicht im ersten Augenblicke sonderbar vorkommen. Ging es mir doch selbst erst mit Ihren Gedichten so! Wie ich mich aber mehr hineinlebte, nahm auch meine Musik einen immer fremdartigeren Character an. Also, an Ihnen liegt die Schuld allein. Ander-sen'sche Gedichte muß man anders componiren, als 'blühe liebes Veilchen'.[14]

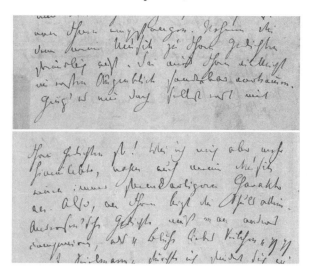

Abb. 2. Faksimile des Briefs von Schumann an Andersen vom 1. Oktober 1842 (Det Kongelige Bibliotek, Kopenhagen).

Sonderbar, fremdartig, anders – Schumann schreibt hier seiner Musik Attribute zu, bei denen der historisch-interpretativ ausgerichtete Musikwissenschafter hellhörig wird. Um herauszufinden, was in diesem Fall das Fremdartige in den Kompositionen

---

13 Brief vom 14.4.1845, zit. nach Erler, *Schumanns Leben*, 320; Jansen, *Schumann's Briefe*, 246.
14 Vgl. Fußnote 10, außerdem Erler, *Schumanns Leben*, 287; Jansen, *Schumann's Briefe*, 242.

Schumanns ist, muss jedoch zunächst der Umweg über eine andere Frage genommen werden: was ist denn überhaupt an Andersens Texten so anders?

Vergleicht man Andersens Märchen mit zeitlich parallelen Textphänomenen wie den Volksmärchen der Brüder Grimm oder der relativ neuen Gattung des romantischen "Kunstmärchens" mit ihren Exponenten Tieck und Brentano, so ist es insbesondere die zutiefst selbstreflexive Gestaltung der Andersenschen Texte, die sie so sonderbar erscheinen lässt. Ob es um Enten, Seejungfrauen oder redendes Spielzeug geht, fast immer ist Andersens Erzähltexten noch ein zusätzliches Thema eingeschrieben: das Erzählen selbst. Das Gros der *Märchen und Geschichten* bietet über die oft genug mit wunderbaren Requisiten und toposhaftem Personal ausgestattete Märchendiegese hinaus eine weitere Verständnisebene an, indem es ebenso als allegorische Verarbeitung verschiedenster Metathemen der künstlerisch-literarischen Produktion verstehbar ist. Andersens Geschichten sind in der Regel nicht nur poetisch gestaltete Handlungsberichte, sondern darüber hinaus auch Kommentare über ihre eigene Zuständlichkeit als verfasste und von einer ordnenden Erzählerinstanz durchwaltete poetische Erzeugnisse und über die Rahmenbedingungen, unter denen ihre Entstehung möglich wird – Beispiele werden folgen. Sollte es tatsächlich dieser selbstreflexive Grundzug sein, der Andersens Texte buchstäblich so "anders" macht, so stellt sich daraus resultierend natürlich eine weitere dringliche Frage: sind analoge Prozesse im musikalischen Werk ebenfalls denkbar?

Wenn nun vermehrt von Selbstreflexivität die Rede ist, so soll dieser Begriff hier nicht als ein feststehendes und schematisch anwendbares Verfahren begriffen werden, sondern vielmehr als ein Konglomerat von Techniken, mittels derer ein Text seinen Kunstcharakter, seine Fiktionalität und den kreativen Prozess, der zu seiner Erzeugung führte, offen zur Schau stellt. Der Produktionsverlauf wird somit, ganz im Sinne der von Andersen wie Schumann gleichermaßen indirekt rezipierten frühromantischen Kunsttheorie,[15] selbst zum Inhalt des ästhetischen Produktes. Es ist dies natürlich ein genuin literarisches Konzept, dessen Übertragung auf absolute Musik nicht ganz ohne Schwierigkeiten ablaufen kann, die sich durch den Metho-

---

15 Die These der 'indirekten Rezeption' frühromantischer Kunsttheorie ist im Falle Schumanns zwar gängig, wird aber durchaus nicht einhellig akzeptiert. Da bis dato Schumanns Lektüre programmatischer Theorieschriften der Frühromantik nicht nachzuweisen ist, wird ihr Einfluss vor allem an seiner ebenso begeisterten wie intensiven Rezeption der Erzähltexte Jean Pauls und E.T.A. Hoffmanns festgemacht, in denen sich zahlreiche theoretisch formulierte Ideen der zeitgenössischen Ästhetik umgesetzt finden – allen voran das prägende Postulat, romantische Poesie habe "das Produzierende mit dem Produkt" darzustellen, wie Schlegel im berühmten 238. Athenäums-Fragment schreibt (*Kritische Friedrich-Schlegel-Ausgabe. Band 2: Charakteristiken und Kritiken. Erster Teil*, hg. von Hans Eichner (München, 1967), 204). Vgl. dazu John Daverio, 'Schumann's "Im Legendenton" and Friedrich Schlegel's *Arabeske*', *19th Century Music*, 11/2 (1987), 150–63, hier 151 f.: "And although it cannot be shown that Schumann was directly influenced by the critical theories of Friedrich Schlegel, we can be sure that their artistic and intellectual dispositions revolved around the same spiritual center". Im Falle Andersens stellt sich die Situation ähnlich dar – seine frühe Begeisterung für die literarischen Texte Schlegels und Hofmanns ist ebenso nachzuweisen wie seine Beschäftigung mit ihren theoretischen Schriften Spekulation bleiben muss. Vgl. dazu Anna Harwell Celenza, *Hans Christian Andersen and Music. The Nightingale Revealed* (Aldershot, 2005), 24–26.

dentransfer auf ein grundlegend andersartiges, weil nichtreferentiell organisiertes Medium notgedrungen ergeben. Dennoch ist zu beobachten, dass in der Musik des 19. Jahrhunderts und insbesondere bei Schumann ein vergleichbares Phänomen anwächst, nämlich die Erzeugung einer Art "musikalischer Sollbruchstellen": merkwürdig aus dem Satzkontinuum herausfallende musikalische Ereignisse, die als Markierungen für das verstanden werden können, was Werner Wolf die "implizite musikalische Metareferenz"[16] nennt: ein im Medium der Musik latent angelegter Kommentar, ihre eigene Verbindlichkeit betreffend und von einem die Markierungen erkennenden Rezipienten zu dechiffrieren. Eine derartige Deutung kann sich vor allem auf die Beobachtung stützen, dass bei Schumann zunehmend Phänomene zu ästhetischen Leitkategorien werden, die in einer auf die Herstellung von Kontinuitäten und die Rekonstruktion von Prozessen der Vereinheitlichung bedachten Analyse bis heute notgedrungen zu kurz kommen: das Disparate, das Heterogene, die narrativ-strukturelle Inkonsequenz. Und genau darin liegt auch die Nähe zu Andersen, dessen "poetische Sprachmusik immer dissonant, unstimmig, gebrochen, zerrissen, gesprungen"[17] erscheint.

Ich möchte nun im Folgenden zwei Besonderheiten der Andersenschen Textorganisation aufzeigen und im Anschluss jeweils an einem Beispiel aus dem Werk Schumanns diskutieren, warum mir der Gedanke, dass beide trotz der medialen Differenz durchaus vergleichbaren Problemstellungen nachgehen, nicht allzu abwegig erscheint. Zu diesem Zweck soll dort begonnen werden, wo beide sich treffen: bei Schumanns *Fünf Liedern* op. 40.

DER VERDOPPELTE SPIELMANN

Die Thematisierung der Textentstehung und -erzeugung erfolgt in vielen der *Märchen und Geschichten* Andersens durch ein einfaches Spiegelverfahren auf Handlungsebene: oft sind die Protagonisten selbst Geschichtenerzähler und der Akt des Erzählens hat Relevanz für den Verlauf der Handlung oder ist sogar ihr recht eigentliches Thema. Beides ist der Fall im Märchen vom *Fliegenden Koffer*: der Protagonist muss sich durch die Erzählung einer besonders gelungenen Geschichte als Schwiegersohn beim Königspaar qualifizieren, was ihm dann mit einem poetologischen Märchen gelingt, in dem verschiedene Küchengeräte ein parodistisches Kunstgespräch miteinander führen. Durchaus vergleichbar ist in dieser Hinsicht *Der Schatten*, wo anhand der Hauptfigur, erneut ein Geschichtenerzähler, und seines sich verselbständigenden Schattens Probleme von Originalität und Plagiarismus verhandelt werden. In *Was man erfinden kann* geht es um Schwierigkeit der Lehr- und Lernbarkeit des Dichterberufs am Beispiel eines ideenlosen Studenten mit begrenzter Wahrnehmungsfähigkeit –

---

16 Werner Wolf, 'Metafiction and metamusic: Exploring the limits of metareference', in Winfried Nöth und Nina Bishara (Hg.), *Self-reference in the media* (Berlin, 2007), 303–24. Ebenfalls zugänglich auf www.wordmusicstudies.org/Wolf%20metamusic-2.pdf.

17 Heinrich Detering, 'Nachbemerkung', in Hans Christian Andersen, *Schräge Märchen*, hg. und übers. von Heinrich Detering (Frankfurt am Main, 1996), 314–18, hier 318.

allein der Einleitungssatz spricht hier Bände: "Es war ein junger Mann, der studierte Dichten und wollte bis Ostern fertig sein".[18] Das Thema Schreibblockade prägt das (schon in seinem Titel auf einen Sprechakt verweisende) Märchen *Die Irrlichter sind in der Stadt, sagte die Moorfrau* und Geschichten wie *Ole Lukøie* oder *Der Wind erzählt von Valdemar Daae und seinen Töchtern* entwerfen in ihren jeweiligen Rahmenhandlungen konkrete Bilder der Situationen, in denen sich der Erzählvorgang der Binnengeschichte ereignet. Ohnehin ist die verschachtelte Rahmenstruktur charakteristisch für Andersens Texte: zahlreiche Märchen sind nach dem Prinzip ineinandergreifender Binnen- und Rahmenerzählung gebaut. Zuweilen ist es nur ein einziger Satz, der darauf hinweist, dass die erzählte Geschichte von einer im Text präsenten Erzählsituation abgehoben erscheint und somit eine zweite Zeitebene eröffnet, wie wiederum der Schluss von *Was man erfinden kann* zeigt: "Wir haben es von der klugen Frau, sie weiß, was man erfinden kann".[19] Auch fingierte Schwierigkeiten der Textüberlieferung werden zuweilen durch den für romantische Erzählliteratur charakteristischen Trick der Herausgeberfiktion Anlass zu satirischen Kommentaren über das Literatursystem, so etwa zu Beginn von *Tante Zahnweh*: "Woher haben wir die Geschichte? Willst du es wissen? Wir haben sie aus der Tonne mit den alten Papieren. ... Oft ist im Eimer, was nicht im Eimer landen sollte".[20]

Solcherlei spielerisch den poetischen Illusionsanspruch destabilisierende Schreibverfahren bleiben jedoch nicht auf Andersens Erzählliteratur beschränkt: im von Schumann vertonten Gedicht vom *Spielmann* bedient er sich vergleichbarer Techniken. Was sich in den fünf Strophen vollzieht, ist nicht allein die Bewusstmachung der Konstruktion des lyrischen Äußerungsvorganges, sondern vielmehr das selbstreflexive Spiel mit dessen Zuschreibung zu einer Erzählerinstanz:

Der Spielmann	Spillemanden
Im Städtchen giebt es des Jubels viel,	I Landsbyen gaaer det saa lystigt til,
da halten sie Hochzeit mit Tanz und mit Spiel.	Der holdes et Bryllup med Dands og Spil.
Dem Fröhlichen blinket der Wein so roth,	Der drikkes Skaaler i Viin og Mjød,
die Braut nur gleicht dem getünchten Tod.	Men Bruden ligner en pyntet Død.
Ja todt für den den nicht sie vergisst,	Ja død hun er for sin Hjertenskjær.
der doch beim Fest nicht Bräutigam ist;	Thi han er ikke som Brudgom her,
da steht er inmitten der Gäste im Krug,	I Krogen staaer han med Sorgen sin,
und streichet die Geige lustig genug.	Og spiller saa lystigt paa Violin.
Er streichet die Geige, sein Haar ergraut,	Han spiller til Lokkerne blive ham graae,
es schwingen die Saiten gellend und laut,	han spiller saa Strængene briste maae,

18 Hans Christian Andersen, *Märchen und Geschichten*, hg. und übers. von Gisela Perlet (Reinbek bei Hamburg, 1998), Bd. 2, 266.

19 Ebd., 270.

20 Ebd., 294 f.

er drückt sie ans Herz und achtet es nicht,	til Violinen med Sorg og Gru,
ob auch sie in tausend Stücken zerbricht.	han trykker mod Hjertet reent i itu.

Es ist gar grausig, wenn einer so stirbt,	Det er saa tungt saa knusende tungt,
wenn jung sein Herz um Freude noch wirbt.	At døe mens Hjertet endnu er ungt!
Ich mag und will nicht länger es sehn!	Jeg mægter ei længer at see derpaa!
Das möchte den Kopf mir schwindelnd verdreh'n!	Jeg føler det gjennem mit Hoved gaae.

Wer heisst euch mit Fingern zeigen auf mich?	See Mændene holde ham fast i Favn –
O Gott bewahr' uns gnädiglich,	Men hvorfor nævne I mig ved Navn?
dass Keinen der Wahnsinn übermannt.	Vor Herre bevare Enhvers Forstand!
Bin selber ein armer Musikant.	Jeg selv er en fattig Spillemand.

Die ersten drei Strophen konfrontieren den Rezipienten mit einem ebenso trostlosen wie toposhaften Bajazzo-Bild: der arme Musikant, der bei der Hochzeit seiner verlorenen Braut zum Tanz aufspielen und gute Miene zum betrüblichen Spiel machen muss. Nach drei Strophen der distanzierten Schilderung dieses "Zerbrechens am Dienst" überrascht die artikulierte Teilnahme der lyrischen Sprechinstanz in Strophe 4. Wer immer sich hier auch zu Wort melden mag, erstaunlich ist, dass er mit den Worten "Ich mag und will nicht länger es seh'n!" plötzlich Partei gegen seine eigene Zuständigkeit ergreift – der "affektive Wechselstrom ... zwischen dem momentanen Hier des Vortrags und dem fernen Dort des vorgetragenen Wundergeschehens"[21] zerreißt unversehens. Bezeichnenderweise geschieht dies in direktem Anschluss an den letzten Vers der dritten Strophe, in dem ein intradiegetischer Illusionsbruch zwar nicht explizit vollzogen, aber doch zumindest angedeutet wird: die Gefahr der Zerstörung des Instruments des Spielmanns offenbart die Labilität des Klangs als primäres Medium zur Aufrechterhaltung der Illusion künstlerischer Versenkung und damit einhergehender persönlicher Unbeteiligtheit.

Der Bruch, der hier durch den Text geht, ist ebenso deutlich wie bedeutsam, denn das, was der Spielmann "lustig genug" auf der Geige zum Besten gibt, ist doch nur von ausgestellter und artifiziell erzeugter Lustigkeit, deren Kenntlichmachung als Täuschung sofort das Risiko der Zerstörung der ästhetischen Illusion heraufbeschwört, symbolisch dargestellt im Zerspringen des Instruments "in tausend Stücken". Die musikalisch vermittelte Emotion ist offenbar keine ehrliche und unverfälschte, sondern ebenso sehr den Gegebenheiten von Herstellung und Gemachtheit unterworfen wie der literarische Text.[22] Der Spielmann innerhalb des Rahmens zerbricht also die performative Vereinbarung zwischen sich und dem Publikum, was

---

21 Volker Klotz, *Das europäische Kunstmärchen. Fünfundzwanzig Kapitel seiner Geschichte von der Renaissance bis zur Moderne* (München, 2002), 246.

22 Das Motiv der technisch verfertigten und daher in der Täuschung perfekten, aber letztlich emotional nicht überzeugenden Kunst ist in vielen Texten Andersens aufzufinden, etwa in *Die Nachtigall*, wo ein mechanischer Vogel das als Sängerin am Königshof gehaltene echte Tier ersetzt und mit seinem perfekten, aber eben technisch hergestellten Klang zunächst die Sympathien des Publikums gewinnt. Eine ähnliche Situation liegt Andersens vielleicht berühmtestem Märchen zugrunde:

sich in der Struktur des Gedichts spiegelt, indem nun wiederum der rahmenbilden-
de Erzähler die ästhetische Illusion aufhebt und sich selber wertend zu Wort meldet:
"Es ist gar grausig, wenn einer so stirbt".[23] Doch die Quittung für dieses ostentative
Heraustreten aus der Vorspiegelung eines die Geschehnisse aus räumlicher wie zeit-
licher Ferne emotional distanziert wiedergebenden lyrischen Ichs folgt sogleich sei-
tens eines imaginären Publikums, das scheinbar seine eigenen Schlüsse gezogen
hat.[24] Die die Ereignisse ordnende und wiedergebende textinterne Erzählinstanz
gerät auf einmal unter Rechtfertigungsdruck und lässt der zunächst noch erstaunten
Reaktion auf die offensichtlich von mitkonzipierten Rezipienten vorgenommene
Gleichsetzung mit der geschilderten Figur ("Wer heisst euch mit Fingern zeigen auf
mich?" bzw. in der genaueren Übersetzung von Irmgard Knechtges-Obrecht "Warum nennt ihr mich beim Namen?")[25] das schlussendliche Eingeständnis "Bin selber
ein armer Musikant" folgen. Nach der dritten Strophe nimmt das Gedicht also einen
gewichtigen Richtungswechsel vor: nicht mehr das dargestellte, sondern vielmehr
das darstellende Subjekt steht im Zentrum der Aufmerksamkeit. Beide wegen der im
letzten Vers eingestandenen gemeinsamen Profession gleichzusetzen würde meines
Erachtens zu kurz greifen, vielmehr problematisiert Andersen in den letzten beiden
Strophen gezielt die Abgleichung von im Text vorhandener Erzählinstanz mit dem

in *Die Schneekönigin* unterliegt der kleine Kay dem Zauber der Titelfigur, zu dem u.a. gehört, dass er
die synthetische Künstlichkeit der Eiskristalle über die angebliche Unvollkommenheit naturhafter
Bildungen stellt: "'Siehst du, wie kunstvoll!' sagte Kay. 'Die [mikroskopisch vergrößerten Schnee-
flocken] sind viel interessanter als die wirklichen Blumen, und an denen ist kein einziger Fehler,
sie sind ganz akkurat, wenn sie nur nicht schmelzen'"; Andersen, *Märchen und Geschichten*, Bd. 1,
198. Vgl. zu diesem Motiv auch das Kapitel über Andersen in Torsten Voß, *Die Distanz der Kunst
und die Kälte der Formen* (München, 2007), 191–202.

23 Zwar ist es nicht üblich, im Rahmen einer Gedichtanalyse von einem Erzähler oder (wie es später
geschieht) einem Protagonisten zu sprechen, dennoch sehe ich die terminologische Problematik
hier durch die offenkundige Ähnlichkeit zu bereits geschilderten narrativen Verfahren in den Erzähltexten Andersen abgemildert.

24 Dass die Stimme eines mitkonstruierten Lesers im Text wirksam wird, ist ein häufig anzutreffen-
des Charakteristikum in Andersens Textorganisation. So postuliert auch der bereits zitierte Beginn
von *Tante Zahnweh* ("Woher haben wir die Geschichte? Willst du es wissen?") einen imaginären
und im Textvollzug mitzudenkenden Rezipienten, dessen Wissbegier es zu verdanken ist, dass die
Erzählung überhaupt ihren Lauf nimmt. Der Text ist somit in der Tat "polyphonic in a very tricky
way"; Jacob Bøggild, 'Framing the frame of H.C. Andersens *Auntie Toothache*', *Fabula. Zeitschrift
für Erzählforschung*, 46 (2005), 17–28, hier 19.

25 Tatsächlich ist dieser Vers im dänischen Text, den die Erstausgabe der zusätzlichen Absetzbarkeit
in Dänemark wegen parallel zur vertonten Übersetzung abdruckt, nicht enthalten, sondern durch
eine Verdopplung des vorletzten Verses ersetzt. Vgl. Knechtges-Obrecht, *Die doppelte Wort-Text-
Unterlegung*, 193: "Der Schreiber des dänischen Textes konnte im Entwurf Vers 18 nicht unterle-
gen, da Chamisso die letzte Strophe nur teilweise übernahm. Der dänische Vers 17 (= Die Männer
halten ihn fest umarmt) fällt bei ihm ganz weg, Vers 18 (= Warum nennt ihr mich beim Namen)
ist völlig frei ins Deutsche übersetzt. Durch Hinzufügen eigenen Textes erweitert Chamisso die
deutsche Version dann wieder auf vier Verse. Der Schreiber der dänischen Worte im Entwurf
entschloß sich daher, Vers 19 einfach zu wiederholen". Die Auslassung des signifikanten Verses in
der Druckversion der Erstausgabe ist also sicherlich eher durch die Probleme der nachträglichen
Unterlegung des dänischen Originaltextes zur primär vertonten deutschen Übersetzung zu erklären und lässt keine Rückschlüsse auf eine willentliche Streichung zu.

im Zentrum der poetischen Diegese stehenden Protagonisten – mithin vergleichbar dem Verhältnis von Autor und Werk, das gerade im Falle Andersens bis heute vornehmlich als eines der autobiographischen Sublimierung begriffen wird.[26] Das sprechende Subjekt ist zwar auch, wie zahlreiche zentrale Figuren in Andersens Texten, ein glückloser Musiker, aber die übereilte Ineinssetzung mit dem poetischen Protagonisten weist es eben doch entschieden zurück: "Oh Gott, bewahr uns gnädiglich, dass Keinen der Wahnsinn übermannt".[27] Ob es sich bei diesem Wahnsinn nun um denjenigen des liebeskranken Hochzeitsmusikers oder eher denjenigen des allzu schnell Rückschlüsse auf die Zusammenhänge zwischen den literarischen Vermittlungsinstanzen Erzähler und Autor ziehenden Rezipienten handelt, mag als gezielte Mehrdeutigkeit begriffen werden.

Schumann hat das vielleicht nicht unbedingt genauso gehört, aber er hat doch sicher bemerkt, dass an einer Stelle ein deutlicher Bruch durch den Text geht, denn die letzte Strophe seiner Vertonung ist ganz im Sinne der entsprechenden Briefstelle im Vergleich zum Vorangehenden tatsächlich "anders komponiert". Das Lied wird somit, wie John Daverio bemerkt hat, zur "Projektion des dissoziativen Zustands, der innerhalb des Gedichts zum Ausdruck kommt".[28] Schon die ersten drei Strophen demonstrieren die langsame Ablösung von der zunächst deutlich vorgestellten Strophenform. Das melodische Material der ersten Strophe ist regelmäßig viertaktig strukturiert und stets auf die Ausgangsphrase des ersten Verses (T. 4–8) rückbeziehbar, die Zwischenspiele des Klaviers jedoch funktionieren als retardierendes Moment, indem ihr Umfang stetig anwächst: jeweils zwei Takte zwischen dem ersten und zweiten sowie dem zweiten und dritten Vers, vier Takte zwischen dem dritten und vierten Vers, schließlich sechs Takte als Überleitung zur nächsten Strophe (siehe Notenbeispiel 1).

Im weiteren Verlauf trüben die fortwährenden Tonartwechsel ebenso wie die auf die Pausen verzichtende Melodieraffung in der dritten Strophe in zunehmendem Maße das Bild regelmäßiger Ausgewogenheit, das der Anfang des Stückes noch vermittelt haben

---

26 Vgl. beispielsweise Heinrich Detering, *Das offene Geheimnis. Zur literarischen Produktivität eines Tabus von Winckelmann bis zu Thomas Mann* (Göttingen, 1994).

27 Die Argumentation will keineswegs den Umstand außer Acht lassen, dass Schumann insbesondere an dieser Stelle eher Chamisso als Andersen vertont. Der sich über zwei Verse erstreckende Ausruf in der Übersetzung ist bei Andersen wesentlich geraffter und nüchterner im vorletzten Vers enthalten. Die wörtliche (aber leider deutlich sprödere) Übersetzung der Schlussstrophe wäre in etwa folgende: "Die Männer halten ihn fest umarmt –/Warum nennt ihr mich beim Namen?/Gott bewahre jeden vor seinem Verstand./Bin selber ein armer Spielmann". Schumann war sich der Freiheit der von ihm vertonten Übertragung offensichtlich bewusst, erwähnte er sie doch im Widmungsbrief an Andersen: "Im 'Spielmann' fürchte ich, findet sich ein Versehen, zu dem die Chamisso'sche, nicht ganz auf ihre Verse passende Uebersetzung Anlaß gab. Ich habe die Stelle auf S. 16 angezeichnet." (zit. nach Erler, *Schumanns Leben*, 287 f.). Tatsächlich stellt das in der Königlichen Bibliothek Kopenhagen vorliegende Widmungsexemplar unter Beweis, dass Schumann hier auf die genannte Stelle Bezug nimmt, beginnt seine Eintragung doch genau vier Takte vor T. 111 (Ausschnitt des Originals zugänglich auf http://www2.kb.dk/kb/dept/nbo/ma/nyhbre/jun05.htm).

28 John Daverio, *Robert Schumann. Herald of a "New Poetic Age"* (New York, 1997), 208. Übersetzung RM.

Notenbeispiel 1. *Der Spielmann*, T. 1–34.

mag. Der Wendepunkt ist dann jedoch in T. 111 mit der bezeichnenderweise zu früh einsetzenden und das Klavierzwischenspiel harsch unterbrechenden Fingerzeigfrage erreicht, die zudem auch noch *Wild* vorzutragen ist. Hier nimmt die Musik einen gänzlich anderen Charakter an, der Tonfall ändert sich auffällig, obwohl das melodische Ausgangsmaterial in Phrasenbau und charakteristischer Punktierung weiterhin präsent ist. Signifikant ist jedoch vor allem die unerwartete Gestaltung der Klavier-

Notenbeispiel 2. *Der Spielmann*, T. 111–34.

begleitung: die Textverse werden nun im Klavier nicht mehr mittels aus dem Melodie-
verlauf ableitbarer Einsprengsel, sondern vielmehr durch *pianissimo* zu spielende Fel-
der der harmonischen und bewegungstechnischen Stagnation miteinander verbunden,
wobei vor allem das über den eigentlich aus der Erfahrung des Vorangehenden heraus
erwarteten Harmoniewechsel durchgehaltene c-Moll in T. 125–31, das überdies auch
noch *ritardando* zu spielen ist, für eine deutliche Distanz zu den deskriptiven Strophen
1 bis 3 sorgt (siehe Notenbeispiel 2).[29]

29 Daverio hebt als Besonderheit dieser Stelle das plötzliche Umschlagen des poetischen Modus vom
   narrativen Bericht in der dritten Person zur lyrischen Bestandaufnahme der eigenen Befindlichkeit
   hervor: "Then, to articulate the wrenching shift in poetic mode during the final verses, the music
   abruptly switches into a prayerful tone when the speaker voices his entreaty for delivery from
   impeding insanity"; Daverio, *Robert Schumann*, 208.

Die elegischen Schlusstakte folgen dem für Schumanns Liedschaffen charakteristischen Prinzip des kommentierenden Klaviernachspiels[30] und verstärken nur das Gefühl der zunehmenden Entfernung vom Vorgeschehen, woran insbesondere der tonartlich unerwartete Beschluss in G-Dur massiven Anteil hat. Schumann komponiert hier keinen artikulierten Bruch, vielmehr erscheinen die wesentlichen Elemente, die zuvor das Stück geprägt haben, wie etwa der charakteristische punktierte Rhythmus im Klavier oder die Melodieführung der Singstimme, in der fünften Strophe zwar weiterhin, aber nurmehr noch in verzerrter Form. Die Musik ist zu sich selbst in Distanz getreten. Klangcharakter und Tonfall der ersten drei Strophen erscheinen so in einem zweifelhaften Licht, ihre Organisation in ihrer Tragfähigkeit in Frage gestellt – durchaus korrespondierend mit dem Verdacht der Unehrlichkeit, den der Text über die vom Spielmann dargebotene Musik nahe legt. Bausteine wie der Achtelrhythmus im Klavier wirken nun beliebig austauschbar und erscheinen somit in ihrer klangmalerischen Konkretion geschwächt. Schumann folgt Andersens Tendenz zur selbstreflexiven Infragestellung von Verbindlichkeiten im Vollzug des Textes, so dass seine Vertonung als Bewusstmachung des dem Stück einkomponierten ordnenden und verbindenden "ästhetischen Subjekts"[31] (Carl Dahlhaus) verstanden werden kann, das hier gleichsam an die klangliche Oberfläche tritt und sich als musikalisches Pendant zum auch bei Andersen häufig anzutreffenden *unreliable narrator* entpuppt.

Die Stimme aus dem Hintergrund

Andersen setzt jedoch noch weitere Mittel ein, um, wie es Jens Tismar formuliert, "den individuellen Erzähler in der Ansprache an Leser und Hörer stets [zu] vergegenwärtigen".[32] So ist es vor allem der seine Märchen und Erzählungen prägende Sprachstil der fingierten Mündlichkeit, über den die Erzählsituation nicht nur auf Handlungs- sondern auch auf Sprachebene immer wieder im Text repräsentiert wird. Oft durchbrechen rhetorische Fragen und Höranweisungen, Ausrufe und Wiederholungen die Kontinuität der Narration, Sätze enden nicht kongruent zu ihrem Beginn oder überlange Parenthesen drohen das Satzgefüge zu zerreißen. Als Beispiel mag der Anfang von *Ole Lukøie* dienen – wiederum ein Märchen, welches insbesondere das Erzählen von Märchen zum Inhalt hat: "Niemand auf der ganzen Welt weiß so viele Geschichten wie Ole Lukøie. Der kann wirklich erzählen! Wenn es Abend wird und die Kinder noch brav am Tisch sitzen ... ; dann öffnet er ganz sacht die Tür, und witsch! sprüht er den Kindern süße Milch in die Augen, ganz fein, ganz fein, aber immer noch so viel, dass sie die Augen nicht mehr aufhalten und ihn deshalb nicht sehen können".[33] Zudem wird, oftmals nur in Nebensätzen, immer wieder eine intradiegetisch konzipierte Zuhörerschaft angesprochen, wie beispiels-

---

30 Vgl. Beate Julia Perrey, Kap. 'The ironic glance back: The last postlude', in *Schumanns 'Dichterliebe' and Early Romantic Poetics. Fragmentations of Desire* (Cambridge, 2002), 208–21.
31 Carl Dahlhaus, *Ludwig van Beethoven und seine Zeit*, 3. Aufl. (Laaber, 1993), 61.
32 Jens Tismar, *Kunstmärchen*, 3. Aufl., erweitert von Mathias Mayer (Weimar, 1997), 108.
33 Andersen, *Märchen und Geschichten,* Bd. 1, 137.

weise im *Fliegenden Koffer,* wo es an einer Stelle heisst: "'Jawohl!' sagte der Kaufmannssohn und erzählte – und jetzt muß man gut zuhören!"[34] oder in *Das Feuerzeug*: "Der Schusterjunge wollte gern die vier Schillinge haben, stürzte davon, brachte dem Soldaten das Feuerzeug und – ja, jetzt werden wir hören!".[35] Zuweilen führt dies zu einem verwirrenden Wechselspiel zwischen nachzuvollziehender Erzählerstimme und mitzudenkenden Zuhörereinwürfen, wie beispielsweise der umständliche Beginn des Märchens *Eine gute Laune* zeigt: "Das beste Erbteil, das ich von meinem Vater habe, ist eine gute Laune. Und wer war mein Vater? Ja, mit der Laune hat das nichts zu tun. … Und was war sein Amt, seine Stellung in der Gesellschaft? Ja, wenn man das aufschreiben und gleich zu Anfang eines Buches drucken wollte, dann würden wohl mehrere Leser das Buch weglegen und sagen: 'Das sieht mir so unheimlich aus, davon will ich nichts wissen'. Und doch war mein Vater weder Schinder noch Scharfrichter … – er war Leichenwagenkutscher! Jetzt ist es heraus! … Siehst du, von ihm habe ich meine gute Laune".[36]

Was zunächst als schrullig-kindgezieltes Schreibidiom erscheinen mag, offenbart seine Relevanz im Blick auf Grundgegebenheiten der Gattung Kunstmärchen, die sich vor allem durch das "Moment des Gemachten"[37] vom sogenannten Volksmärchen der "Gattung Grimm"[38] (André Jolles) mit seinem "vermeintlichen 'Sichvonselbstmachen'"[39] abzuheben versucht: "Das Bewusstsein eines Abstands konstituiert das Kunstmärchen".[40] Dass in jedem schriftlich fixierten Märchen ein Akt subjektiver Erfindungskraft und keineswegs nur einer der Vermittlung eines als naturwüchsig gedachten Volksstoffes vorliegt, wird gerade durch die kaum überhörbaren und zuweilen (wie im Falle von *Tante Zahnweh*) nicht gerade verlässlichen Erzählerstimmen fast aller Andersen-Märchen immer wieder aufs Neue manifestiert. Im Text ist somit eine ordnende Instanz präsent, die stets darauf verweist, dass die präsentierte Fabel selbst im Falle einer der Verschriftlichung vorangehenden Überlieferungsgeschichte Konstruktion eines schöpferischen Subjekts und originäre Leistung eines Autors ist. Dazu äußert sich in bezeichnender Weise der Erzähler der äußerst knappen Rahmenhandlung des Märchens *Der Marionettenspieler*, dessen Schlussrahmung nach dem ausführlichen Bericht der Titelfigur aus einem einzigen Satz besteht: "Und ich, als sein Landsmann, erzähle es natürlich gleich weiter, *nur um zu erzählen*".[41]

In der Musikforschung sind der Problematik von Oralität und Schriftlichkeit analoge Fragestellungen insbesondere in der Diskussion um das Phänomen *Volks-* bzw. *Naturton* aufgekommen.[42] In der Schumann-Forschung ist dies bereits produktiv

---

34 Ebd., 132.

35 Ebd., 14.

36 Ebd., Bd. 2, 31.

37 Tismar, *Kunstmärchen*, 1.

38 Zit. nach Stefan Neuhaus, *Märchen* (Tübingen, 2005), 2.

39 Tismar, *Kunstmärchen*, 1.

40 Ebd., 2.

41 Andersen, *Märchen und Geschichten*, Bd. 2, 256. Hervorhebung RM.

42 Vgl. z.B. Hans Heinrich Eggebrecht, Kap. 'Naturlaute', in *Die Musik Gustav Mahlers* (München, 1982), 127–68.

diskutiert worden,[43] daher möchte ich einen anderen Weg wählen und zur Aus-
gangsfrage nach der Narrativität zurückkehren. Wie kann im musikalischen Text eine
vernehmbare Erzählerstimme präsent sein? Dieser Frage ist zu Beginn der 90er Jahre
die amerikanische Musikologin Carolyn Abbate nachgegangen und herausgekommen
ist ihr relativ bekanntes Buch *Unsung voices*, in dem sie für einige seltene Momente in
der Instrumentalmusik des 19. Jahrhunderts die Offenlegung und Hörbarmachung
eines das musikalische Material ordnenden und strukturierenden Kompositionssub-
jekts postuliert – einer Instanz, die für gewöhnlich versteckt und unhörbar operiert:
"Such moments seem like voices from elsewhere, speaking (singing) in a fashion we
recognize precisely because it is idiosyncratic. … A musical voice sounds unlike the
music that constitutes its encircling milieu. The narrative voice is defined not by
what it narrates, but rather by its audible flight from the continuum that embeds it.
That voice need not remain unheard, despite the fact that it is unsung".[44] Ich glau-
be, dass solche Momente in Schumanns Musik zwar durchaus nicht omnipräsent,
aber doch immer wieder und in allen Schaffensperioden aufzufinden sind. Als Beispiel mag, natürlich nicht grundlos gewählt, das zweite der vier *Märchenbilder für
Klavier und Viola* op. 113 von 1851 dienen. Der Aufbau der Komposition ist denkbar
einfach: ein rondoartiges Charakterstück in F-Dur mit zwei kontrastierenden Episoden in der Anordnung A – B – A – C – A – Coda, wobei sich in den Ritornellen so
gut wie gar keine Variation ereignet, sie sind vielmehr abgesehen von der unterschiedlichen harmonischen Gestaltung der Überleitungen identisch. Die Episoden B
(T. 51–70, im parallelen d-moll) und C (T. 119–42, in der Subdominanttonart B-Dur)
könnten jedoch uneinheitlicher kaum sein: ebenso offensichtlich wie der B-Teil ein
Musterbeispiel an periodischer Ausgewogenheit und Ebenmaß ist, läuft der C-Teil
aus dem Ruder. In Teil B ist alles quadratisch regulär und klar nachvollziehbar: die
Ausgeglichenheit der Melodieführung (zwei Takte sprunghafter Abstieg – zwei
Takte gradliniger Aufstieg), die dialogische Viertaktstruktur zwischen Klavier und
Bratsche, die mittelteilartige Zusammendrängung der Motive in T. 59–62 (siehe
Notenbeispiel 3).

Was aber geschieht in Teil C? Man könnte wohl sagen das genaue Gegenteil: die
offenkundig zuerst anklingende Absicht zur kanonischen Führung der beiden Instrumente erweist sich als problematisch in der Umsetzung. Die Imitation der Viola
steigt in T. 120 auf verschobener Taktzeit ein, zum Zielton in T. 125 fehlt der fundie-
rende Akkord, die in T. 119 exponierte Figur bleibt wirkungslos und zeitigt keine
Fortentwicklung mit der Ausnahme von fortwährenden sequenzierten Wiederholungen auf verschiedenen Stufen, in T. 132 lässt die Bratsche den Zielton aus, in T. 135
fehlt gleich die zweite Phrasenhälfte, woraufhin das Klavier die immerfort stur
perpetuierte Sechzehntelphrase wieder zu ihrer Ausgangsposition im Taktgefüge
zurückverschiebt. Als wäre die Verwirrung nicht schon groß genug setzt nun auch

---

43 Vgl. Helga de la Motte-Haber, Kap. 'Erfundene Natur', in *Musik und Natur. Naturanschauung
und musikalische Poetik* (Laaber, 2000), 160–98.
44 Carolyn Abbate, *Unsung Voices. Opera and Musical Narrative in the Nineteenth Century* (Princeton,
1991), 29.

Notenbeispiel 3. *Märchenbilder für Klavier und Viola*, op. 113, Nr. 2, T. 51–66.

noch eine überraschende Wiederholung ein, die den Binnensatz zum formsymmetrischen Kuckucksei werden lässt. Zusammen mit den Auftakten in T. 128 und T. 143 kommt der mit T. 129 ansetzende Teil nach dem Wiederholungszeichen stets auf den ungeraden Umfang von 15 Takten und die Reminiszenz an den Beginn des Abschnitts in T. 135, die sich eigentümlich mit den plötzlich abbrechenden Geschehnissen der vorangehenden Takte überlappt, kann ebenfalls nicht den Eindruck einer strukturschaffenden Rückführung zum Anfang des Formteils erzeugen, erst recht nicht in der Wiederholung, deren unmotiviertes Zurückspringen mitten in den Satzprozess keinerlei Zäsur schafft, sondern vielmehr die formale Konfusion nachhaltig verdoppelt (siehe Notenbeispiel 4).

Teil B und Teil C dieses *Märchenbildes* lassen ein grundlegendes musikalisches Gestaltungsprinzip – dasjenige der korrespondierenden Dialogführung zweier Instrumente nämlich – in denkbar unterschiedlichem Licht erscheinen. Hier tritt es geordnet und nachvollziehbar auf, dort chaotisch und verwirrend, als regelrechtes "Zuviel an Ereignis". Beide Ansätze aber scheinen durchaus gleichwertig veranschlagt zu sein, verletzen sie doch die Rahmenbildung durch die Ritornellteile

Notenbeispiel 4. *Märchenbilder für Klavier und Viola*, op. 113, Nr. 2, T. 119–43.

keineswegs – ganz anders als im *Spielmann*, wo die Musik nach dem entscheidenden Wendepunkt ein komplett anderes Gepräge annimmt. Man könnte – unter bewusster Eingestehung des metaphorischen Aktes, den man damit vornimmt – behaupten, hier werde eine ähnliche Geschichte auf zwei grundlegend unterschiedliche Arten erzählt. Die beiden Binnenepisoden der Komposition stehen dabei in einem Verhältnis der wechselseitigen immanenten Kritik zueinander. Sie lassen sich gegenseitig in kritischem Licht erscheinen, ohne dass jedoch eine von ihnen den Anspruch auf

größere "Richtigkeit" oder "Angemessenheit" dem Rahmen gegenüber erheben könnte – die Komposition bleibt vielmehr, ganz im Sinne der Romantischen Ironie, durch-
lässig für ein alternatives Sagen.[45] Schumann exponiert hier die verschiedenen Kon-
struktionsmöglichkeiten, die dem Komponisten in der Behandlung einer dialogisch
organisierten Passage zu Gebote stehen, offen vor dem Zuhörer. Die Gemachtheit
musikalischer Charaktere wird so der Wahrnehmung eines (wohlgemerkt durchaus
speziellen) Rezipienten gegenüber freigelegt, der erst dadurch, dass etwas aus der
Ordnung herausfällt, diese als eine konstruierte erkennen kann. Ebenso wie Andersens Texte wird Schumanns Musik oft so *anders* und *fremdartig*, weil sich eine ordnende Präsenz aus dem Hintergrund immer wieder zu erkennen gibt und so auf den
Akt der Verfertigung des Materials verweist. Mit Carolyn Abbate gesprochen, wird
"the sound of speaking one's art into being"[46] hörbar, indem die Anwesenheit eines
ansonsten unbemerkt operierenden diskursiven Subjekts klanglich enthüllt wird.
Wenn es, wie es Carl Dahlhaus formuliert hat, in der Musik nach Beethoven vornehmlich darum geht, "dass Komponist, Interpret und Publikum die Übereinkunft
treffen, 'Selbstausdruck' ... als ästhetisches Postulat anzuerkennen",[47] so findet sich
genau diese eben doch nicht immer so leicht vonstatten gehende Übereinkunft bei
Andersen wie Schumann im Hinblick auf ihre respektiven Medien problematisiert
und in den Text bzw. in die Komposition hineingespiegelt. Einen klar festzumachenden Inhalt transportiert die Erzählerstimme natürlich nicht, obwohl ich eine Idee
habe, was sie sagen könnte – vielleicht ja nichts anderes als *Ich erzähle – und jetzt
muss man gut zuhören!*

Summary

The text takes a closer look at the relationship between Robert Schumann and Hans Christian Andersen – two artists of the mid-nineteenth century, who shared mutual admiration for
each other. After summarizing how Schumann and Andersen got in contact through letters in
1842 and finally met in 1844, the article seeks to pin down structural relations between Andersen's texts and Schumann's compositional practice. Starting with a close examination of Andersen's poem *Der Spielmann* and the special way Schumann set it to music in his *Five Songs*
op. 40, and continuing with a comparison of techniques of framing in Andersen's fairy tales
as well as Schumanns *Märchenbilder* op. 113, it turns out that both the composer and the
writer share a common goal: the exposition of an aesthetic illusion through activation of the
reader-listener's awareness of its modes of construction within the work. Taking its clues from
textual procedures in Andersen's work and the way Schumann deals with them in his compositions, the article also argues for genuine modes of musical self-reflexivity.

45 Vgl. Heinz J. Dill, 'Romantic Irony in the Works of Robert Schumann', *The Musical Quarterly*,
   73/2 (1989), 172–95; Christine Moraal, 'Romantische Ironie in Robert Schumanns "Nachtstücken"
   op.23', *Archiv für Musikwissenschaft*, 54/1 (1997), 68–83.
46 Abbate, *Unsung Voices*, 56.
47 Dahlhaus, *Beethoven und seine Zeit*, 63.

'And Incidentally, the Score is Quite Beautiful'
– *Work conceptual reflections on the phonographic remediations of Max Steiner's symphonic film score for 'Gone with the Wind' (1939) as soundtrack album*

STEEN KAARGAARD NIELSEN

In 1954 RCA Victory released a 10" vinyl album entitled *The complete film music from 'Gone with the Wind'*, the first substantial phonographic release of music from Max Steiner's landmark score for David O. Selznick's film version of Margaret Mitchell's epic novel. When Max Steiner (1888–1971) had scored the movie in 1939 the hundreds of scores of predominantly symphonic underscoring produced annually by contract composers within the music departments of the Hollywood studio system were not considered a potential source of income away from the screen and were therefore only rarely recorded for commercial release. Thus before the beginning of the end of the studio system in the late 1940s, short selections from less than twenty re-recorded[1] scores were released as separate score albums, and only in 1949 the first American album with actual music track recordings from the original recording sessions for Miklos Rozsa's score for MGM's *Madame Bovary* was issued by the recently founded MGM Records.[2]

---

1 Throughout this article the terms 're-recorded' or 're-recording' refer to later studio re-recordings, and not the initial proces of recording music tracks for film use, also known as 're-recording' or 'dubbing'.

2 However, as *Gone with the Wind* was the most anticipated American film of the year, shortly before its premiere in December 1939 producer David O. Selznick approached Williams S. Paley, president of CBS, which included Columbia Records and other labels: 'The thought occurs to me that you might like to have one of your record companies get out one or more records of the musical score of *Gone with the Wind*. I know that under ordinary circumstances the musical score of a picture couldn't be expected to sell records, but everything in connection with *Gone with the Wind* is apparently attracting such unprecedented attention that this may be the exception. And incidentally, the score is quite beautiful'; quoted from Rudy Behlmer, 'The Saga of *Gone with the Wind*' [sleeve-note essay], *Original Motion Picture Soundtrack 'Gone with the Wind'* (TCM/Rhino R2 72269, 1996), 32. But nothing came of the suggestion. Four years later Max Steiner commented on the film producers' to him incomprehensible lack of interest in recording and publishing film music in the early film music periodical *Film Music Notes*: 'Conservatively speaking, at least one half of all the movie-goers in the country are musical minded. I get between two and three hundred letters a week from fans. And immediately a picture is released the studio gets requests from all over the country asking where recordings or the sheet music can be purchased. Yet neither the studios nor the exhibitors are doing much to take advantage of the fans' interests'; quoted from Bill Wrobel, *Film Score Blogs*, http://www.filmscorerundowns.net/blogs/32.html, accessed on 18 February 2008. Apart from a few recordings of popular arrangements of the Tara theme issued in the late 40s and early 50s (cf. Table 1), the *Gone with the Wind* score went unrecorded until 1954.

However, in the wake of the phenomenal popularity of Dmitri Tiomkin's folk-style ballad 'Do not forsake me, oh my darling' written for *High Noon* in 1952, one of the early consequences of the radical and financially challenging re-structuring of the American film industry in the 50s was a producer-led demand for scores with a prominent title theme or song that had obvious promotional and commercial potential. At the same time a new generation of often free-lance film composers better attuned to and more sympathetic towards new developments within popular music and jazz (or even contemporary art music) caused an explosion in the stylistic diversification of film scoring that brought an end to the so-called golden age of symphonic film scoring while adding to the profitability of film music as a phonographic product. 'Good old-fashioned' symphonic scores would still be part of the stylistic palette, in particular lending grandeur to the prestigious wide-screen epic dramas (usually biblical or historical) with which the major studios tried to counter the invading success of television throughout the 50s and well into the 60s. By the mid-50s the new extended and long playing formats (EP and LP) introduced by Columbia in 1948 were becoming more regular vehicles for film scores to serve as a promotional tool for the latest studio productions.

The 1954 *Gone with the Wind* album was emblematic of this development. Although an anomaly, dedicated as it was to a fifteen-year old film score, the album was produced to coinside with another theatrical re-release of the still phenomenally successful film in June 1954, and thus fit the bill as a topical soundtrack album, reflecting the birth of a new phonographic album genre: the soundtrack album.

In this article I want to explore this coming together of the traditional American symphonic background score and the phonographic album format, primarily to discuss the work-conceptual themes at play in the various strategies of remediation that inform the re-conceptualizations of the symphonic film score as a phonographic product from the early formation of the soundtrack album in the 1950s and onward. I shall focus on soundtrack albums devoted to only one score to highlight how the initial 'fit' between the newly introduced LP formats (later the CD) and the film score became and has remained a key work representation for an essentially unpublished musical genre. To serve as an exemplary but also somewhat unique illustration throughout the article I have chosen the numerous phonographic mediations of Max Steiner's monumental three-hour score for *Gone with the Wind* released as albums between 1954 and 1996 (cf. Table 1, pp. 54-55); it is through this recurring prism that I pursue the historically evolving character of this soundtrack sub-genre.[3]

---

3 For a general outline of the history of soundtrack recordings, see Jon Burlington, *Sound and Vision. Sixty Years of Motion Picture Soundtracks* (New York, 2000), 1–32. An elaborate treatment of the classical Hollywood film score can be found in Kathryn Kalinak, *Settling the Score. Music and the Classical Hollywood Film* (Madison, 1992) and in Royal S. Brown, *Overtones and Undertones. Reading Film Music* (Berkeley, 1994).

BRIEF REMARKS ON THE WORK AS CONCEPTUAL CONSTRUCT, THE FILM SCORE AND THE PHONOGRAPH RECORD

Within Western musical culture the conceptual construct of the musical work is primarily associated with the tradition of so-called art music and has been extensively theorized in relation to that empirical framework.[4] To conjure up some of the most common notions associated with the idea of 'the work' and thus provide a theoretical frame of reference for my reflections on the work-conceptual re-conceptualization of the symphonic film score, I turn to David Horn's article 'Some Thoughts on the Work in Popular Music'. Before discussing the concept in relation to popular music, he outlines nine interrelated senses or shades of meaning attached to the term in Western aesthetic discourse. The following quotation amounts to a somewhat condensed version of Horn's listing:

1. The PIECE of music: the discrete, identifiable musical object.
2. A piece of music with its own IDENTITY, or … 'character'.
3. An ACHIEVEMENT, the outcome of endeavour.
4. The endeavour is that of an identifiable AUTHOR, or of a collaboration between authors. … The author has shown CREATIVITY, and the result of that creativity lends AUTHORITY to both the piece and its author.
5. As the end product of an often individual-centred creative process with its own identity, the work can be said to have ORIGINALITY.
6. Originality in its turn bequeaths two things. The first is the potential to obtain STATUS or rank. … One feature of the ranking system is the practice of CANONIZATION.
7. The second gift of being considered original is that works … may be thought … to exude a hard-to-define sense of artistic sanctity, the phenomenon that Walter Benjamin termed the AURA.
8. At the same time, in the everyday world where music is a means of making a living, a work is a piece of PROPERTY.
9. In order to ensure that the individuality of the musical work, both as a property and as artistic expression, can always be recognised, the work's existence incorporates some form of BLUEPRINT or template for performance.[5]

Although hardly exhaustive, as Horn himself is careful to point out, this pragmatic mosaic does suggest a wealth of themes and debates to be pursued when exploring

---

4   For a key contribution to an exploration of the historical genesis of the musical work-concept, see Lydia Goehr, *The Imaginary Museum of Musical Works: An Essay in the Philosophy of Music* (Oxford, 1992). In a more recent symposium anthology, Michael Talbot (ed.), *The Musical Work: Reality or Invention?* (Liverpool, 2000), the work-concept is the subject of various thematic approaches in relation to a variety of also contemporary empirical contexts.

5   David Horn, 'Some Thoughts on the Work in Popular Music', in Talbot (ed.), *The Musical Work: Reality or Invention?*, 18–19. Emphasized words are retained from the original.

Table 1. Chronological listing of major commercial soundtrack albums of Max Steiner's score for *Gone with the Wind*.

YEAR	FILM	ORIGINAL MGM MUSIC TRACK RECORDINGS (*) AND VARIOUS RE-RECORDINGS
1939	US premiere 15 December	
1947	US theatrical re-release 21 August	*Gone with the Wind,* Themes [side A only] Al Goodman and His Orchestra Victor 28-0419, 12" Recorded 30 September. Side B: 'Fantasia Mexicana' from MGM film *Fiesta* based on Copland's *El Salon Mexico*. Tracks re-released in 1951 as part of album *Theme Music from Great Motion Pictures* (RCA Victor LPT 1008).
1952		*Love Themes from the Motion Pictures* Victor Young and His Orchestra Decca DL-5413, 10" LP album Album includes track 'Theme from MGM Picture *Gone with the Wind*'. Another popular arrangement of the Tara theme.
1954	US theatrical re-release 3 June	*The Complete Film Music from 'Gone with the Wind'* *Composed and conducted by Max Steiner with Symphonic Orchestra under the direction of the composer* Max Steiner/studio orchestra RCA Victor LPM-3227, 10" LP album Obviously not the complete score, but a symphonic suite arrangement conceived by the composer in 1943 for a New York concert at Lewisohn Stadium. Recorded in June 1954.
1959		*Music from 'Gone with the Wind'* *Commemorates 20th anniversary of the world's most popular motion picture* Muir Mathieson/Sinfonia of London Warner Bros. WS-1322, LP album First stereo recording of music from *Gone with the Wind* based on Steiner's published 1943 symphonic suite.
1961	US theatrical re-release 10 March	*Music from the Soundtrack of the Warner Bros. Motion Picture Parrish* *Composed and conducted by Max Steiner with the Warner Bros. Orchestra* Max Steiner/Warner Bros. Orchestra Warner Bros. WS-1413, LP album Album includes track 'Tara's Theme', a popular arrangement with pianist George Greeley as soloist.
		* *The Music from the MGM Motion Picture Release 'Gone with the Wind'* *Commemorating the Civil War Centennial* Cyril Ornadel and Starlight Symphony MGM SE-3954, LP album This the first MGM album with music from *Gone with the Wind* is a typical 'themes' album with new arrangements and orchestrations.
		'Gone with the Wind' The Authentic Original Score Recording *Composed and authorized by Max Steiner* *The Only Official Centennial Full Range Recording* Muir Mathieson/Sinfonia of London Warner Bros. WS-1322, LP album Re-release of the 1959 album with identical catalogue number. Usually referred to as first release.

1967	US theatrical re-release ('widescreen') 10 October	*A Spectacular New Recording [of] Max Steiner's Complete Original Score 'Gone with the Wind'* Walter Stott/London Symphonia Orchestra Pickwick SPC-3087 (UK release), LP album Another recording of Steiner's 1943 symphonic suite.
		* *'Gone with the Wind'. The Original Sound Track Album* *Music composed and conducted by Max Steiner* Max Steiner/MGM Studio Orchestra MGM S1E-10, LP album First release of selection of original MGM music track recordings recorded November and December 1939. Electronically re-channelled for stereo effect.
1974	US theatrical re-release 18 September	*Max Steiner's Classic Film Score 'Gone with the Wind'* *New Expanded Version Authorized by the Composer which includes music* *never before recorded* Charles Gerhardt/National Philharmonic Orchestra RCA Victor ARL1-0452, LP album A revised and expanded version of Steiner's 1943 symphonic suite arranged in consultation with the composer. This version includes several at the time 'unreleased' original music cues. Gerhardt had already recorded a shortened and re-sequenced version of Steiner's suite in the late 1960s with the National Philharmonic Orchestra released as part of Reader's Digest 4 LP box-set *Great Music from the Movies*. The only album in RCA's influential *Classic Film Scores* album series dedicated exclusively to one score.
1976	US network television debut on NBC, 7–8 November	
1983		* *'Gone with the Wind'. Music from the Original Motion Picture* *Soundtrack As Monophonically Recorded in 1939* *Music composed and conducted by Max Steiner* Max Steiner/MGM Studio Orchestra Polydor 817 116-2, CD First official mono release of (expanded) selection of MGM music track recordings.
1989	US theatrical re-release 3 February	
1990		* *'Gone with the Wind' Original MGM Soundtrack* Max Steiner/MGM Studio Orchestra CBS Special Product AK 45438, CD This expanded album includes three 'scenes' drawn from the composite soundtrack, thus including dialogue and sound effects: 'Scarlett returns to Tara', 'Melanie's death' and 'Finale'. Only album to include 'Overture' and 'Exit music'.
1996		* *Original Motion Picture Soundtrack 'Gone with the Wind'* *Music composed and conducted by Max Steiner* Max Steiner/MGM Studio Orchestra TCM/Rhino R2 72269, 2CD First close to complete release of the original MGM music track recordings, including a selection of extended versions and other recorded cues not used in the final film.
1998	Latest US theatrical re-release, 26 June	

the status and/or effect of the work-concept in other musico-cultural contexts than that of art music. In his discussion of its apparently much more ambiguous and debatable presence in popular music culture, Horn nevertheless singles out the phonograph record as a musical artefact that can be associated with most of the work-conceptual aspects outlined above, even if it is to be regarded not itself a piece, but the bearer of one. Thus it can

- possess identity
- be seen as a completed achievement
- become part of a canon
- acquire auratic qualities; and
- certainly, be exploited as property.[6]

Unlike the record the symphonic film score in its 'original' form is traditionally viewed as a poor contender for appreciation as a discrete object, the most fundamental work-conceptual requirement, for at least two reasons:

1. The music is basically conceived as a functional adjunct, and at that the very last element to be added to a film.
2. The intermittent nature of the score lends it a fragmentary on–off character. In addition to a functional musical framing of the film (main title and end title),[7] the score is made up from a series of separate elements, discrete music cues preventing an overall structural coherence and integrity.[8]

These work-conceptual 'defects' may partially account for the general exclusion of film music within traditional musicology despite the fact that the practice of symphonic underscoring can be viewed as a direct outgrowth of the post-Romantic tradition of Richard Strauss and Gustav Mahler. Given the Viennese origins of early Hollywood film composers like Max Steiner and Erich Wolfgang Korngold and the European backgrounds of Franz Waxman, Dmitri Tiomkin and Miklos Rozsa it only makes good sense that it was through American film production and distribution that the late-tonal musical idiom would achieve its widest dissemination and remain a vital and popular musical style throughout the twentieth century.

It is the historical fusion in the soundtrack album of the problematic (i.e. integrated and fragmented) symphonic film score with the work-conceptually alluring

---

6 Ibid. 33.
7 Especially in connection with more prestigious productions, the traditional film score may even include a meta-framing of the film in the form of an overture and exit music, plus intermission and entr'acte music in the case of double-length films.
8 The employment of an overall tonal design, which is not unknown in traditional film scoring, may be viewed as an attempt to secure a structural score coherence, symbolic rather than functional in nature. For a discussion and exemplification of this topic, see David Neumeyer and James Buhler, 'Analytical and Interpretive Approaches to Film Music (I): Analysing the Music', in K.J. Donnelly (ed.), *Film Music. Critical Approaches* (Edinburgh, 2001), 26–36.

artefact of the new long-playing phonograph record that provide the starting point for the following exploration of the various strategies of remediation that have affected our view of the film score as a musical work for more than half a century.

TOWARDS A PHONOGRAPHIC AUTONOMIZATION OF THE FILM SCORE: THE RE-RECORDED SOUNDTRACK ALBUM

In a 1943 interview for the early film music periodical *Film Music Notes*, Max Steiner touched upon the potential of film music scores as concert music, here paraphrased by the interviewer:

> Mr. Steiner believes that much of the music being written for background scores could, if it had the opportunity to do so, 'stand alone' — in other words, that it has merit as 'pure' music. Eventually, he hopes that music publishers will recognize this, and make the best of it available for concert hall performance.[9]

That same year Steiner arranged a concert suite from the *Gone with the Wind* score for a New York concert. According to film historian Rudy Behlmer,[10] it is this 30-minute concert suite that Max Steiner recorded when given the opportunity by RCA Victor in 1954 in conjunction with the first theatrical re-release of the film since the introduction of the LP format. Thus this initial attempt to elevate this particular film score from its integrated and subordinate position in the soundtrack hierarchy through phonographic remediation and thereby liberate it from its formal and narrative functions within an audio-visual whole – its original *raison d'être* – was no more than the reproduction of a score re-conceptualization already realized for the concert hall, neatly fitted to the LP format by dividing the suite into two parts of equal length.

Considering the classical background of this Austrian-born composer the use of the concert suite as a formal template was of course an obvious choice. This pragmatic form had become a conventional vehicle for the recycling and autonomization of other primarily stage-related music genres like ballet, incidental music, and even opera, and had also already been used by other Western (film) composers, like Florent Schmitt (*Trois Suites d'Orchestres*, op. 76 (1925) based on his *Salammbô* score), Hanns Eisler (several orchestral suites, including *Suite Nr. 3*, op. 26 (1932) culled from *Kuhle Wampe*) and Erich Wolfgang Korngold (*The Adventures of Robin Hood* (1938), based on the score for the Errol Flynn swashbuckler).

As raw material for his concert suite Steiner selected a number of individual music cues that only necessitated minimal re-arrangement to combine them into an almost unbroken flow of music, not unlike a symphonic poem. This strategy fitted his extremely flexible and fluent composition style – the result of his early formal training at the Imperial Academy of Music in Vienna – that he exploited in his overall approach

---

9 Quoted from Wrobel, *Film Score Blogs* (accessed on 18 Feb. 2008). The name of the interviewer is not given.
10 Rudy Behlmer, untitled sleeve-note essay, *Max Steiner's Classic Film Score 'Gone with the Wind'* (RCA Victor GD80452, 1990), 11.

to film scoring characterized by close synchronization (so-called 'mickey-mousing').[11] At the same time he was obviously careful to give prominence to more 'static' mood cues that dwelled on key leitmotifs, whether for characters (Melanie, Belle Watling), love relationships (Ashley and Melanie, Ashley and Scarlett) or places (Tara). Considering his approach to the scoring process, which he always initiated by composing leitmotifs and other thematic material on which to base the temporally constricted 'close-scoring' of single cues, it is likely that he regarded the leitmotivic 'raw material' as such (and not its actual cue setting) as key work-defining elements conceived in an atmosphere of relative creative freedom and therefore of particular importance when 'distilling' the score. In this light the rather ludicrous title given the LP album, *The complete film music from 'Gone with the Wind'*, could almost begin to make sense.

Viewed as a formal whole the sequencing of cues can be read as a balancing act between two different objectives: on the one hand the suite seems conceived as an autonomous musical work entity with a structural integrity of its own that conforms to the well-established suite convention of inter-movement variety; and on the other the selection and sequencing of cues act as a reflection of the overall narrative progression of the film. However, as the criss-crossing of lines in Table 2 shows, Steiner's construction of a musical narrative is not necessarily dictated by the original placement of individual cues within the filmic context. By sometimes using 'just' their thematic content or general character as a guideline for assembling the musical narrative,[12] Steiner was more free to work out a 'meaningful' musical combination of single cues. The cues selected were renamed to provide an additional discursive anchoring of the unfolding story, although these titles are actually quite difficult to match exactly to individual cues in the mostly unbroken flow of music.[13] Apart from referring to characters, locations, events, and actions, two of the titles refer directly to the leitmotivic character of the music itself ('Melanie's Theme' and 'Bonnie's Theme').[14] The overall framing of the suite by the fanfarish overture character of

11 For a contemporary and richly detailed account of his approach to film scoring in the early days of Hollywood sound film production, see Steiner's own description written a year before his work on *Gone with the Wind*, in Max Steiner, 'Scoring the Film', in Nancy Naumburg (ed.), *We Make the Movies* (London, 1938), 216–38.

12 For instance, the use of a musical cue for 'Bonnie's Death' originally written to underscore Scarlett's discovery of her mother's death on her return to Tara during the Civil War. This cue was actually discarded and not used in the film, and thus essentially an 'unheard' cue.

13 The two sides of the 1954 album is not divided into single tracks corresponding to the cue titles given (perhaps retained from the original concert suite). However, a pairing of titles and timings is attempted in Table 2. In the expanded 1974 recording of the suite the original music cue titles are used according to Rude Behlmer's notes. However, a comparison to the music cue titles given by the same writer in the complete 1996 soundtrack album results in only a partial match, which only adds to the confusion. The present author has not had the opportunity to check the music cue titles against Max Steiner's original manuscripts.

14 The widespread use of the term 'theme' (e.g. 'Tara's Theme' or 'Love Theme') in track titles on film music albums is an early genre convention. Compilations of popular arrangements of film themes was undoubtedly the most popular type of film music album throughout the 1950s and 1960s. Cyril Ornadel's *Gone with the Wind* album from 1961, the first official MGM release of music from the film, is a heavily re-arranged theme album, cf. Table 1.

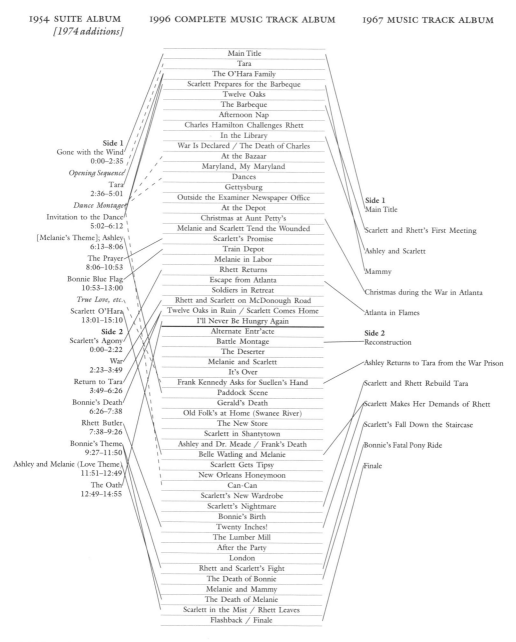

1954 SUITE ALBUM *[1974 additions]*	1996 COMPLETE MUSIC TRACK ALBUM	1967 MUSIC TRACK ALBUM
	Main Title	
	Tara	
	The O'Hara Family	
	Scarlett Prepares for the Barbeque	
	Twelve Oaks	
	The Barbeque	
	Afternoon Nap	
	Charles Hamilton Challenges Rhett	
	In the Library	
Side 1 Gone with the Wind 0:00–2:35	War Is Declared / The Death of Charles	
	At the Bazaar	
Opening Sequence	Maryland, My Maryland	
Tara 2:36–5:01	Dances	
	Gettysburg	
Dance Montage	Outside the Examiner Newspaper Office	**Side 1** Main Title
Invitation to the Dance 5:02–6:12	At the Depot	
	Christmas at Aunt Petty's	Scarlett and Rhett's First Meeting
[Melanie's Theme]; Ashley 6:13–8:06	Melanie and Scarlett Tend the Wounded	Ashley and Scarlett
	Scarlett's Promise	
The Prayer 8:06–10:53	Train Depot	Mammy
	Melanie in Labor	
Bonnie Blue Flag 10:53–13:00	Rhett Returns	Christmas during the War in Atlanta
	Escape from Atlanta	
True Love, etc.	Soldiers in Retreat	
Scarlett O'Hara 13:01–15:10	Rhett and Scarlett on McDonough Road	Atlanta in Flames
	Twelve Oaks in Ruin / Scarlett Comes Home	
	I'll Never Be Hungry Again	
Side 2 Scarlett's Agony 0:00–2:22	Alternate Entr'acte	**Side 2** Reconstruction
	Battle Montage	
War 2:23–3:49	The Deserter	
	Melanie and Scarlett	Ashley Returns to Tara from the War Prison
Return to Tara 3:49–6:26	It's Over	
	Frank Kennedy Asks for Suellen's Hand	Scarlett and Rhett Rebuild Tara
Bonnie's Death 6:26–7:38	Paddock Scene	
	Gerald's Death	Scarlett Makes Her Demands of Rhett
Rhett Butler 7:38–9:26	Old Folk's at Home (Swanee River)	
	The New Store	Scarlett's Fall Down the Staircase
Bonnie's Theme 9:27–11:50	Scarlett in Shantytown	
	Ashley and Dr. Meade / Frank's Death	Bonnie's Fatal Pony Ride
	Belle Watling and Melanie	
Ashley and Melanie (Love Theme) 11:51–12:49	Scarlett Gets Tipsy	Finale
	New Orleans Honeymoon	
The Oath 12:49–14:55	Can-Can	
	Scarlett's New Wardrobe	
	Scarlett's Nightmare	
	Bonnie's Birth	
	Twenty Inches!	
	The Lumber Mill	
	After the Party	
	London	
	Rhett and Scarlett's Fight	
	The Death of Bonnie	
	Melanie and Mammy	
	The Death of Melanie	
	Scarlett in the Mist / Rhett Leaves	
	Flashback / Finale	

Table 2. A comparison of cue selection and programming between two key *Gone with the Wind* soundtrack albums, the 1954 suite album and the 1967 music track album. For want of a complete music cue sheet, the strictly chronologically programmed track titles of the close to complete 1996 music track album is used as a convenient frame of reference. The three track titles in italics indicate the additions to the suite on the 1974 album.

the opening main title cue ('Gone with the Wind') and the finale character of the concluding grandiose cue ('The Oath') that ends the first part of the film, works as a conventional structural and narrative device and thus satisfies both objectives.

In its phonographic version the linking of the suite to the film was stressed by the use of back cover notes and a promotional film still of Scarlett and Rhett on the album front cover, no doubt dictated by the commercial interests of the producers (perhaps shared by the composer) in making this tie-in product an even more attractive souvenir of the film experience. But viewed as a separate work representation this marriage of the LP album format to an at least semi-autonomously conceived distillation of a single film score also resulted in a work-conceptual 'enhancement' that fulfilled the composer's desire to see his music stand on its own as 'pure' music. Over the next twenty years this suite would be re-recorded several times by various conductors and orchestras, often coinciding with the regular and always successful theatrical re-releases of the film, only adding to its status as an authoritative work representation.

Apart from the suite being arranged by the composer himself, another factor lent authority to this phonographic re-recording. To quote the strangely tautologically phrased cover announcement: 'Composed and conducted by Max Steiner with Symphonic Orchestra under the direction of the composer'. To a far higher degree than the cult of the composer-conductor within art music culture – Igor Stravinsky and Benjamin Britten are revered examples – the composer-conductor bestowing interpretational authority on his or her own work on the recording stage is a pivotal figure in American film music, a practice convention going back to the pioneering years of sound film scoring within the studio system and including most of the later canonized film composers of the golden age like Max Steiner, Alfred Newman, Erich Wolfgang Korngold, Dmitri Tiomkin, Franz Waxman, Miklos Rozsa and Bernhard Herrmann.[15]

Later re-recordings by other conductors can buy into this in the course of time still stronger aura of authenticity by adhering to original arrangements and join the ranks of canonized recordings by achieving the seal of approval from the (supervising) composer as announced on two of the later re-recordings of the *Gone with the Wind* suite (cf. Table 1): the first album is the first stereo recording of Steiner's suite from 1959 conducted by Muir Mathieson, an absolute key figure within British film music. When re-issued in 1961 the title read: *'Gone with the Wind'. The Authentic Original Score Recording. Composed and authorized by Max Steiner* and the back sleeve-notes read in part: 'According to no less critical an authority than Steiner himself, Mathieson gave the *Gone with the Wind* score a reading such as Steiner never dreamed possible. "It was a completely beautiful performance", says Steiner. "The Sinfonia orchestra is just fantastic. It's magic!"'.[16] The second album is a seminal 1974 record-

---

15 Quite unlike the mostly unsung orchestrators, of which no less than five worked on *Gone with the Wind*: Hugo Friedhofer, Maurice de Packh, Bernhard Kaun, Adolph Deutsch, and Reginald Bassett. According to Rudy Behlmer, because of time pressure, Hugo Friedhofer, Adolph Deutsch, and Heinz Roemheld actually contributed a small amount of material composed in the manner of Max Steiner; Behlmer, 'The Saga of *Gone with the Wind*', 29.

16 Max Steiner, *'Gone with the Wind'. The Authentic Original Score Recording* (Warner Bros. WS-1322, 1961).

ing of the suite in a 'New Expanded Version Authorized by the Composer'.[17] Before Steiner's death in December 1971 conductor Charles Gerhardt had met with the composer on three occasions to discuss the concept of a new recording. In the words of Rudy Behlmer from the original sleeve-note essay:

> At their last two meetings on *Gone with the Wind* Gerhardt proposed another dream: a new expanded version [of the 1943 suite], which would include all of the themes [the composer] wrote for the picture. Recording the entire score Steiner felt would be totally impractical and unmusical because some of the melodies occur in incomplete or rearranged ways – sometimes as often as 20 times during the picture – and he saw no need for this repetition. The new version eventually worked out with Mr. Steiner contains, in the composer's preferred settings, all of the major thematic material he wrote for the film and it is performed by the same size orchestra as that used for the film rather than the somewhat reduced orchestra used in earlier recordings. The objective was to offer a longer, more inclusive and permanent memento of the original film that would stand on its own and to present a substantial work in the form of a one-movement symphony or symphonic poem based on the music from *Gone with the Wind*.[18]

In this paraphrase all the work-conceptual themes outlined above are obviously rehearsed: the album would offer a phonographic score distillation ('contains ... all of the major thematic material') cast in a classical mould ('a substantial work in the form of a one-movement symphony or symphonic poem') adhering to the composer's authoritative arrangements ('in the composer's preferred settings') and using the same size orchestra as the original MGM Studio Orchestra, which would amount to an autonomous work with souvenir potential ('[a] permanent memento of the original film that would stand on its own'). And it would seem that Steiner's insistence on theme prominence (e.g. anchoring the suite on themes given in their 'original' complete form) may have ruled out a perhaps more 'radical' re-conceptualization of the score. Apart from three additional cue-blocks inserted into the first part of the original suite (cf. Table 2), the 1974 album basically adheres to Steiner's original design and thus adds to its canonization as *the* work representation best suited to strengthen the work-conceptual character of the score.

Although it is hardly possible to give a single exhaustive definition of the work-conceptual nature of the early soundtrack album devoted to the symphonic film score, Steiner's 1954 album is in many ways typical of the most prominent type: a re-recording matching the LP format. The phonographic re-mediation was conceived as a work entity with formal integrity, and the suite format was quickly established as a still operative genre convention that secured the re-mediated score a work character of its own. But unlike the unbroken flow of the Steiner suite, many suites were based on an autonomization of single re-arranged cues presented as well-formed character pieces, to draw on another classical analogy, unlike the filmic cue that typically trails off or falls silent when it had served its narrative purpose. The sequencing of single cues/tracks would be an overall reflection of the progression of the film

17 Max Steiner, *Max Steiner's Classic Film Score 'Gone with the Wind'* (RCA Victor ARL1-0452, 1974).
18 Behlmer, untitled sleeve-note essay, 12.

framed by a prelude or main title and a finale or end title, depending on terminological preferences, but would also conform to the well-established audio cultural convention of the concert hall that carefully planned programme variety provides the best listening experience. In the phonographic distillation of the score this was secured through careful selection and sequencing of cues playing mood, location, character, and/or action.

But while the overall enhancement of the work-conceptual character of the film score in its new phonographic presentation did potentially embody most of the shades of meaning listed by David Horn, it was not until the late 1960s and onward that the symphonic film score would be associated with (or recognized for) the characteristics most commonly conjuring up the art work: originality, status, canonization, and aura.

RECYCLING THE ORIGINAL MUSIC TRACK RECORDINGS: THE ORIGINAL SOUNDTRACK ALBUM

Contrary to popular belief the classic soundtrack album was not typically drawn from edited original optical music track recordings, the recordings made for the film, but as outlined above based on re-recordings of a selection of cues in amended arrangements and orchestrations. The release of original music track recording in the first half of the 1950s was at best sporadic. The most prominent example is three 10" albums issued between 1951 and 1953 by MGM Records with selections from scores by Miklos Rozsa for MGM's epic historical dramas: *Quo Vadis* (MGM E-103, 1951),[19] *Ivanhoe* & *Plymouth Adventure* (MGM 179, 1952), and *Julius Caesar* (MGM E-3033, 1953, with dialogue and narration).[20] By 1956 the release of instrumental soundtrack albums devoted to one score was becoming more regular, but due to poor annotation it can be difficult to determine the source of the content. Thus the conventional and strangely alluring sleeve announcement 'original soundtrack' or 'original soundtrack recording' should never be taken at its face value by researchers. Although one of the most successful MGM soundtrack albums when released in 1960, an original music track album of Miklos Rozsa's epic *Ben-Hur* score would not be released until 1996, perhaps because Rozsa as a commercially shrewd composer-conductor would keep feeding the market with his own re-recordings of score suites on different record labels.

The first official release of *Gone with the Wind* music tracks from the original recording sessions in November and December 1939 did not occur until 1967 coinciding with the perhaps most spectacular theatrical re-release of the film in an 'updated' widescreen format and in six-track stereo. By then developments in recording and sound technology reflected in the 'state of the art' re-recordings of the suite had rendered the old optical music track recordings, which had been rediscovered in

---

19 Also issued as a two 10" album with dialogue (MGM E-134, 1951).

20 It lies outside the scope of this article to address the work-conceptual questions raised by the early production of soundtrack albums that included spoken dialogue as a major or even the major sound component.

1965, hopelessly outdated, hence so-called stereo 'enhancement' was applied in a rather futile attempt to overcome what was now viewed as technical limitations.

Compared to the re-recorded suite album, the work-conceptual nature of the music track album produced by Jesse Kaye is strikingly similar: its suite-like programming framed by 'Main Title' and 'Finale' is based on a comparable selection and combination of music cues (cf. Table 2 for a comparison) retaining less than 20 percent of the complete music track recordings and adding up to a total length close to that of the suite.[21] Unlike the 1954 album the programme is divided into thirteen separate tracks (most, as must be expected, with typical musically unmotivated cue endings simply trailing off or even fading) and with only two exceptions, the sequencing of the chosen cues follow the chronology of the film, which is reflected in the chosen track titles that read like a story outline. Compared to the extensive re-sequencing and free re-naming of cues in Steiner's own suite version, the 1967 album producer hardly deviates from the original underscoring function of each cue, perhaps out of respect for the composer or loyalty to the film fan.

This album was a major success spending 36 weeks in the Billboard album charts peaking at number 24, easily outselling other contemporary recordings. Apart from the obvious 'souvenir' value of this album (containing the music actually heard in the cinema) at least part of its success must be ascribed to the special aura associated with original music track recordings, in particular by film music lovers and enthusiasts, linked to the already mentioned art cultural notion of the composer-conductor bestowing interpretational authority on his or her work on the recording stage in an almost symbiotic relationship with the studio orchestra.[22] It is this very moment of the score's first realization, comparable to the highly symbolic first performance of new works within contemporary art music culture, that is heard captured in the music track recordings, and subsequently celebrated in the 'true' original soundtrack album. In the case of the *Gone with the Wind* album this sense of aura was only compounded by the 28-year gap between the by then historical date of recording and the 'belated' release allowing nostalgia for a bygone era to become an important part of the equation.

However this album dedicated to a historical score was an exception at the time owing its existence primarily to the unique longevity of this particular film. Still, it can be viewed as a precursor of the coming rise of the historical soundtrack album.

21 I have not been able to ascertain whether the composer was in any way involved in the production of the album. The fact that special thanks are extended to the film's assistant musical director Lou Forbes on the album's back sleeve, but not to Steiner himself, may indicate that he was not involved.

22 The symbiotic relationship between certain free-lance film composer-conductors and their orchestras created a uniquely distinct sound impossible to 'imitate'. In the words of film score restorer John Morgan: 'There is a great deal of wonderful film music from the '60s and later that I think is among the best written, but it is so "player" dependent, or dependent on technology, it would be impossible to do it justice. Henry Mancini wrote some fine scores, but so much of his work – whether original tracks or album re-recordings done at the time – are so unique that they would be impossible to match ... unless you "concertized" them'; John Morgan, 'Memo to "FSM" – Re: Re-recordings', *Film Score Monthly*, 9/6 (2004), 29.

FILM MUSIC ARCHAEOLOGY: 'RESTORING' THE ORIGINAL FILM SCORE

When Charles Gerhardt recorded the expanded suite six years later in September 1973, it was as part of an RCA Victor series of film music albums begun in November 1972 called *Classic Film Scores* celebrating the golden age of symphonic film scoring. Until the series was cancelled in 1978 a total of 13 albums, all produced by Georg Korngold, was dedicated to the mostly unavailable and even forgotten symphonic film music of composers like Erich Wolfgang Korngold (father of the producer), Max Steiner, Alfred Newman, Bernard Herrmann, Franz Waxman, Miklos Rozsa and Dmitri Tiomkin. This pioneering and both commercially and critically successful effort would prove instrumental in generating renewed interest in the legacy of symphonic film scoring that would eventually change the phonographic mediation of this historical repertoire.

However, viewed as an album concept the series broke with the score concept of the traditional soundtrack album, with the *Gone with the Wind* album as the sole exception. Each album was thematic, dedicated to the music of a single composer or the music of films associated with major actors/actresses (like Bette Davis and Humphrey Bogart), and consisted of short suites and single cues from a variety of scores, a compilation concept that was not new but as always popular. More significant in regard to a score oriented concept, but much less prominent, was a subscription series, *The Film Music Collection*, begun in 1974 by Elmer Bernstein, a stylistically eclectic film composer-conductor with symphonic inclinations. Each of the resulting fourteen albums[23] was dedicated to one or two unrecorded scores from the 40s and 50s written by largely the same film composer-conductors anthologized in the Gerhardt–Korngold series, and only original arrangements and orchestrations were used for re-recording a substantial selection of music cues. The Bernstein series was clearly aimed at film-music enthusiasts with elaborate sleeve-notes that signalled artistic dedication to a neglected cultural heritage and an almost scholarly approach to the existing score material. Also, a quarterly film music journal, *Film Music Notebook*, containing composer interviews and scholarly articles was published in conjunction with the albums.[24] In hindsight this private and basically non-profit enterprise, which 'stayed in business' until 1979, can be seen as part of a then burgeon rescue operation focused on the preservation of the totally neglected film music material still existing in studio archives and private collections, coinciding with the establishment of what today is known as *The Film Music Society*.[25]

This new era of film music archaeology, preservation, historization, and canonization accelerated a process towards the recognition and institutionalization of film

---

23 The series was re-issued in 2006 as a CD-boxset entitled *Elmer Bernstein's Film Music Collection* (FSM BOX 01).

24 A complete edition of this journal was published by *The Film Music Society* in 2004 under the title *Elmer Bernstein's Film Music Notebook. A Complete Collection of the Quarterly Journal, 1974–1978* (Sherman Oaks, 2004).

25 For information on this still active society, see http://www.filmmusicsociety.org.

music as art,[26] and also had a profound effect on the album concept within the commercial production of soundtrack albums dedicated to historical scores as small independent record companies like Varèse Sarabande sprang up to cater to a growing specialist's or collector's market devoted to historical film music.[27] As to the score album two distinct types would prevail: one represents an attempt to roll back time by creating the original soundtrack albums that never were, using unearthed original music track recordings made commercially presentable by means of digital audio restoration. The most recent effort in this category is a considerable and ongoing series by the American film and TV music periodical *Film Score Monthly* called 'Golden Age Classics' begun in 1998. The other type brings the historical scores into the present by way of new state-of-the-art re-recordings, as exemplified by the ambitious classic film music series by Varèse Sarabande and Marco Polo. All efforts are dedicated to present the composer's score in what is considered its most pure, authentic and complete state. As Marco Polo's score restorer John Morgan put it in 2004:

> First, my loyalty is always with the composer's music, not with what ends up in the film. In all of our re-recordings, I have returned to primary sources: the composer's original sketches. Ideally, I would only refer to these sketches, the original orchestrations, the original parts, the original conductor parts and a music-only track. Unfortunately, this is usually not the case. For more than 50 percent of the music we choose to record, no full scores survive; we must orchestrate the music from original sketches or conductor-piano scores. When a composer writes music to a timing sheet, this reflects the cut or edit of the film at that time. By the time the music was ready for orchestration, more often than not, editing changes had occurred within the film that forced the composer to cut bars or add repeats. This re-editing of film often continues after the orchestrations are prepared and even after the score is recorded, which further changes the composer's original music. With very few exceptions, I find the music that the

26 This renewed 'academic' interest in the classic symphonic film score is also seen as a major incentive behind the post-modern revival of symphonic film scoring, usually attributed to John Williams' 'archaeological' approach to the scoring of the first *Star Wars* trilogy, a compositional tribute to the adventure scores of Erich Wolfgang Korngold if you will, released between 1977 and 1983. (In fact Charles Gerhardt dedicated what would be the last album in his *Classic Film Scores* series to two John Williams-scores, *Star Wars* and *Close Encounters of the Third Kind*.) The unprecedented commercial success of the three original soundtrack albums, with the first album spending a whole year in the Billboard album charts peaking at number two, helped pave the way for a producer-sanctioned renaissance of more or less 'old-fashioned' symphonic scoring taken up by a new generation of film composers including names like James Horner and Danny Elfman, and on British ground Patrick Doyle, all three born in 1953. Thus since the late 1970s the phonographic revival of the classic film scores has run parallel to a renewed blooming of the symphonic scoring tradition.

27 Jay Alan Quantrill has suggested that this repertoire of symphonic film music appealed especially to classical music aficionados who were disappointed in the radical experimentation embraced by modern composers; Jay Alan Quantrill, 'The Archeology of Film Music', sleeve-note essay for *Elmer Bernstein's Film Music Collection* (FSM BOX 01, 2006). David Horn concludes that 'in the case of film music, authorship is important within the film-making industry and within academic writing, but, with a very few exceptions, is almost entirely absent from the language of the audience'; Horn, 'Some Thoughts on the Work in Popular Music', 23. The album production and consumption dedicated to a canonized selection of first generation sound film composer-conductors is indeed such an exception.

composer originally wrote to be the best and most interesting presentation of the music. At least 80 percent of the music we have recorded would not fit the film's final timings. These additional edits are made strictly for filmic reasons at the expense of the music. Often entire cues are dropped because a scene was cut or the producer or director just didn't think the music was right. Well, when we re-record, if the music feels 'right' as music, we'll do it.[28]

The dedication to 'Werktreue' expressed here obviously entertains the notion of a creative 'purity' in the early stages of the scoring process, where the composers realizes the full potential of his or her creative 'genius' in isolation before the outcome of 'pure' music ('music [that] feels "right" as music') is compromised in the collaborative machinery of film production. The parallel to the art cultural cult of the isolated composer genius is of course striking. And although presented as acts of preservation and necessary re-construction, the archaeological quest for the composer's so-called original artistic intentions and their realization in a complete phonographic presentation entail no less work construction than that found in the classic suite-based soundtrack albums of the 1950s and 1960s.

So far no attempt has been made to re-record the mammoth score of *Gone with the Wind* in its 'original and complete form'.[29] In fact Gerhardt's expanded suite album of 1974 still constitutes the latest substantial re-recording. But a series of no less than three distinct official original music track albums issued between 1983 and 1996 illustrate how the era of film music preservation has affected the commercial phonographic mediation of Steiner's score, with each instalment in this ongoing serial raising new and different issues.

In 1983 an expanded version of the 1967 music track album, adding four 'unreleased' music cues plus the Selznick International music trademark[30] preceding the main title, marked the first release of a selection of the original music track recordings in original mono sound (cf. Table 1). In his sleeve-note, album supervisor Ron Eyre points out that 'all of the selections heard on this album were taken directly from the original optical music track as recorded by the orchestra.' However, 'in order to maintain the exact sequence of this magnificent score as heard in the picture and to keep "Tara's Theme" intact', the source for two tracks are 'less than optimum sound quality taken directly from a print of the film'. Thus ultimately this remediation of the selected music tracks aims at being true to the film experience (i.e. the album as faithful and exact souvenir),[31] which is also reflected in Eyre's conclusion: 'It was felt that you, the buyer ..., would prefer to have the original, albeit with poor sound, rather than any substitutions'. Still, there is no mistaking the overall

28 Morgan, 'Memo to "FSM"', 27–28.
29 According to Rudy Behlmer, Max Steiner composed 99 separate music cues for the film based on his own 11 primary leitmotifs and 16 additional melodies and adaptions of folk and patriotic material; Behlmer, untitled sleeve-note essay, 10.
30 This music trademark was written by Alfred Newman in 1937.
31 Also, the two-part structure of the film is retained on the original LP. Thus side two opens with the previously unreleased 'Intermission Music'.

discursive wrapping of the project as an act of restoration and preservation when Eyre sums up: 'We have attempted to create, from those elements still available, the best possible authentic reproduction of the original soundtrack'.[32]

Only seven years later an expanded music track album approaching a full hour in length was issued in the CBS Special Products series, with album supervisor and annotator Bruce Eder proclaiming:

> For fans of *Gone with the Wind*, this specially expanded and restored soundtrack repre-sents a chance they've never previously had – to hear the screen's most legendary film score properly for the very first time.[33]

Apart from expounding the sound technical clean-up of the sound material in a process 'usually regarded as "impossible" in music engineering circles'[34] allowing unheard musical details to surface, Eder is referring to the album programming: included for the first time is the conventional musical meta-framing of this epic movie (overture, entr'acte music and exit music) plus music cues from Scarlett's oath scene at the end of part one (used as a finale in Steiner's suite) and Melanie's death followed by Rhett's departure towards the end of the film. For these three additional cues/tracks only, Eder decided to use the composite soundtrack including dialogue and sound effects. Thus almost halfway through the album spoken dialogue in the form of Scarlett's passionate oath suddenly invades the 'abstract' sound world of music with rather startling effect. When experiencing the film, the score will 'natu-rally' blend in with the other sound elements in a complex sonic collage, but a key work-conceptual strategy in the autonomization of the film score is to extract and isolate the sound of music from its noisy environment and present it as (a) pure sound undisturbed by so-called extra-musical or worldly noises.[35] Still, Eder's deci-sion is far from pointless, as he argues: 'Since Steiner wrote this music to fit the dialogue, it was felt that listeners would appreciate a crisp, clean recording of the entire sequence'.[36] In other words, this particular music underscores another 'supe-rior' sound element, the dialogue, and is less suited to stand on its own, an impor-tant factor to consider when rescuing the score from the mire of functionality to extoll it as art in its isolated glory. Scarlett's famous oath scene in the fields of war-ravaged Tara can serve as a useful illustration.

Scarlett's spoken lines occur towards the end of the scene and are framed by the Tara theme. But between these two thematic statements the composer sets up the protagonist's spoken statement, mirroring her determined effort to get her worn-

---

32 Ron Eyre, untitled sleeve-note, *Gone with the Wind* (Polydor 817 116-2, 1983), no page numbers.
33 Bruce Eder, untitled sleeve-note essay, *Gone with the Wind. Original MGM Soundtrack* (CBS Spe-cial Product AK 45438, 1990), no page numbers.
34 Ibid.
35 For a discussion of the artistic practice of separating musical sound from sound as such even within 20th century avant-garde music, see Douglas Kahn, 'The Sound of Music', in Michael Bull and Les Back (eds.), *The Auditory Culture Reader* (Oxford, 2003), 77–90.
36 Eder, untitled sleeve-note essay, no page numbers.

out body off of the ground in a sequence of rising violins before announcing her oath with two fanfarish orchestral chords. As Scarlett speaks ('As God is my witness … I'll never be hungry again!') the music duly recedes into the background, although Steiner does suspend the moment musically by sustaining a discreet violin line that eventually leads to the almost apotheosic return of the Tara theme ending the first part of the movie.[37] When recycling this music cue as the grandiose finale of his symphonic suite, Steiner was obviously well aware of the anti-climatic audio void left by the 'missing' dialogue, and simply resolved the problem by recasting the music itself as protagonist: by intensifying both tempo and dynamics and 'dramatizing' the arrangement the background violins are brought centre stage singing out almost as passionately as had the now silenced Scarlett. This, of course, is not an option when limited to the original music track recordings. However, Eder's momentary breach of the longstanding convention of separating music from all other sound elements in the remediation of film music as soundtrack album can hardly be considered a convincing solution to this apparent dilemma. On the contrary, it could be argued that the defilement of the musical soundspace with the entrance of the word undermines the work-conceptual enhancement of the score that the rest of the album seems to procure. It may be no coincidence that this inconsistent mixing strategy has remained an anomaly in the remediation of the *Gone with the Wind* score.

The latest chapter in the ongoing history of *Gone with the Wind* soundtrack albums was added in 1996 when Turner Entertainments, as part of an ongoing series of historical MGM soundtrack albums, released a close to complete two-CD music track album (cf. Table 1) containing almost 150 minutes of original music cue recordings. The cues are programmed in strict chronological order and sometimes stitched together two or three at a time to generate musical flow. Again the two-part division of the overall programme mirrors that of the film, but curiously neither overture nor intermission and exit music is included, contrary to several extended cues written by the composer but not included in their entirety in the final film. Yet, this album is representative of the still prevalent completist trend to excavate all surviving music track recordings and issue them in more or less unedited form. Thus for the first time the film music lover is invited to engage with the entire film score as an uninterrupted and purely musical listening experience, the only way to truly experience and appreciate musical works worth our time, as art culture conventions will have it. But rather than simply unveiling the 'true' score in its most original and authentic state through what is usually perceived as an act of re-construction, this phonographic representation is a very recent work construct appealing primarily to completists and musical purists.[38] Ironically, this the undoubtedly most venerating work conceptual strategy presents the score in a manner that the composer being honoured felt would be 'totally impractical and unmusical'.[39]

37 For Steiner's own advice on the scoring of dialogue, see Baumburg (ed.), *We Make the Movies*, 225–26.
38 A single CD version with 'highlight' selections was issued in 1997 to cater for a broader market segment (TCM/Rhino/Warner 8122 72822-2, 1997).
39 Behlmer, untitled sleeve-note essay, 12.

IN CONCLUSION

It has been the primary objective of this article to discuss the soundtrack album as a both artistically, commercially, and even academically convenient work-conceptual vehicle for the symphonic film score to stand on its own. Although creators, proprietors, and later advocates may have had partly conflicting interests and goals in re-launching the classic film score as a phonographic album (as a work of 'pure' music, as a film promotional tool, or as an act of cultural heritage preservation), the commercial longevity of this specific album genre has no doubt had a profound effect on our perception of film music not just as a commodity but as a music worth engaging with away from the dark of the cinema.[40] Today the soundtrack album remains the primary outlet for the symphonic film score, both old and new, as a distinct work object in various guises.

SUMMARY

The article discusses key work-conceptual themes at play in the various re-mediations of the classic American symphonic film score as a phonographic product from the early formation of the soundtrack album in the 1950s and onward. Released between 1954 and 1996, the numerous soundtrack albums dedicated to film composer Max Steiner's canonic score for David O. Selznick's *Gone with the Wind* (1939), based on either the original optical music track recordings or later studio re-recordings, serve as an exemplary but also somewhat unique illustration throughout, as the historically evolving character of this phonographic sub-genre is pursued.

40 The same is true of phonographic album genres related to music drama. For a discussion of the formation of the 'original Broadway cast' album, see Steen Kaargaard Nielsen, 'A change of scene. On the phonographic reconceptualization of the Broadway musical in the 1940s as reflected in commercial Kurt Weill cast recordings', in Alf Björnberg et al. (eds.), *Frispel. Festskrift till Olle Edström* (Göteborg, 2005), 581–95.

Reports

Research Projects

EMS: Two Music Cultures – One Institution.
Swedish electro-acoustic music from 1965 to the late 1970s

The current Ph.D. project (2006–9, Musicology, Department of Arts and Cultural Studies, University of Copenhagen, funded by The Danish Councils for Independent Research) focuses on EMS (Electro-acoustic Music in Sweden) which is an institution with studios for producing electro-acoustic music and sound art. It was first established in 1965 under the Swedish Radio, where an old radio-theatre studio was opened up to composers and other artists wanting to experiment with sound. The first studio, later named the 'Sound Workshop' ('klangverkstaden'), was intended solely for contemporary work. Very high investments were allocated to a prestigious computer music studio, which opened in 1970. The computer music studio was, for its time, highly advanced and even before its opening very famous, but also difficult to work with for various reasons. The Sound Workshop was available to the artists 24 hours a day and much easier to handle. Therefore most of the pieces from this period were produced in the Sound Workshop.

In the early 1970s a conflict emerged between the composers and the studio director, Norwegian composer and pianist Knut Wiggen (b. 1927). Wiggen was idealistic and in his eager search for 'the music of the future' he believed in continuing the earlier experiments within *musique concrète* (Radiodiffusion Francaise's *Studio d'Essai* in Paris) and *elektronische Musik* (Westdeutscher Rundfunk's *Studie Akustische Kunst* in Köln) through research into sound and sound perception. Most of the composers and artists, on the other hand, wanted to produce pieces that could be performed 'here and now'. These composers – with Sten Hanson, Bengt Emil Johnson, Lars Gunnar Bodin, and Åke Hodell as the leading figures – were mainly from the Swedish 'Text Sound' milieu, which aesthetically is related with intermedia artforms such as concrete poetry, sound poetry, *Neues Hörspiel*, performance, and political art. They were too impatient to wait for Wiggens' results in the computer-music studio and they wanted investments to renovate and update the Sound Workshop. Wiggen did not agree to this and in the early 1970s the composers boycotted the studio. After many discussions Wiggen was dismissed in 1975, in 1976 Jon Appleton was appointed new director and in 1979 he was followed by the Swedish composer Lars Gunnar Bodin.

The artistic material produced at the institution during these years varies from so-called abstract electronic music produced mainly in the computer-music studio, to performance-related and political text-sound pieces created and produced in the Sound Workshop. So far, there has been very little academic writing about this, and the writing that has been done is mainly by the composers themselves. Going into the conflict and the very broad and heterogeneous material, many questions appear which I believe have not been raised properly in earlier writings on electro-acoustic music and sound art. To the extent they have been dealt with, it has been done within separated traditions of either historiography or analysis.

Sanne Krogh Groth

HIP HOP CULTURE AS MUSICAL PRACTICE: ANALYSES AND DISCUSSIONS

Hip hop culture may in a very direct manner be understood as multi-dimensional or syn-aesthetic, composed by at least four cultural forms of expression. That is, rap, dj'ing, break dance, and graffiti, to which one might add slang, fashion, hand signs, etc. This line of cultural expressions and their relations play a key role in participants' understanding of and identification with hip hop, and they pose a challenge to analysts' attempts to characterize hip hop in relation to other musical cultures or (to be concrete) to describe, what is going on at for instance a hip hop jam, that is a concert or party traditionally involving break dance and graffiti along with music.

In this postdoc-project – with the working title *Hip Hop Culture as Musical Practice: Analyses and Discussions* (Department of Musicology, Institute of Aesthetic Studies, University of Aarhus, 2007–10) – I try to contribute to an analytical understanding of hip hop culture, through an interdisciplinary approach to a series of case studies focusing on musical practice, as what may be said to connect the culture's expressions in specific situations. I take as the outset for my understanding of practice a combination of discourse analysis and cultural sociology, theorizing how musical practice may be seen as an articulation (or mediation) of certain personal, social, discursive, material (e.g. sonic) conditions constituting a given situation (e.g. that of a jam). Music is thus understood in a rather broad sense, and a key question is exactly how what one might term different ontologies of music seem to coexist in our perception and understanding of different kinds of music and music cultures. Following this I do not consider either multi-dimensionality or syn-aesthetics as something exclusive to hip hop. On the contrary these features may be viewed as characteristic features of music culture in general, making hip hop culture, however, a very obvious case – and one which is lacking in academic interest compared to the rather dominating position claimed by the genre in popular music today.

The case studies I undertake focus on three very basic types of action in connection to hip hop culture, namely the production of a rap music album (by different rap groups in Århus), the staging and celebration of hip hop at concerts (at the yearly festival *Århus Took It!*) and the reception of hip hop in journalistic popular music criticism and public debates about the genre. While the first case studies rely on auditive analysis along with interviews and observations, the last case study takes on a more text analytical approach. I try in all instances to show how the articulation of hip hop at one level (as for instance a sonic phenomena) implies the construction of other aspects of the situation (e.g. social and discursive conditions) and, connecting the case studies, how for instance social conditions and values articulated in the production and reception of the music correspond with (or diverge from) the staging of hip hop as a concert phenomenon. My case studies do not comprise all, of course, but are merely a frame for discussing musical practice as central to participants' understanding along with analysts' characterization of hip hop and perhaps in a broader sense of popular music culture.

The project is funded by the The Danish Research Council for the Humanities as well as The Faculty of Humanities, University of Aarhus.

Mads Krogh

SKANDINAVISCHE SYMPHONIK IM WILHELMINISCHEN KAISERREICH

Ausgangspunkt dieses Dissertationsprojektes ist die auffallende Begeisterung für den skandinavischen 'Norden' im deutschen Kaiserreich zur Regierungszeit Wilhelms II (1888–1918). Die bisherige Forschung hat gezeigt, dass sich altnordische Sagen sowie skandinavische Literatur und Malerei im Kaiserreich großer Beliebtheit erfreuten. Eng verknüpft mit der Vorstellung vom 'Germanisch-Nordischen' trug die deutsche Skandinavien-Rezeption zur Konstruktion einer deutschen Identität nach 1870/71 bei. Die Bedeutung der wilhelminischen Norden-schwärmerei für die Rezeption skandinavischer Musik, speziell der Symphonik, wird im Projekt mit dem Arbeitstitel *Skandinavische Symphonik im wilhelminischen Kaiserreich* beleuchtet. Weiterführend wird zudem gefragt, ob es möglich ist, die Werke mit ihrer wilhelminischen Rezeption als 'nordisch' zu verknüpfen, ohne in das alte Denkmuster zu verfallen, das nach einer 'nordischen Substanz' sucht.

Entsprechend diesen zwei Fragestellungen umfasst das Projekt zwei Aspekte: erstens eine Studie zur Rezeption skandinavischer Musik im musikbezogenen Schrifttum des wilhelmi-nischen Kaiserreichs. Ausgehend von der Tatsache, dass skandinavische Musik überwiegend als 'nordisch' charakterisiert wurde, stehen hier die Images vom Norden im Blickpunkt, die in den Texten formuliert werden. Obwohl grundsätzlich symphonische Werke im Zentrum des Interesses stehen, bezieht sich die Rezeptionsstudie auch auf allgemeinere Veröffentlichungen zu skandinavischer Musik.

Zweitens werden einige der als 'nordisch' rezipierten Symphonien in Fallstudien unter-sucht. Den Fallstudien liegt die Hypothese zugrunde, dass Werk und Rezeption auch ohne einen substanziellen Begriff vom 'Nordischen' miteinander in Verbindung gebracht werden können. In einem ersten Schritt wird auf werkanalytischem Weg die Stellung der Werke zur Gattungstradition herausgearbeitet. Anschließend wird geprüft, ob die Passagen, in denen die Werke von Standards dieser Tradition abweichen, mit zentralen Begriffen der Rezeption in Einklang gebracht werden können. Ästhetische Kategorien wie die des Erhabenen stellen bei diesem Schritt eine vermittelnde Instanz dar, die gleichzeitig direkte Semantisierungen einzel-ner musikalischer Merkmale verhindert.

Die Dissertation entsteht seit Winter 2005 und voraussichtlich bis 2009 bei Prof. Dr. Siegfried Oechsle am Musikwissenschaftlichen Institut der Christian-Albrechts-Universität zu Kiel. Das Projekt ist Teil des DFG-geförderten interdisziplinären Graduiertenkollegs *Imaginatio borealis. Perzeption, Rezeption und Konstruktion des Nordens* (1999–2008), das nach Vorstellungen vom Norden zu verschiedenen Zeiten und an verschiedenen Orten fragt. Weitere musikwissenschaftliche Schwerpunkte innerhalb des Kollegs sind beispielsweise Jean Sibelius' Symphonien und deren Rezeption sowie Dieterich Buxtehude und das 'nor-disch Phantastische'. Für weitere Informationen zum Graduiertenkolleg siehe www.uni-kiel.de/borealis.

Katharine Leiska

Transformations in Russian Popular Music of the Post-Soviet Era – Case study St Petersburg

The Ph.D. project explores the production of popular music in St Petersburg (Russia) and how it is embedded in global flows, concentrating on the post-Soviet diaspora community in Berlin. Combining ethnomusicology and popular music studies, the project is based at the Section of Musicology, University of Copenhagen. It is financed through a three-year grant (2007–9) from the university's Faculty of the Humanities.

During the Soviet period, Leningrad (now St Petersburg) was one of the major centres of Soviet popular music, a position it has retained until today. Applying the theoretical concept of scenes to delimit the field, the project's first part examines local dynamics in St Petersburg, the musicians' and groups' relationships to the city, musical resources they draw on, and how they construct their musical identities. Special attention will be given to the discourse on the (perceived) genre 'russkii rok' and, using a post-colonial lens, the relationship between the former Soviet Socialist Republics, Russia and Ukraine.

Due to extensive emigration following the disintegration of the Soviet Union the post-Soviet diaspora in countries like Germany, Israel, and the United States has grown. This has created a burgeoning market for music from the former Soviet Union. The project's second part examines how post-Soviet popular music from St Petersburg through the dynamics of global flows resurfaces within and extends beyond diasporic communities. These processes will be discussed using the popular Berlin night life event 'Russendisko' (run by the emigrants Wladimir Kaminer and Yuriy Gurzhy) as an example.

The project's research is based on fieldwork (interviews and participant observation) conducted from 2004 until 2006 in St Petersburg, Berlin, and New York. More information can be obtained at http://phd.d-ew.info.

David-Emil Wickström

Conferences

ZOLTÁN KODÁLY SYMPOSIUM, COPENHAGEN 2007

On the occasion of the 125th birthday of the Hungarian composer, ethnomusicologist, and music pedagogue Zoltán Kodály, a three-day symposium was held in Copenhagen, 22–24 November 2007. The symposium presented workshops and lectures on Kodály at the Royal Academy of Music and at the Section of Musicology, University of Copenhagen, which were organizing the event in cooperation with the Danish Cultural Institute, The Hungarian Embassy and the Danish Kodály Society.

The first two days were dedicated to working with students at the Royal Academy and the University. Key figures were the two guests from the Kodály Institute in Kecskemét, Hungary, Mihály Ittzés and Szuszanna Kontra. On the first day, Ittzés gave a lecture at the Royal Academy of Music on Kodály as a folk music researcher. The second day he was lecturing at the University on Kodály the composer. On the same day Szuszanna Kontra gave two workshops at the University, in the morning conducting and introducing choir works of Kodály with the choir of first year students of musicology, and in the afternoon introducing to the Kodály solfege method. For both of these workshops the students had been preparing for several weeks.

The final day was a public symposium at the Royal Academy of Music. Mihály Ittzés gave a lecture on the three main topics of Kodály's work, his collection and study of folk music, his compositions inspired by these studies, and his effort to bring good music, classical as well as folk music, to a wide range of people, not least the children. Later we were introduced to the impact of Kodály pedagogics in Denmark by the Kodály Society and Mette Storgaard Nielsen presented the concept of 'color strings', a Kodály-inspired method for teaching string instruments to children. The programme also contained live music: the choir of musicology students conducted by Szuszanna Kontra presented three choir pieces prepared during the workshop; Morten Zeuthen and Elisabeth Zeuthen-Schneider performed Kodály's Duo for Piano and Cello; and Thomas Vetö and Hedwig Rummel gave a short recital with Kodály songs.

The value of such a symposium, besides the very interesting contributions from the Hungarian guests, is to a large extend to be found in the fact that it brings students to work with international scholars and that it brings together the factions of Danish musical life: the researchers, the musicians, and the pedagogues. In that regard Kodály might inspire us to recognize the importance of working together within the field of music.

Michael Fjeldsøe

Passagen – 18th Congress of the International Musicological Society (IMS), Zurich 2007

The Congresses of the IMS every fifth year ought to be the grandest musicological event in the world. It is a unique opportunity to gather the scholars in every field of the subject and to make fruitful discussions for the development of the discipline.

Therefore the expectations were high, when I went to the 18th congress, which this year was held 10-15 July at the largest university of Switzerland. My expectation of Swiss perfectionism and wealth did not seem to be exaggerated. The whole conference was well organized and the facilities were new and professional. This basis gave the optimal options for the many seminars and papers, and I was impressed by the capacities of the Institute of Musicology at Zurich University. Perhaps this is also an outcome of the facility problems from the last conference?[1]

It is a good opportunity to get the impressions of the 'hot topics' in international musicology right now.[2] It is also a possibility to get feedback on one's own research, and to discuss specific issues with likeminded people.

Though this is one of the biggest international musicological congresses in the world with many participants from other continents like America and Asia, German musicology this year seemed to dominate the days. I got the impression that musicology in Zurich is closely linked to the German tradition. The editor of the latest edition of *Musik in Geschichte und Gegenwart*, Professor Ludwig Finscher, initiated the keynote speeches with a promotion of research in *Gattungsgeschichte*, and many of the seminars were dominated by subjects and agendas related to recent German musicology; an exception was the area of musical semantics. The subject was represented on a high level by the Harvard professor, Kofi Agawu, and on several well-attended symposia.

The dominance of Continental European musicology is to be expected at a musicological congress in the heart of Europe, but the lack of papers in the field of ethnomusicology and other systematic disciplines (with the field of notation as one exception) was a problem. It is sad, if this indicates a great gab between systematic and historic disciplines and their scholars. The overlapping days of other conferences seemed to confirm this tendency. The 39th World Congress of the International Council of Traditional Music in Vienna took place at the same time, and the conference of The International Association of Music Libraries was held in Australia the week before. If the reason for this is found in the lack of contact between these organizations, there is still work to be done in the future. Musicology is not a large discipline, and the lack of cooperation will undoubtedly weaken the field in the long term.

With the exception of the excursions on Saturday, the days were all organized with keynote speeches in the morning followed by symposia and free papers from 10 a.m. to 6 p.m. It is highly relevant to organize the papers in symposia, when it is possible. The size of the conference and the large number of papers demands a strong organization in smaller units, and I think this will be crucial, if the congress, which becomes bigger and bigger, is to survive.

Some of the symposia had a tendency to be forced. This is of course the price to pay, when so many different papers have to follow same directions, and when the programme-committee has to do a great puzzle. In many cases this problem could be partly solved, if the keynote

1 See Thomas Holme Hansen's report from the 17th congress in *Dansk Årbog for Musikforskning*, 30 (2002), 96–99.

2 An overview and presentation of the papers can be found in Hans-Joachim Hinrichsen and Laurenz Lütteken (eds.), *Passagen – 18. Kongress der Internationalen Gesellschaft für Musikwissenschaft Zürich, 10. bis 15. Juli 2007. Programm* (Kassel, 2007).

speakers in their preparation not only concentrated on their paper, but also on organizing the symposia. An example of this was the well-organized symposium 'Zwischen "U" und "E" – Grenzüberschreitungen in der Musik seit 1950', where there was planned a later, following meeting, and the participants were invited to join an organized dinner afterwards.

Six excursions were arranged Saturday, and they went to different cities in Switzerland. I went to Basel and was introduced to institutions like the *Paul Sacher Stiftung* and *Schola Cantorum Basiliensis*. The tour was well organized, and we once again got the impression of a country, which has the money and is not afraid of spending it on culture.

The City of Zurich and its musical institutions were closely involved in the programme of the conference, and I found this symbiosis fruitful and got the impression of a town with a living and dynamic music life. The annual festival of new music was present at the same time, and it was therefore possible to hear performances of new Swiss music every day. There were also possibilities to get introductions to Zurich's music history. An exhibition at the Public Library and a city tour to historical places were organized. It is a great pleasure when scholarship, musical performance, and political goodwill are able to cooperate. The days in Zurich showed us a significant example of this.

In these years, politicians seem to be more focused on visible outputs and the ability of public attention, when research appropriations are distributed. The collaboration between scholarship and performance in making cultural events seems to be an obvious place to respond to these demands. The next congress of the IMS will take place in 2012.

Peter E. Nissen

DIGITAL EDITIONS. PERSPECTIVES FOR EDITORS AND USERS, UNIVERSITY OF COPENHAGEN, JANUARY 2008

On Saturday 19 January 2008 the Section of Musicology, University of Copenhagen held a symposium on the subject *Digital Editions. Perspectives for Editors and Users*. Ph.D. students Bjarke Moe and Axel Teich Geertinger had taken the initiative to this arrangement with the following four keynote speakers and demonstration of projects: Paul Vetch (London), 'CFEO and OCVE as digital editions: models, methods and Outcomes' (demonstration of Chopin First Editions Online, CFEO (2004–7): http://www.cfeo.org.uk; Online Chopin Variorum Edition, OCVE (2003–8): http://www.ocve.org.uk); Frans Wiering (Department of Information and Computing Sciences, Universiteit Utrecht), 'Digital editions of Renaissance polyphony and lute tablatures: the model and the scholar' (demonstration of Electronic Corpus of Lute Music, ECOLM (1999–): http://www.ecolm.org; Corpus Mensurabilis Musicae Electronicum, CMME (1999–): http://www.cmme.org); Peter Woetmann Christoffersen (Department of Arts and Cultural Studies, University of Copenhagen), 'Publishing 15th-century music: Open Access and Digital Editing'; Johannes Kepper (Universität Paderborn), 'The Edirom tools as an approach to digital editions of music from the Common Western Notation period' (demonstration of Edirom Digitale Musikedition (2004–): http://www.edirom.de).

These four papers gave a splendid overview of the phenomenon Digital Editions, and the rapid development which takes place these years in this field. First of all it was emphasized that a digital edition is more than a digitized version of a traditional printed score on a CD ROM or at the Internet. The digital medias contains undreamt possibilities when it comes to editing and publishing music, e.g.: reproduction of the complete source material (manuscripts, printed editions, letters, and other documentation); presentation of different layers in the sources (e.g. later additions in a manuscript); extended possibilities for the user to compare different sources on the screen; critical notes placed as a separate layer directly connected to the music; and search function tools (within the text as well as in the music).

Thus digital editions are very well suited to illustrate difficult editorial problems, which in a printed edition would have been very complicated to explain. No doubt the digital editions in many ways are superior to the printed editions. Nonetheless, till now it has been a problem that digital editions have not been regarded as a serious alternative to the traditional printed critical editions. But at the *Edirom*-project, however, there has recently been established a collaboration with the Weber and Dvorak Editions, and thus proved how a conventional critical 'Gesamtausgabe' can be united with a modern digital edition. Therefore it does not seem as if the digital editions will force out the printed editions; rather it is likely that in the future digital editions will be an unavoidable supplement to printed editions.

Digital editions are still a relatively new phenomenon. All the projects mentioned are less than ten years old. Frans Wiering compared the development of the digital editions with the evolution of the car and he concluded that in this comparison the digital editions have reached the time around 1910.

Niels Bo Foltmann

MUSIC, MEDIA & EMOTIONS, UNIVERSITY OF AARHUS, OCTOBER 2007

The seminar, *Music, Media & Emotions*, affiliated to the research network, *Emotion, Knowledge & Culture*, took place on 11 October 2007 at the Institute of Aesthetics, Aarhus University. The seminar was arranged and organized by Charlotte Rørdam Larsen, Department of Musicology and Iben Have, Institute of Information and Media Studies, University of Aarhus. One of the primary intentions of the network is to bring emotions on the agenda of research in the humanities. Such a project needs interdisciplinary approaches and the seminar contributed to the project by illuminating intersections and interventions between musicology and media in research as well as in practice by discussing the subject from different viewpoints.

Iben Have introduced the seminar by outlining the three concepts and their intersection and called attention to a growing mediatization of emotions through the use of music and sound in different media. The seminar's most dominant subjects were related to music and sound in film and television. Torben Grodal (Department of Film and Media Studies, University of Copenhagen) discussed some basic biological characteristics of emotions and related these to the perception of film music in his paper, 'Emotions, Film and Music'. Birger Langkjær (Department of Nordic Philology, University of Copenhagen) introduced in his paper, 'Now I feel, now I do not feel!', different approaches of musicology and film studies, and discussed critically the prevailing idea of emotions as something that can be switched on and off concurrently with the use of music in films. Nicholas Cook's concepts of *similarity*, *emergence*, and *perceptual selection* were applied to a detailed analysis of a Danish television commercial in Nicolai Graakjær's (Institute of Communication, Aalborg University) paper on 'Music in Relation to Moving Images'. The leader of sound editing at The National Film School of Denmark, Per Meinertsen, pleaded for a more reflected, sparse, and moderate use of music, illustrated by examples from film and television productions.

Charlotte Rørdam Larsen's paper 'Get out in that kitchen and rattle those pots and pans – auditive staging of the experience of taste' analysed the use and function of music in food programmes on television and related this to the sound of television lifestyle programmes and their handling of food and emotions. Concerning emotions and the use of media, Even Ruud (Department of Musicology, University of Oslo) discussed in his paper 'The MP3-player

– our new home pharmacy' the use of music as soothing, relieving, and stimulating. Finally, from the field of practice, sound designer Karsten Kjems (*Sonic Branding*) talked about music and sound in relation to commercial product and business branding – a new and upcoming area.

The seminar was organized as collaboration between Institute of Aesthetic Studies and Institute of Information and Media Studies and addressed students and researchers from both institutes with more than 100 participants and will be followed by more.

Charlotte Rørdam Larsen & Iben Have

SOUND, ART, AUDITORY CULTURE, UNIVERSITY OF COPENHAGEN, 28–30 NOVEMBER 2007

Hosted by the Copenhagen Doctoral School at the Department of Arts and Cultural Studies, University of Copenhagen, the three-day conference *Sound, Art, Auditory Culture* constituted the first major presentation on Danish ground of the multible interdisciplinary research activities that explore a wide range of themes and debates in what is emerging as an ever more important international field of research on sound and aural experience. This advocacy of an aural turn, if you will, has attracted various headings like 'auditory culture', 'acoustemology' and 'aural history' and has, particularly since the turn of the century, resulted in a number of groundbreaking anthologies, among them *The Auditory Culture Reader* (Oxford: Berg, 2003) edited by Michael Bull & Les Back and *Hearing History – A Reader* (Athens, GA: University of Georgia Press, 2004) edited by Mark M. Smith.

The conference organizers had invited papers on all aspects of sound studies but singled out four areas of particular interest: 1) the mediation of bodily presence and the role of the body in aural experience; 2) the voice and its mediations; 3) the interplay between sound and spatial experience; and 4) the significance of instrumental timbre. While all of these topics were addressed in varying degrees, the some thirty short papers that made up the afternoon parallel sessions constituted an impressively gaudy quilt of theoretical and methodological approaches to a very broad range of sound-related topics, which rendered the attempted thematical grouping somewhat meaningless. Still, viewed as a network of specifically positioned examples of interdisciplinarity at work various and sometimes surprising dialogues between apparently unrelated papers kept emerging, which may at least in part have been responsible for the often lively informal debate and exchange between sessions.

By contrast every morning provided thematic common ground for all delegates in the form of two-part plenary sessions, each beginning with a keynote lecture: The first, an explicitly philosophically informed talk, was given by Christoph Cox (Hampshire College, MA) under the title 'Sound Art and the Ontology of the Audible', in which he argued for and explored 'a conception of sound as a continuous, anonymous flux to which human expressions contribute but which precedes and exceeds these expressions'. In her keynote paper 'Sound Experience, Sound Culture, Sound Studies', Sabine Breitsameter (Faculty of Media, Hochschule Darmstadt), gave a historical outline of how sonic phenomena within German thought have been 'perceived, categorized and analyzed by paradigms closely related to music', which has led to the marginalization or even exclusion of sound in cultural, artistic, and academic discourses. Finally Allen S. Weiss (Performance Studies and Cinema Studies, New York University), offered a fascinating but grim tour through 'Impossible Audio Worlds', audiophonic representations of the *danse macabre* in twentieth century art focusing on the unsettling glissando as a major trope.

Each keynote speaker was supplemented by shorter presentations by the four organizers. Apart from Søren Møller Sørensen's introductory remarks, all addressed different aspects of the voice: 'The Electronic Voice' (Torben Sangild), 'Solitary Voices. Glenn Gould's *The Idea of the North*' (Erik Granly Jensen) and 'Speaking Volumes. A Geography of the Voice' (Brandon LaBelle).

The appreciable presence of sound-art artists and performers was highlighted by an evening's relocation of the conference to the Academy of Arts for a sound event with work presentations and performances by Aeron Bergman & Alejandra Salinas, Shinji Kanki, Lawrence English, and Brandon LaBelle. And throughout the conference delegates could experience *Soundwalkers*, a 2007 work by Portuguese sound artist Raquel Castro.

From the point of view of a musicologist, part of a minority group among other minority groups at this 'multi-cultural' conference, the opening-up of the concept of sound and aural experience through a wealth of often disparate theoretical contextualizations and empirical grounding offers an opportunity or challenge to engage with our 'own' rather stale Western concept of music from within a different and fresh intellectual framework – that of an outsider perhaps – to address the many unexplored 'interrelationships' between music and sound, obviously so much more than simply a question of acoustics. With the emergence of research groups and networks, also in Denmark, the prospect of new 'hearings' seems promising.

At all events, this conference was an unqualified success in demonstrating the potential in re-mapping the academic soundscape in its present state. That it is indeed possible to change your tune by hearing it differently.

Steen Kaargaard Nielsen

Danish Musicological Society, 2007

BOARD

Associate professor, Ph.D., Thomas Holme Hansen, University of Aarhus, chairman
Research librarian, cand.mag., Anne Ørbæk Jensen, The Royal Library
Associate professor, Ph.D., Morten Michelsen, University of Copenhagen
Ph.D. fellow, Ingeborg Okkels, University of Copenhagen
Associate professor, cand.mag., Peder Kaj Pedersen, University of Aalborg
Cand.mag., Fie Skovsbøg Thaning
Research librarian, cand.phil., Kirsten Flensborg Petersen, The Royal Library, deputy

At the Society's annual general assembly, held on 21 March 2007, the board was re-elected in toto. Following the assembly cand.mag. Valdemar Lønsted – writer and programmer at the Danish National Radio – gave a presentation of his recent book, *Mahler* (København: Gyldendal, 2006). During 2007 Morten Michelsen has acted as the Society's representative in the programme committee for the *15th Nordic Musicological Congress* which will take place in Oslo, 5–8 August 2008.

Like the preceding years the main event of 2007 was the Society's one-day symposium, which was held on 21 April at the Department of Musicology, University of Copenhagen. This fourth symposium centered on the subject *Musicology between visibility and professional legitimacy* and was joined by around 40 participants. The initial lecture, 'Musicology tomorrow', was presented by Lars Lilliestam (University of Gothenburg) and was followed by six papers which lead to a concluding plenary debate on the main topic. The day was rounded off by a short recital by mezzosoprano Trine Bastrup Møller and pianist Julie Andkjær Olsen. Abstracts and some full-length papers were subsequently published on the Society's web-site (www.hum.au.dk/musik/dsfm/dsfm_m/dsfm1.html).

Once again, a revised membership directory was included in the autumn letter to the members of the Society along with preliminary information on the Society's fifth symposium, *Danish Musicologies 2008*, which is scheduled for 26 April 2008 (general information on the society can be found on pp. 132–33).

Thomas Holme Hansen

Book Reviews

Musik og psykologi, Psyke & Logos, 28/1 (2007)
ed. Lars Ole Bonde
Copenhagen: Dansk Psykologisk Forlag, 2007
640 pp., illus.
ISBN 978-87-7706-457-9
DKK 235

'… the most extensive Danish publication on the subject of music and psychology' (p. 17). In this manner, the *Psyke & Logos* issue, *Musik og psykologi* (Music and Psychology), is introduced by Lars Ole Bonde, the guest editor of this issue. No need to object to this introduction. Certainly, it is the first time for this subject to be put that thoroughly on a Danish research agenda, and the issue includes an impressive number of 26 articles, written in Swedish (1), Norwegian (1), English (3) and the remaining in Danish. Previously in the history of *Psyke & Logos*, music has been discussed only sporadically (cf. *Art and Psychology*, 1993/2, and *Competence*, 1998/2), thus it is the first time for the psychological journal, *Psyke & Logos*, that music plays a decisive part. Considering the 30 year history of *Psyke & Logos*, this present issue is definitely the most extensive, and moreover some of the articles are highlighted by additional website material.

It has been a premise when demarcating the content of the issue that music psychology and music therapy as two related fields of research should be more or less equally represented (p. 6). As it turns out, the first 15 articles are representing music and psychology in a broad sense (p. 17), and in continuation of this, the last 11 articles are representing a so-called 'applied music psychology' in a narrow sense, that is music therapy. Besides music therapy, applied music psychology also includes educational music psychology and music in media and commercials (p. 17), but these subfields seem to be somewhat marginalized. For example the field of music in media and commercials is only considerably dealt with in two articles (directly in Iben Have's analysis of underscores in audiovisual media texts and indirectly in Martin Knakkergaard's discussion on music and time). Regarding the use of music in everyday life, this marginalization of specific subfields could seem misrepresentative. However, from the viewpoint of the editor the present emphasis is both justifiable and intelligible: it is precisely within the area of music therapy that music psychological research in Denmark appears strongest and most concerted, and the prized research environment within music therapy at Aalborg University seems to be a natural and very productive nucleus (the last 11 articles are all written by researchers with current or previous affiliation to the research environment in Aalborg).

Judging by the methodological and theoretical positions involved in the 26 articles, it is no exaggeration to say that they are wide-ranging. Both poles of the spectrum in 'music psychology of today' are presented; 'a humanist-ethnological-psychodynamic pole as opposed to a scientific-neurological-experimental-psychological pole' (p. 27). In serving the occasion, these poles appear somewhat crude (for instance there is not always convergence between humanist and psychodynamic schools of thought). Still, they make good sense in pointing out main views within the field of research. An observation is made regarding the historical and international relation of the poles moving from a clear separation toward what might be called an interdisciplinary and multi-paradigmatic situation (p. 23). However, the *Psyke & Logos* issue indicates that the present Danish music psychology (as it is here proposed and supplemented with a few noticeable foreign researchers) appears not to be affected by this interdisciplinary situation. For example, discussions concerning *intersubjectivity* (Kirsten Fink-Jensen), *mimesis* (Klaus Nielsen) and *technologies of the self* (Tia DeNora) are brought up mutually independent of discussions concerning *functional cerebral organization* (Alice Theilgaard), *lateral asymmetries of auditory stimulus* (Peter Vuust), and *mere exposure effect* (Anders Christian Green). True enough, interdisciplinary initiatives are not in all instanses relevant or productive, but in the present case it seems that research is carried out 'side-by-side' to a greater extend than 'across'. Therefore, the article 'Introduction to Music Psychology and Music Therapy' by Lars Ole Bonde should be consulted before reading the other articles. Bonde's article offers both concise definitions and a qualified and very extensive overview of historical and current research initiatives.

Summing up, the field of research in Denmark indeed represents variety over unity (p. 23). One thing that contributes to a sense of unity is the inspiration that many authors have found in the developmental psychological theories of Daniel Stern. Half of the articles are referring to his work and for several of them Stern's theories are pivotal. This probably has to do with Stern's relatively broad theoretical and methodical scope; his analysis of emotions and interactions between child and primary caretaker seems appropriate for the understanding of the complex relationship of music and experience. However, it should call for further consideration whether it is reasonable for instance to refer to children's preverbal communication with primary caretakers as 'musical communication' (p. 95) – a consideration which the author (Sven-Erik Holgersen) also shortly hints.

This example pinpoints another characteristic feature of the issue, namely the tendency to have 'music' include a very wide variety of auditory phenomena and functions; for example: 'the chirping of birds can be understood as a musical sequence' (p. 106), and when it comes to music as an applied phenomenon the following descriptions appear among many others: 'Music can reach deep inside us' (p. 65), 'communication can be established by the aid of music' (p. 135), 'music ... can afford social participation' (p. 284), and often the metaphor 'music as medicine' is referred to (see p. 527) – all these qualifications seem of interest and are all well argued for, even if the limits of the music-as-medicine metaphor are left unidentified (cf. Is music in effect a biochemical stimulus? Are there any adverse effects of music? Can music exceed a use-by date?).

This many-stringed description of music still holds one common denominator in that music is nearly glorified. The tone is set already in the preface where the editors of *Psyke & Logos* explains that 'music is a dearly beloved leisure time activity among psychologists' (p. 5). Such a preoccupation with music as a desirable object with undreamt-of possibilities and positive ability to function is partly a result of the aforementioned narrow focus within applied music psychology and partly a manifestation of a broader tendency. Thus it seems symptomatic that there has been no obvious need within musicology or music psychology to establish a counterpart to what has become *Positive Psychology* within psychology (e.g. Martin Seligman and Mihaly Csikszenmihalyi, 'Positive Psychology – An Introduction', *American Psychologist*, 55/1 (2000), 1–14). However, it is doubtful whether this entails a forthcoming explicit *Negative Musicology* even if recent publications in different ways come close (e.g. Christopher Washburne and Maiken Derno, *Bad Music – The Music We Love to Hate* (New York: Routledge, 2004), and Steven Brown and Ulrik Volgsten (eds.), *Music and Manipulation – On the Social Issues and Social Control of Music* (New York: Berghahn Books, 2006)).

In conclusion, it seems clear that there is no shortage of research interest, competence, and relevance within the field of music psychology. Internationally, this has been evident for long, and the field of research has been acknowledged for at least 100 years. In recent years, the field of research has even been subjected to increased attention. In Denmark, however, music psychology has until now lived a rather obscure and fragmented life, and there is no educational or research institution focusing on music psychology, for example. This issue on 'Music and Psychology' shows the fertile ground for changing that condition.

Nicolai Jørgensgaard Graakjær

Jens Henrik Koudal, *Grev Rabens dagbog.*
Hverdagsliv i et adeligt miljø i 1700-tallet
Folkemindesamlingens kulturstudier, 10
Odense: Syddansk Universitetsforlag, 2007
318 pp., illus., ISBN 978-87-7674-173-0
DKK 275

Jens Henrik Koudal fandt i 1991 en betydelig nodesamling på Ålholm Slot på det sydlige Lolland – en nodesamling, der har tilhørt grev Otto Ludvig Raben (1730-91), og som Koudal i de mellemliggende år har præsenteret på tryk i bl.a. *Cæcilia* (1992-93) og *Siden Saxo* (1992) samt i flere udsendelser i Danmarks Radio. Desuden er en del af musikken på Koudals foranledning blevet indspillet på cd af Concerto Copenhagen. Sammen med noderne fandtes også grev Rabens dagbog, ført fra nytår 1749 til kort før hans død i 1791, og den foreligger nu udgivet. Jens Henrik Koudal har med vanlig omhu givet dagbogen en grundig præsentation i et fornemt layout. Omslaget på bogen prydes af et diskret nedtonet portræt af greven, der på grå baggrund med et venligt imødekommende men samtidig uudgrundeligt blik byder læseren indenfor til at kigge med i optegnelserne om hans liv. Han synes på en gang at være nærværende som person, og så alligevel ikke rigtig til at blive klog på.

Koudal har da også haft sine betænkeligheder ved at udgive dagbogen, for "hvorfor skrive om en ukendt greve fra 1700-tallet?", spørger han i sin indledning. Og er det overhovedet interessant at læse 42 års faktuelle registreringer af hændelser i et ikke særlig begivenhedsrigt liv, når dagbogsskriveren næsten intet røber om sine tanker og følelser? Som man kan regne ud, er overvejelserne mundet ud i, at Koudal trods alt fandt det umagen værd at udgive dagbogen, for skønt Otto Ludvig Raben måske ikke i sig selv var så fascinerende som f.eks. tidens store kunstnere og videnskabsmænd, giver hans optegnelser et indblik i, hvordan han reagerede på sin tid og sine omgivelser. Dagbogen betragtes altså som et redskab til at se på et udsnit af historien fra en bestemt persons synsvinkel, og som sådan er den meget velkommen. For at få dagbogsskriveren til at fremstå mere vedkommende supplerer Koudal grevens optegnelser med studier i godsets øvrige arkivalier og en mængde faglitteratur, hvad der ikke bare er nødvendigt i betragtning af karakteren af grevens optegnelser, men også gør udgivelsen mere til en biografi end til en publiceret selvbiografi. Eller som det mere præcist hedder på omslaget til "en kulturhistorisk skildring af et delvis ukendt hverdagsliv i Rabens aristokratiske miljø".

Dagbogen præsenteres i 38 korte kapitler med betegnende overskrifter som "Pilgrimsrejsen", "Ulykkesåret", "Forlovelse og Bryllup", "Musik", "Livet på landet", "Tjenestefolkene". Optegnelserne kan altså ikke læses i deres helhed fra begyndelsen til slutningen, men når man ser, hvor kortfattet og lejlighedsvis indforstået, greven skrev, – hans egne ord sættes med kursiv – er man formentlig også bedre hjulpet med således at få indholdet præsenteret tematisk. Kapitlerne indledes med livskloge eller kulturhistorisk perspektiverende betragtninger, hvor man får mangt og meget at vide, f.eks. om standssamfundet og rangvæsenet, om betingelserne for at få oprettet et grevskab, om disciplinering af legemsbevægelserne og om bordskikke ved hoffet.

Fremstillingen bærer præg af, at udgiveren har kunnet bearbejde sine data elektronisk. For netop ved at kunne holde styr på "personer, steder og aktiviteter" har Koudal kunnet få øje på mønstre, der tegner sig i grevens adfærd, hvilket igen har ført til tematiseringer i fremstillingen.

Dagbogen blev ført på fransk, men er i udgaven oversat til dansk og gengivet med moderne retskrivning. Det gælder også andre samtidige kilder – hvad enten de er på fransk, tysk eller dansk – at de citeres på dansk med moderne retskrivning. En undtagelse fra den ellers konsekvent gennemførte modernisering af sproget er dog Rabens "Uddannelsesprogram" for sønnen Frederik Christian Raben, der er gengivet som bilag 3. Det er affattet på dansk, formentlig i årene 1774-76, og originalens ordlyd og stavemåde er bevaret i udgaven, hvorved man får et glimrende indtryk af grevens sprog, tænkemåde og verdensbillede samtidig med, at man får illustreret hans tidsbundne formuleringer:

"Af det *Latinske* Sprog behöves Hand kuns at lære saa meget, at det paa dend Lætteste og beqvemmeste maade, som for Hans bestemmelse kand agtes nogenledes fornöden [i det mindste saa meget, at han ikke i *Assembleer* eller andre honnette Selskaber skulde staae som en Hest eller Stud naar Han hörte en eller anden latinsk *Phrase*], mens udj Det Tydske maae hand flittig öfves og vel fatte *Ortographien*, særdelis maae hand erhverve dend största muelige Færdighed i Fæderne-Lands Sproget og med Tiden i begge sidste Sprog anföres til at opsætte Forestillinger Betragtninger *etc*: i en sammenhængende og Grundig *Deduction* om Een eller anden forelagt *Materie*, samt En kort og Net Brevstiil" (s. 270, det i skarp parentes indföjede er tilföjet i det originale manuskript i fremmed hånd).

Det er behageligt og letter læsningen, at udgiveren har gjort sig ulejlighed med at oversætte sådanne formuleringer, når de forefindes på fremmedsprog; de kan være vanskelige nok at forstå på gammelt dansk. Men oversættelsen kan på den anden side komme til at berøve dagbogen noget af dens sproglige atmosfære i den forstand, at flersproglighed var et karakteristisk træk for dannede folk i det meste af 1700-tallet. Der er en nøje sammenhæng mellem sprog, begrebsdannelse og omgangsformer, hvad det oven for citerede turde illustrere, og et af formålene med den store europæiske dannelsesrejse, som også Raben blev sendt ud på, var vel ikke mindst, at man fik lejlighed til at tilegne sig andre landes sprog og konversationstone *on location*. Man fik herved mulighed for at erfare, hvordan visse emner bedst lod sig debattere på ét sprog, konversationer føre på et andet og ordrer udstede på et tredje. Vigtige nuancer risikerer at gå tabt, når man oversætter de originale formuleringer til nudansk. Således var der en temmelig frivol omgangstone i de franske saloner ved midten af 1700-tallet, hvad Koudal forsigtigt antyder ved at sætte overskriften "Farlige forbindelser" over kapitlet med Rabens oplevelser i de parisiske saloner. Netop i denne del af dagbogen er adskillige sider dog skåret ud, så hvorvidt greven under dette ophold opførte sig mere naivt eller mere dristigt end han senere brød sig om at tænke på, får vi ikke at vide. Begge dele antydes i de gengivne brevuddrag (skrevne af andre) omhandlende Rabens færden blandt de letsindige franske kvinder. Koudal tager diskussionen om grevens flersproglighed op i kapitlet "Sprog og vurdering", hvor han beskriver grevens fransk som "forholdsvis stereotypt og helt uden litterære ambitioner" (s. 213), mens den lejlighedvise brug af tysk i dagbogen viser, at tysk lå lige under overfladen. Der gives tillige eksempler på, hvilke ord og navnlig stillingsbetegnelser, greven især benyttede på tysk.

Et andet markant valg – eller rettere fravalg – udgiveren har foretaget, er, at dagbogen ikke er forsynet med et register over personer eller sagsforhold. Dagbogsindføringerne og den uddybende litteratur, der er anvendt for at sætte den pågældende oplysning i perspektiv, er meddelt i slutnoterne, mens en række faktuelle oplysninger, herunder en stamtavle over Rabenslægten, opregnes i bilag. Man får altså grundig besked om, hvem de enkelte medlemmer af slægten var, og hvem de gennem afstamning eller ægteskab var beslægtet med, men man kan altså ikke bare lige foretage et opslag i bogen for at se, om greven måtte have nævnt denne eller hin person – eller for den sags skyld: et bestemt musikværk. Det sidste er et større savn end det første, men hvis man vil vide noget om grevens personlige omgangskreds eller musikalske repertoire må man altså læse hele bogen eller ty til de systematisk opbyggede bilag bag i bogen. Her får man til gengæld overordentlig præcis besked, f.eks. om at Otto Ludvig Raben i årene 1757-86 noterede sig, at han spiste 1243 gange hos sine forældre (bilag 4), mens de i årene 1759-83 spiste 12 gange hos ham (bilag 5). Statistikken kan ved første øjekast synes meningsløs, for mon ikke greven spiste sammen med sine forældre i de fleste af sine 27 første leveår? Men grevens omhyggelige opregning af måltider, han indtog hos andre eller selv indbød gæster til, har givet Koudal anledning til at skrive et kapitel om måltidets betydning som et socialt anliggende. Det var åbenbart magtpåliggende for greven at notere sig, hvem han spiste med og ved hvilket bord, når det foregik ved hoffet, så det er en fin pointe at gøre opmærksom på, at det var selskabeligheden omkring måltidet snarere end det kulinariske aspekt, der havde grevens opmærksomhed.

Ligeledes opregnes (i bilag 6) den fløjtespillende greves mange koncert- og operabesøg i ind- og udland. Man kunne ønske sig, at han havde været langt mere meddelsom med hensyn til det selskabelige aspekt af de mange koncerter, han overværede eller deltog i i private sammenhænge. For eksempel var han i året 1756 til koncert hele 79 gange hos sin far på dennes gods Bramsløkke eller om vinteren i hans palæ i Stormgade. Det er et imponerede antal, men var der mon i alle tilfælde tale om koncerter, der blev udøvet for et inviteret eller subskriberende publikum (hvad der i hvert fald i nogle tilfælde er dokumentation for), eller bruges ordet koncert mon også om langt mindre prætentiøse musiksammenkomster, hvor de tilstedeværende musicerede med og for hinanden under afslappende former? Det er påfaldende, at greven selv noterede sig for at have holdt et så beskedent antal koncerter på Ålholm (seks i 1772 og en i 1785). Havde han mon ikke anledning til at afholde flere, eller er musikdyrkelsen efterhånden blevet en så integreret del af det daglige liv på Ålholm, at det ophørte med at være en noteringsværdig begivenhed, at der blev musiceret? Der var ikke ansat musikudøvende lakajer på Ålholm, så betingelserne for at afholde mere organiserede musiksammenkomster i form af koncerter var måske meget begrænsede, eller fik greven mon sin lyst til musik styret ved udelukkende selv at være udøvende i familiens eller venners kreds? Der er fortsat mange ubesvarede spørgsmål at stille til det rige nodefund på Ålholm, herunder hvem der anskaffede noderne og af hvem og under hvilke omstændigheder, der blev musiceret efter dem. Men takket være udgivelsen af Otto Ludvig Rabens dagbog er vi da nu blevet lidt klogere på den person, der i en periode ejede (eller måske arvede?) en meget stor del af samlingen, og med Koudals gennemarbejdede præsentation er der frit spil til mere perspektivrige spekulationer over, om grevens altoverskyggende musikinteresse trådte i stedet for den naturvidenskabelige interesse, som både hans far og hans søn var kendetegnet af, eller om den erstattede den filosofiske og politiske interesse, som mange af hans standsfæller var så optaget af i det brogede oplysningsårhundrede.

Få år efter, at dagbogen blev draget frem i lyset, blev den sammen med det meste af det øvrige indbo fra Ålholm bortsolgt på auktion, og den er i dag kun tilgængelig som mikrofilm på Det Kongelige Bibliotek, mens originalens opholdssted er ukendt.

Til slut skal nævnes en pudsig ombrydningsfejl side 281-82, som viser at selv den skarpeste korrekturlæser kan løbe sur i arbejdet med at spotte fejl i de faktamættede bilag. En side i bilag 5 – indholdende en fortegnelse over alle personer der har spist mere end én gang hos Otto Ludvig Raben – er blevet trykt to gange med forskelligt sidetal.

Lisbeth Ahlgren Jensen

 Henrik Glahn, *Supplement til Salmemelodien i dansk tradition 1569–1973.*
Registrant vedrørende melodisamlinger til 'Den danske Salmebog 2002' samt
rettelser til 'Salmebogen i dansk tradition 1569–1973', ed. Inge Bønnerup
København: Forlaget Anis, 2007
31 pp., ISBN 978-87-7457-466-0
DKK 125

In 2000 the grand old man of Danish hymnody Henrik Glahn published his study *Salmemelodien i dansk tradition 1569–1973*. The book is an index of hymn melodies which have occurred in important Danish hymn books and melody collections from the first official Danish hymn book, *Hans Thomissøns Psalmebog 1569*, to the second edition of *Den danske Koralbog* of 1973. In addition to the detailed tabulated information on the sources and provenance of the various melodies the book also contains an invaluable, well-written, and pedagogical introduction to the history and development of the large and very diverse repertory of hymn tunes in Danish tradition.

Glahn was for a time a music consultant to the select committee on church music in the latest Danish hymn book commission, and he was a critical participant in the long debate which accompanied the preparation and publication of the latest official hymn book, *Den Danske Salmebog 2002*, and its accompanying melody collection, *Koralbog til Den Danske Salmebog 2003*.

At his death in 2006 he left the finished manuscript of a supplement for his melody index which includes the melodies in the new *Salmebog* and *Koralbog*. The new repertory consists of 568 tunes, 393 of which also appeared in the older *Koralbog* whereas 175 are 'new', although some of them have at different times had a certain dissemination in Danish hymn singing. The majority of these new melodies are written in the twentieth century. Glahn classifies and comments on the melodies in accordance with the system of the original book.

Apart from the classifying overview and some statistics, the book contains little information which cannot be found in the annotations of the melodies in the new *Koralbog*.

For a large part of the twentieth century the study of hymn melodies was a central issue in Danish musicology, not least through the contributions of Glahn which began with his university dissertation on the treatment of rhythm in the hymn tunes of the Reformation period (1947) and his doctorate thesis of 1954, *Melodistudier til den lutherske salmesangs historie fra 1524 til ca. 1600*, and continued in a long series of special studies. For many reasons hymnody now holds a more inferior position in Danish research, and it seems unlikely that it will ever again receive the passionate, detailed, and scholarly attention it had in the hands of Henrik Glahn. It is all the more satisfying that we now have the completion of his index of what he termed 'the collected, relevant Danish hymn material'.

Henrik Palsmar

 Harry R. Graversen, Peter E. Nissen, and Claus Røllum-Larsen (eds.)
Efterklange af romantikken i dansk orgelmusik. Tre komponister og en
repertoireundersøgelse
Det Danske Orgelselskabs Skriftserie, 1
Jelling: Det Danske Orgelselskab, 2007
120 pp., illus., music exx., ISBN 978-87-88238-10-5
DKK 125

The high romanticism of organ music had a very short period of flowering in Denmark. The romantic organ types and the musical styles appropriated to them were only hesitatingly introduced in the country as late as the last decade of the nineteenth century. And they were quickly suppressed again when the so-called Organ Movement conquered the land from the 1920's onwards. The composers fell into oblivion. However, today's rekindling of interest in the period has caused some publishing of music and CDs, and now the Danish Organ Society has published the book *Efterklange af romantikken i dansk orgelmusik. Tre komponister og en repertoireundersøgelse* (*Echoes of Romanticism in Danish Organ Music. Three composers and a survey of repertory*) – a collection of four excellent articles on the period. Composers Gottfred Matthison-Hansen, Otto Malling, Gustav Helsted and Johan Adam Krygell are the protagonists, but they are treated from quite different points of view: one as a concert organist, others as composers with substantial work analyses, and the last-mentioned as a biography with a relevance to the understanding of the social conditions of organists at the time.

Claus Røllum-Larsen researches the repertoire played at Gottfred Matthison-Hansen's (1832–1909) organ recitals in Trinity Church, Copenhagen, between 1882 and 1902. The concept of organ recitals was a novelty in Copenhagen musical life at the time, and at these concerts a large number of contemporary French and German organ works were introduced to the audience in Copenhagen. In the beginning, the recitals focused on Bach and Handel (the latter with transcriptions of the organ concerti), but in time Matthison-Hansen more and more turned his interest especially towards the new French repertoire with works by among others Alexandre Guilmant, César Franck, Théodore Dubois, Charles Marie Widor, and Théodore Salomé. His own works and those of his father, Hans Matthison-Hansen, figured prominently in the programmes too. He may have had the inspiration for the organ recitals from William Best's concerts in Liverpool or those of Alexandre Guilmant in Paris. He was friendly with the latter, as is documented by various dedications.

The recitals were exclusive subscription concerts at ticket prices of as much as two Danish kroner. In return, the public could hear 'our first organ player' in a repertoire which was to a large extent new to a Danish audience. Furthermore, as an organ teacher at the Copenhagen conservatory Matthison-Hansen had significant influence on the next generation of organ players – including the three other composers discussed in the book. Another student was P.S. Rung-Keller, who later became famous as organist at Our Saviour's Church, Copenhagen. In his recollections of Gottfred Matthison-Hansen he consistently refers to him as 'master'. One readily believes this designation when examining the impressive repertoire of his organ recitals, which must be considered an extraordinary pioneering effort.

Swedish professor Sverker Jullander gives a well-informed introduction to the substantial organ production of Otto Malling (1848–1915), about 60 pieces mostly collected in cycles of biblically inspired tone-pictures. This is sacred music which is almost completely separated from the traditional forms of church music, and was therefore later bound to arouse the wrath of the followers of Thomas Laub. However, Jullander analyses the music on its own premises, which leads to many interesting conclusions. Malling was an original composer, not only as far as his favourite genre is concerned, for which there are not many models, not even abroad, but also in regard to many traits in the music: the use of programmes, the 'oriental' colouring, his personal way of quoting hymn tunes, and not least the music's purpose of expressing and vitalizing the biblical Word. At the same time, Malling's music is almost too traditional: 'it does not break borders, but rather makes it a point of honour to be a strictly controlled "Kleinkunst", with complete mastery of the means of expression within closely-drawn limits', as Jullander puts it (p. 69).

Jullander shows his knowledge of Malling's production, which is probably matched by very few others. You feel inspired to go exploring – even if he may overplay Malling's importance a bit with his final comparison to Olivier Messiaen. Fortunately, most of Malling's organ compositions are in print, and Helge Gramstrup has recorded a CD of *St Paul* and *The Saviour's Seven Words on the Cross*.

Gustav Helsted's (1857–1924) output for the organ was far smaller than Malling's, even though he worked as an organist from 1891, where he was appointed organist at the newly inaugurated Cavaillé-Coll organ in the Jesus Church in Valby, until his death in 1924, when he had become Malling's successor as cathedral organist in the Church of Our Lady in Copenhagen. In his article 'Gustav Helsted ved orglet' (Gustav Helsted at the Organ) Peter E. Nissen partly occupies himself with the Cavaillé-Coll organ and its significance for Helsted and Danish organ culture in general, partly with the changing musical circumstances that caused a leading church musician like Helsted to produce only two major organ works out of an output of 33 opus numbers. His background was the concert music, which is mirrored in the organ pieces *Phantasy in E minor* (Op. 16) and *Sonata in D Major* (Op. 29), which are both analysed. In them, Peter E. Nissen traces the influence of Franz Liszt and César Franck. Like Malling, Helsted was brushed aside after his death, as was his pupil Rued Langgaard.

Finally the book contains a revised excerpt of Jørgen Hansen's MA dissertation *Johan Adam Krygell (1835–1915). En værkfortegnelse med en kort biografi til en afdækning af en kleinkomponists økonomiske forhold i København i slutningen af forrige århundrede* (Johan Adam Krygell (1835–1915). A work-list with a short biography in order to uncover the economic circumstances of a minor composer in Copenhagen at the end of the last century; University of Copenhagen, 1990). The title accurately sums up the contents of the article. Krygell was a provincial, apparently awkward and hardly a man of the world, but an industrious church musician, who was employed at St Matthew's church in Vesterbro in Copenhagen from 1880 until his death. His limited success in his own time is partly explained with his lack of ability to make connections with important people. The thesis – and this article – contains the most substantial evaluation of his life and a detailed list of his many compositions for the organ.

Mikael Garnæs

Nila Parly, *Absolut Sang. Klang, køn og kvinderoller i Wagners værker*
Copenhagen: Multivers, 2007
364 pp.
ISBN 978-87-7917-181-7
DKK 389

Nila Parly has taken on an impressive project and written an impressive book based on her Ph.D. thesis of 2005. In the wake of many years of research and writing about Wagner's operas and music drama she has dared to come out with another book and another angle on the works of the controversial composer. Wagner always provokes very strong views and opinions, and this book is no exception.

The intention of the book is twofold: 1) to save the reading of Wagner's women characters and his operas from the traditional feminist stance which, briefly stated, concludes that Wagner's women always die and are repressed as women, and that this is an indication of Wagner's repressive, patriarchal attitude to the role of woman; and 2) to interpret Wagner's operas and music dramas with a clear focus on the women, their musical *Gestalt* and their active role in the constitution of the drama by way of their musical, textual, and visual-dramatic 'agency' in the operas.

In thorough, but selective and focused analyses, the author interprets the music and singing of the principal female characters in the major operas: Senta in *Der Fliegende Hol-*

länder, Elisabeth and Venus in *Tannhäuser,* Elsa and Ortrud in *Lohengrin,* Brünnhilde in *Der Ring des Niebelungen,* Isolde in *Tristan und Isolde,* Eva in *Die Meistersinger* and Kundry in *Parsifal.* She also points out dramatic, expressive, and structural interconnections among the women characters in the different operas.

Against this background she is able to construct a coherent, quite convincing argument about the creative role of women and Wagner's position in the 'woman question'. To do so, she consults and re-reads Wagner's own writings: his letters, *Mein Leben, Oper und Drama,* and other works. She also discusses the most important interpretations and theoretical discussions of Wagner to date, including those of musicologists, but also those of recent literary, psychological, psychoanalytical, and other traditions: Carl Dahlhaus, Carolyn Abbate, Jean-Jacques Nattiez, Slavoj Zizek, and others.

The analyses and interpretations are mainly close readings of the scores (texts, notes, remarks); but the author also considers the sounds of the characters' voices – that is, how the scores and the Wagnerian voice tradition define how those voices are to sound. And this brings me to some of the problems and the main objection to certain difficulties in the book: 1) the obscurity of the ontological status of the works (objects) analysed; 2) the lack of an explicit account of what the author is doing (the method actually used) and of the underlying theories; and 3) the resulting analytical-interpretative discourse, which unintentionally and perhaps unconsciously results in a closure of the dynamic meaning-production of the operas and the readings of it – a tendency in fact to produce a fixed meaning instead of an analytically open process in a theoretical productive discourse of her own.

The intention is to convince the reader of certain statements and conclusions (meanings, i.e. signifiers, *énoncé*) drawn from the analyses of the operas – as the author herself has been convinced; an intention clearly revealed by the increasing frequency of various qualifying phrases like 'in my view', 'I find', 'I mean', 'personally I (rather) think', 'I do not mean', 'personally I find' and so on, throughout the book. According to the author the analytical process is the difficult but creative way to distil out this operatic 'meaning', gradually formulated as the "essence" of the Wagner work, (pp. 243, 235–36); that is, a concept of the score as an authorized, ideal, and essentialist conception of 'the work' and its meaning.

How attendance to a performance of the operas would operate and work is something the author implicitly addresses by installing 'the audience' as an explicit reference point, a witness to semantic, interpretative 'truth' (pp. 187, 195, 235). But this 'audience' is by no means real or concrete; it is entirely virtual (imagined), although this is never stated or commented on by the author. This notion of the 'audience' might have been given a theoretical basis by theories of reception aesthetics (Hans Robert Jauss, Wolfgang Iser, Umberto Eco) and their notion of 'the implicit recipient', but the author does not do so.

Furthermore, the discursive style of the analyses has a tendency to mythologize the composed musical *Gestalt* of the singing women characters as their own 'compositional activity', interpreting this as if it is some living manifestation of real womens' characters and enabling a feminist reading of those characters (behind Wagner's back!). Even though the author admits that they should be understood as acting on behalf of Wagner himself, this undermines the stringency and authority of the analytical discourse and leaves the impression of a seductive and over-creative interpretation – one that is nevertheless mainly well argued and documented in the score.

This kind of hermeneutic-structural interpretative analysis has a long and strong tradition behind it in musicology, but here it is combined with the latest feminist-inspired opera and narration-theory tradition (Abbate) powered by a strong, but sometimes too literal, bombastic and emotive discourse on female and male in all aspects of life: in opera, in music, in Wagner, in his and our society, and in 'the audience'.

If Nila Parly – on the basis of the score – can read a feminine ending into the first two forte fortissimo staccato semiquavers of the *Trauermusik beim Tode Siegfrieds*, then you can interpret anything as feminism. On the CD interpretation I have (Georg Solti, 1965/97 Decca) I clearly hear the two sounding semiquavers as equally stressed, physically shocking enunciations of death and sorrow, physically affecting and phenomenologically arousing me (the CD listener). Whether this would also be the case for a real opera audience is a matter for the theory of the sounding, performed opera – which would by its nature take a quite different theoretical point of departure where the closure of semantics and meaning is not the main focus.

However, the most original and important achievement of the book is that Nila Parly has managed to focus on the singing women's voices and their articulation ('enunciation') in the tension between text (language) and music as decisive for the understanding of these women characters. The project is important in relation not only to Wagner himself, but also to the understanding of the historical and current reception of Wagner.

The book's title, which means *Absolute Song*, used as a concept for this 'voicing', is problematical and perhaps misleading in relation to Eduard Hanslick's concept of 'absolute music', which he developed precisely in opposition to Wagner's musical aesthetics. An alternative would have been to consult Roland Barthes' classic text, *The Grain of the Voice*, which – inspired by Kristeva and by Benveniste's linguistic enunciation theory – investigates at quite another theoretical level the intertwined voice production of music *and* language as the most profound and complicated creative source for human articulation of body and mind.

Ansa Lønstrup

Finn Egeland Hansen, *Layers of Musical Meaning*
København: Museum Tusculanum Press, 2006
333 pp., music exx.
ISBN 87-635-0424-3
DKK 300

The purpose of the book is clearly stated in the preface: there are 'two approaches to music in need of both supplementary and corrective reflection'. The truth value of hermeneutic interpretations cannot be determined, and structural analysis is not meaningful unless one pays close attention to the underlying codes. The normative character of Egeland Hansen's undertaking is evident throughout, but his attitude towards the two domains is different. Whereas analysis is supplied with a basic theory as well as with inventories of things that he considers necessary to make music inherently meaningful, various attempts to establish extramusical content are severely critized — the reader cannot but get the impression that hermeneutics is a futile activity beyond remedy.

The reason for this condemnation is the author's strong adherence to positivistic principles — 'positivism' taken as a neutral term within the theory of science, of course, not as a trigger of irrational conditioned reflexes. He holds that theories (and by extension findings in general) should be falsifiable, and that unverified results amount to nil in scholarly work. When applied to musical hermeneutics, this guiding rule is bound to yield negative results and — so it seems to this reviewer — practicians of musical analysis have to be careful not to get into credibility problems as well. It does not emerge as altogether clear whether Egeland Hansen's no-nonsense criterion of meaningfulness, strictly implemented, is entirely reasonable within a field like musicology. To the extent that there are things in music that we want to learn about but that are not strictly knowable, we might consider a less rigorous methodology.

Anyway, chapter two disposes of hermeneutics. Quite a few interpretations of Shostakovich's Tenth Symphony are cited (and a number of pages are wasted) just to show how much they diverge in terms of approach and extra-musical content. But Egeland Hansen also offers evaluations of four hermeneutic authorities. In as far as Kretzschmar restricts himself to middle-of-the-road characterizations of themes and motifs — a quite primitive kind of hermeneutics — he is harmless. Schering's way of reading Beethoven's compositions along with works by Shakespeare, Schiller etc. in order to extract musical narratives is exemplified and dismissed without further arguments (which seems both fair and sufficient). The interest is considerably heightened when the attacks are aimed at contemporary big game. Kramer claims that music, like the other arts, bears content, and that this content is accessible if only the analyses are valid. It is convincingly shown, however, that the hermeneutic 'window' through which Kramer observes Beethoven's Op. III is marred by serious errors of refraction. Tarasti's theory of music semiotics is succinctly presented — one cannot but marvel at the richness of musical signification that reveals itself when introspection is unhampered by positivistic control — and the atemporal semiotic square is then found to be too square a straitjacket to capture the essence of Chopin's *Polonaise Fantasy*.

For every strange analysis a counter-analysis should be available. There is much work to be done here — musicology seems self-supporting in this respect — and it is praiseworthy when someone with an unbiased mind sets about to undertake it. The author also warns analysts of the pitfalls associated with establishing motivic affinities (beware of too short and stylistically commonplace items in out-of-the-way corners!). It is indeed quite awkward when one suspects that an analyst has by far out-smarted the composer. But identifying affinities does involve such risks, and turning to the reverse pitfall of triviality, of saying too little, overly circumscribed, pedantic analyses may fail to do justice both to the unregulated creativity of the composers and to the unbridled associations of the listening mind.

Egeland Hansen's theory of the structural meaning of music, music as heard when 'uncontaminated' by irrelevant associations and circumstances, assumes the existence of one 'comparator' for each element in music (rhythm, harmony, melody, etc.) that compares what actually happens in these domains (*parole*) with the codes for such events (*language*), codes that the listener must be in command of as internalized knowledge. The output of these processes serves as input for the 'integrator' having three functions: to establish the interrelationships between the elements, to recognize stylistic patterns, and to determine the relative importance of the elements. This scheme amounts to a quite plausible machinery for informed listening, but it also strikes as being a 'theory' that is too abstract to be strictly testable. Cognitive musicology might shed some light on some of these processes, but the author somewhat rashly adopts a quite negative attitude towards such research since it has a record of not taking due account of musical context and stylistic matters. Meanwhile, nothing prevents the workings of Egeland Hansen's framework from being specified, an endeavour that occupies most of the book and yields a number of pertinent observations that may be shown to agree, not primarily with how music is heard, but with how it is in fact constructed.

Some particulars of his system deserve mentioning and comment. While admitting that repeated listening often makes for more rewarding experiences, the author, wanting to take account of the temporal nature of music and its concomitant effects of expectation, opts for dealing with first-time encounters. And whereas he acknowledges the fact that the listener may in fact choose among several codes, he insists 'that in the ideal listening situation the listener must apply exactly the same set of codes as the composer did when he wrote the piece of music' (p. 14) — otherwise the understanding will be lost. It is regrettable, however, that the best listening is left aside, and that ideal/uncontaminated listening tends to be extremely rare, perhaps unattainable.

In his discussion of Nattiez's concepts of *poiesis* ('the way a musical work is created') and *aesthesis* ('how it is perceived'), Egeland Hansen dismisses the 'neutral level', i.e. the 'level of analysis on which it is not decided *a priori* whether the results ... are pertinent from the aesthesic or poietic point of view': 'In my opinion a strict and mechanical analysis of the musical surface has no great relevance, at least not to the present work' (p. 28). However, already one page later he embarks on an investigation to find out whether the Franconian rule applies in a certain body of works. Intervals are counted and durations are sliced, and it seems that the level is neutral indeed; the statistical method as well as its results would certainly come as a surprise both to the contributors to Codex H 196 and to their listeners, which does not prevent that the findings are pertinent for both. The Franconian test is quite good, and I think that many of the best things in the book derive from such 'neutral' undertakings.

According to the theory, music may be 'represented' by means of notations or sound registrations of various sorts. It can also be 'paraphrased', and this happens as soon as we attach musico-theoretic terms like 'upbeat' or 'triad' to a represented event, thus adding intellectually reliable pieces of experiential content. Finally, music is also 'interpreted' which means, not that we play it, but that we 'attribute specific content to a musical progression', which in turn implies that we have left 'the discipline of musical analysis' which is scholarly and 'therefore objective'. It is the prerogative of any author to stipulate re-definitions of worn-out words, but as far as music analysis is concerned, it is a pity that testability commands such a high price in terms of reduced territory and interest. There are insights to gain already if the restrictions regulating what counts as a permissible description were somewhat less rigid, if the phenomenology of tonal motion were granted some space within 'paraphrasing'. Words like 'upbeat' and 'triad' cannot very well be the outermost boundary marks beyond which the quagmire of hermeneutics necessarily begins.

The larger part of Egeland Hansen's book deals with the codes that we must know in order to understand the various layers of musical meaning. Gregorian chant is used as an example to show the workings of tonality: the author simply gives a short version of his thesis from 1979 — a *tour de force* on the neutral level. Summarizing common knowledge, the chapters on harmony and form are entirely eclectic. Lots of old meat is served, but the chewing is made easier by the clarity of the presentation and the well-chosen music illustrations. As a bonus, the proponents of harmonic dualism (may they otherwise rest in peace) are found guilty of having invented theories that lack support from compositional practice.

Most of the chapter on rhythm is devoted to a discussion of the phenomenon of metric accent, being the main (or only?) material for the comparator dealing with small-scale temporal formats where it gives rise to sensations of tension and release. But what about grouping — is it matter of *parole*, rather than *language*? From the point of view of analytic objectivity, it is worrying that ambiguities turn up already when considering the relative accentual weights between pairs of bars, but Egeland Hansen handles such situations without much discussion. Perhaps the scope and power of the rhythmic comparator is severely restricted when it comes to hypermetric issues? Perhaps some assistance from the integrator is what is needed?

'Stray Reflections on Melodic Codes' is the shortest but most interesting of these chapters — questions and provisional answers provoke thinking. The author suggests that, especially when compared to the orderly and thoroughly studied system of harmony, the relationship between melodic *parole* and *language* (being hard to pin-point) may be different, and indi-

cates some problems to be pursued. What is, for instance, the relationship between interval size and melodic/tonal tension? What is the nature of the symmetry between ascending and descending melodic motions?

Bengt Edlund

Anders Meng, *Temporal Feature Integration for Music Organisation*
Kgs. Lyngby, Danmarks Tekniske Universitet, 2006
IMM-PhD-2006-165

Peter Ahrendt, *Music Genre Classification Systems – A Computational Approach*
Kgs. Lyngby, Danmarks Tekniske Universitet, 2006
IMM-PhD-2006-164

This is not a review proper but merely a brief presentation of two closely related Ph.D. theses from the Technical University of Denmark (DTU).

The subjects of these theses lie within the research area *Music Information Retrieval* (MIR) and aim at a computerized genre recognition mechanism working on the acoustical signal as it appears on a CD or other standard music medium.

The mechanisms developed may be compared with fingerprints and DNA-tests in forensic medicine. These methods may certainly be crucial in establishing 'who did it', but they do not in themselves contribute to our understanding of the crime committed, psychologically or sociologically. In the same way the concepts *Short-time Feature Extraction* and *Temporal Feature Integration* which form the central approaches in both theses may well establish that a given sequence of music belongs to a certain musical genre or that it is written by a certain composer – but they do not tell us anything about music – neither the music analysed nor music in general.

Short-time Feature Extraction consists in cutting the music into overlapping slices of typically 10–40 ms. The slices are then analysed with regard to frequency and intensity. It should be noted, however, that a Fourier transform performed on such narrow time windows yields a very coarse frequency resolution. Consequently the extracted spectra may not be intuitively connected with any normal musical concept such as harmony or timbre. This, however, does not prevent the analyses from yielding useful information in connection with MIR.

Temporal Feature Integration 'is the process of combining (integrating) all the short-time feature vectors in a time frame into a new single feature vector on a larger time scale' (Ahrendt, p. 31). Various, mainly statistical methods are discussed, none of which, however, speak directly to the musician or the musicologist.

The performance accuracy of the systems is tested on two data sets, one of which is made up of 100 songs evenly distributed among the five genres Classical, Jazz, Pop, Rock, and Techno. The other, and much larger set consists of 1,210 songs distributed among 11 genres: Alternative, Country, Easy Listening, Electronica, Jazz, Latin, Pop & Dance, Rap & HipHop, R&B Soul, Reggae, and Rock. The first set is tested on a panel of 22 persons 'without any

specific knowledge of music' between 25 and 35 years of age. With music examples of 10 seconds the accuracy with which the panel could label the examples was 98%. The second data set was tested in a similar fashion. With examples of 30 seconds the accuracy was 57%. When tested by the computerized systems the best hit-rate was 92% for the first data set (as compared with 98% by the human test panel) and 48% for the second (as compared with 57%).

These two theses may well prove to be useful for an uninformed user in search of music in a specific genre – and it must be stressed that this is what the projects aim at. But as contributions to musicology in the traditional meaning of this term they do not contribute at all.

Finn Egeland Hansen

Jens Westergaard Madsen, *Kreativt klaverstudium*
København: Museum Tusculanum Forlag/Københavns Universitet, 2006
2 vols.: i: Tekstdel, 110 pp.; ii: Nodedel, 133 pp.
incl. 1 CD: Jens Westergaard Madsen, *En kort introduktion*
ISBN 87-7289-930-1
DKK 198

Jens Westergaard Madsens *Kreativt Klaverstudium* består af to bind – en tekstdel og en nodedel – samt en CD, hvor forfatteren på godt fyrre minutter i en blanding af spillede musikeksempler og talte kommentarer giver et indblik i bogens sigte og de muligheder bogens arbejdsmetoder åbner for. Og de muligheder er langt mere vidtrækkende end bogens titel lader ane. Bogens sigte er at nedbryde nogle af de eksisterende grænser mellem repertoirespil, improvisation og diverse satslærediscipliner, og det gør *Kreativt Klaverstudium* i lige så høj grad til et kreativt studium af satslæreprincipper – ja, i sidste instans til en kreativ indføring i selve musikkens substans – som et studium i (brugs)klaverspilsteknik. Musikken, der arbejdes med, er den dur-mol-tonale, klassiske musik repræsenteret gennem et begrænset værkudvalg af Bach, Mozart, Beethoven, Chopin og Brahms.

Metoden til dette er at træne sig i bogstaveligt talt at få musikken op i fingrene. Dette forløb har forfatteren tilrettelagt i fire trin: satsreduktion, transposition, sekvensering og modelkomposition.

Første trin, satsreduktion, består i at reducere en given klaversats til dens rene melodiske og harmoniske skelet i en såkaldt 'ageret analyse'. Det 'agerede' er centralt for bogens ærinde: Analysen af musikken sker gennem lige dele finger- og hjernearbejde således, at hjernearbejdet udmøntes i fingrenes bevægelser snarere end i nedskrevne analysesymboler. I en progressivt tilrettelagt, klar og pædagogisk gennemgang viser forfatteren, hvorledes dette kan gøres og hvilke overvejelser og indsigter det kan give anledning til.

Med den reducerede sats er vejen banet for de to følgende trin, transposition og sekvensering. Særlig sekvenseringen af satsen har forfatterens bevågenhed, da en sekvensering af et givent materiale i højere grad end den blot mekaniske transposition kræver stillingtagen til satsudformningen (fx i forbindelse med eventuelle bidominanter, håndtering af tonekøn m.m.). Og som en ekstra bonus medfører dette et kapitel viet til en grundig gennemgang af samtlige dur-mol-musikkens sekvenser.

Musikeksemplerne fra bogens første del genoptages og perspektiveres i disse følgende øvelser, der igen viser sig at fremstå som forberedende for metodens fjerde og sidste del, modelkomposition. Efter indledningsvist at have dokumenteret, hvorledes denne måde at undervise i satslære på har været praktiseret fra 1700-tallet frem til det 20. århundrede, appliceres den på det materiale, læseren (eller rettere: brugeren) har arbejdet med. Model-

komposition består i at benytte en given kompositions harmoniske og formmæssige skelet som grundlag for en 'ny komposition'. Det kan f.eks. gøres, som Westergaard Madsen viser det, ved tage akkordgangen fra Bachs præludium i d-mol (Wohltemperiertes Klavier bind I) og lade det melodiske materiale være figurerne fra præludiet i D-dur fra samme bind. Eller man kan, som forfatteren også viser det, ud fra et intermezzo af Brahms arbejde friere og skabe sine egne melodier indenfor rammerne af en given harmonik og form. Sigtet med dette er for Westergaard Madsen – og det er vigtigt – ikke at lære at komponere, men at opnå en større musikalsk forståelse. Bogen afsluttes da også med en række overvejelser over metodens videre perspektiver.

Fremstillingformen er som nævnt hele vejen igennem ukrukket klar, enkel og meget pædagogisk. Nodeeksemplerne er ligeledes tydelige og hensigtsmæssigt sat op med en god progression nodeeksemplerne imellem. Man kommer takket være den velvalgte koncentration på et begrænset eksempelmateriale, der for hvert trin udbygges, virkelig i dybden med såvel metode som materiale.

Som indledningsvis antydet er bogen langt mere vidtrækkende end titlen antyder. Det er ikke en klaverspilsbog, men en indføring i musikforståelse formidlet gennem klaveret. Og som sådan er metoden oplagt som grundlag for et satslærekursus for pianister. Eller for den sags skyld enhver klaverspillende musikstuderende. Samtidig er den oplagt til brug i arbejdet med brugsklaver. Det er med andre ord lykkedes Westergaard Madsen at formidle mellem musikalsk teori og praksis på en måde, som beriger begge sider. Måtte et kursus i denne disciplin blive et obligatorisk indslag på enhver højere musikalsk læreanstalt!

Svend Hvidtfelt Nielsen

Jane Mink Rossen and Uri Sharvit, *A Fusion of Traditions: Liturgical Music in the Copenhagen Synagogue*
Odense: University Press of Southern Denmark, 2006
156 pp., illus., music exx., incl. 1 CD
ISBN 87-7674-038-2
DKK 200

Music historiography is in the business of breaking silences. *A Fusion of Traditions* is breaking the silence of untold musical pasts, presents, parts and elements of a culture in Denmark, which is only little known: that of the Jewish liturgical music at the Copenhagen Synagogue, in *Krystalgade* (Crystal Street), central Copenhagen.

The study centres around Rossen's recordings made in 1967 of which selections can be heard on the CD accompanying the book. The study is supported by other sources, such as interviews with participants, material from the Danish National Archives and cantorial scores in manuscripts. The book is structured in two individual parts. Part one by Jane Mink Rossen is called 'History of the Cantorate and Choir 1833–2001', and offers a historical account of the Jewish community in Copenhagen and the developments in the Synagogue, and includes biographical information about cantors and choirmasters. Part two by Uri Sharvit has the title 'The music and its socio-cultural role'. It is based on transcriptions and analyses of Rossen's recordings and addresses in detail aspects of the liturgical framework and musical practice.

This study of the liturgical music in the Copenhagen Synagogue is an interesting testimony to the history of the 400 years old Jewish minority in Denmark as a culture influenced by Yiddish- and German-speaking Jews from Central and Eastern Europe. The present musical practice in the Copenhagen Synagogue is comprised of harmonized musical arrangements from the middle of the nineteenth century and is the result of a long process of a 'fusion' of different practices and traditions, of compromises between the Jewish reformist contingent and the traditionalist faction and between Ashkenazic and Sephardic communities, of negotiations with the Danish legislative institutions, as well as cooperation with Christian composers (such as Friedrich Kuhlau and C.E.F. Weyse). A fine point of the importance of understanding music as culture and social phenomenon is provided both in the historical account, but also in the musical analysis – and this is perhaps where the two separate parts actually meet as two fragments making a larger whole: in his detailed musical analysis, Sharvit shows that 'compromises that were adopted following the Reform–Orthodox conflict and the predominance of Eastern European cantors from 1844 onward gave rise to the special character of the liturgical tradition of the Copenhagen Synagogue, namely the combination of German and Polish practices and the amalgamation of their musical styles' (p. 70). Thus peace between reformists and orthodox congregations was eased musically by mixing German style and Polish cantorial recitative that created a 'tolerant atmosphere through acceptance of both styles and the creation of unique features' (p. 111).

In taking part in – if not indeed initiating – the historiography of Jewish liturgical music in Denmark, this fine book offers insight into a culture for a wider public, not least for those of us who have so far been wondering about the musical activities and religious life that went on in the Copenhagen Synagogue behind the massive walls and the security personnel posted outside (a reminder that the lives of the congregation have quite often been at risk during its entire existence in Denmark). The book satisfies the reader with a fascinating and detailed account of names and places that is not in the wider public associated with any positive influence on 'our' society within the Old Danish Kingdom, such as those from Poland and Romania. As a piece of research that speaks a first word, *A Fusion of Traditions* also leaves the reader with many new questions: there is indeed much more to know about Jewry in Denmark and its European heritage. In that sense the book is inspiring and opens up for issues for future research to tamper with.

A Fusion of Traditions also has its few shortcomings, not so much for what it contains, but rather for what is missing. When the book addresses the 'present', it is not always clear exactly *what* present the authors have in mind. The present of 1967 is clearly fundamental to the book. It should be emphasized that 1967 is an important temporal marker of the book's primary material (Rossen's historical recordings) which is presented to the reader (and listener) in both transcriptions and sound. However, the year 1967 is also a past in relation to the tradition that has continued since then. This brings me to another present, namely the historical limit of the book's objective, 2001 that is (Part 1 addresses the time span '1833–2001'), which wisely enough allows for the inclusion of updated and new information (1833 is the year of the consecration of the Copenhagen Synagogue). It would be interesting for future research to focus on what it meant and means to be Jewish in Denmark in various pasts and presents and how sound and music has taken part in forming Danish-Jewish and European-Jewish identities – specially now in the light of the development of the 'New Europe', the European Union, since the end of the 1960s.

For a study of a musical tradition, this reader would have welcomed a discussion of the central concepts of 'tradition' and 'assimilation' in order to facilitate the understanding of the *meaning* of tradition and change in the context of Jewry – not only by the authors, but perhaps also by participants in the Jewish community themselves (the latter would be a clearly defined objective for a future fieldwork). What does assimilation mean in terms of sacred sounds and music? Was Jewish culture merely 'assimilated' in the sense that it was adjusted to fit Danish law and Christian culture? As ethnomusicologist and researcher into Jewish music

Kay Kaufman Shelemay states, 'Melodies can only be borrowed when they are already part of the sound world of the singers who would appropriate them'.[1] In other words, the liturgy also creates contexts in which changes are manifested in action and sound. *A Fusion of Traditions* is a contribution to scholarly knowledge about musical tradition and change in general; however, the discussion throughout the book would have benefited from conferring more closely with the insights of other studies of sacred musical traditions, which would have shown, for example, that the Jewish liturgical musical tradition in Copenhagen is as variegated (though in its own idiosyncratic way) as many other Jewish traditions around the world. Rossen speaks of an 'unbroken' Jewish tradition in Denmark (p. 9) since the first Jews came to the duchy of Holstein in 1584. Whatever 'unbroken' means, it is clear that it does not imply that the tradition is unchanged but the contrary, which is precisely one of the main (and important) points of the book.

As an ethnographic work, *A Fusion of Tradition* places its emphasis on its empirical material and the presentation of its data. It does not aim at discussing the implications of the research methods that have been applied (reflection on fieldwork and the transcription process is absent); neither does it address the theoretical framework that implicitly makes out the bases for the interpretations in the study, as already mentioned. The critique aside, it remains clear that the aim of this book is to document the Jewish liturgical tradition based on unique material and to communicate the historical account to a wider audience also outside academia.

Rossen's and Sharvit's book is important reading and offers important insights into the cantorate and the formation of the Jewish liturgical tradition in the Copenhagen Synagogue. It calls also for future research within its cultural domain from a wide range of approaches including for example minority studies, anthropology, music history, and ethnomusicology. Such research might well be continued at the Danish Folklore Archives, or amongst the congregation in the living tradition in *Krystalgade*.

Tore Tvarnø Lind

Fabian Holt, *Genre in Popular Music*
Chicago and London: Chicago University Press, 2007
221 pp., illus., music exx.
ISBN 0-226-35037-1/978-0-226-35037-0 (cloth),
0-226-35039-8/978-0-226-35039-4 (paper)
USD 50 (cloth) / 19 (paper)

What kind of book is Fabian Holt's *Genre in Popular Music*? Readers usually make such guesses based on the title: for example, it is likely that a text bearing a person's name in the title (like *Oliver Twist, Don Quijote, Madame Bovary* or *Doktor Faustus*) be a novel, unless that person is a king, or an emperor, or a famous politician, in which case we are probably dealing with a tragedy or a historical drama (*Julius Caesar, Oedipus Rex, Richard III*). But sometimes one can be misled. As one of the potential readers of *Genre in Popular Music*, probably very close to Fabian Holt's model reader (as a popular music scholar and musician, and one that started thinking and writing about genre long time ago), I must say I made my guesses and was also partially misled. With a title like that, especially considering that the publisher is the Univer-

1 Kay Kaufmann Shelemay, 'Mythologies and Realities in the Study of Jewish Music', in Lawrence E. Sullivan (ed.), *Enchanting Powers. Music in the World's Religions* (Cambridge, Mass.: Harvard University Press, 1997), 299–315, on 314.

sity of Chicago Press, one is led to think that the text is an essay, or a montage or sequence of short essays, dealing with the issue of genre, and circumscribing it to the field of popular music. Adding some contextual and circumstantial information – Holt already wrote about genre, and I met him on various occasions during conferences on popular music studies – I had reasons to believe that: 1, This would be a kind of *definitive* book about genre, both in the sense that it would include strong theory about the topic (with a clear definition of what a genre is, how it is constituted and works), and that it would cover the topic in ways that previous literature only hinted at, and 2, That the application of the concept to popular music would cover the 'field' extensively, in the broad sense that the term has come to mean not only in common sense, but in the name of a large organization like the International Association for the Study of Popular Music (as a matter of fact, when I first opened the book, I found the name of IASPM at the bottom of page one).

But I was wrong. Because: 1, the author explicitly refuses to build a systematic theory of genre and criticizes any former (or future?) effort to create anything similar: a series of 'weak', fragmented reflections on some aspects of genre seems to him more appropriate to the very nature of the topic; and 2, 'This is a book about the work of genre categories in American popular music', as stated at the beginning of chapter one (p. 1). So, this is not the book a naive reader like me would expect from its title, that is, an essay where a tentative theory of how genre works in musics in general is put to test (for falsification or refinement) with any genre in the worlds' popular music, like Italian *canzone d'autore*, Russian *avtorskaya pesnya*, Greek *néo kyma*, French *nouvelle chanson*, Catalan *nova cançó*, Cuban *nueva trova*, etc., because, according to the author, 1, such a theory cannot be created; and 2, any of the genres/contexts mentioned would require an adjustment, a piece of theory of its own. And the latter is not to say, obviously, that all genres have (or consist in) their own conventions or social norms, but that a theory trying to understand how those categories work should be adjusted to each of them.

That said, it would be silly for a reviewer to criticize a book just on the basis of his/her expectations. Taken for what it is (and according to the author's intentions) it is a serious and useful essay on popular music in the US and on some of the main genre-related contradictions and tensions within that country's musical communities (audience, critics, musicians, producers, record companies, etc.). After a 29-page Introduction (chapter one) that includes considerations on the centrality of the concept of genre, a description of the project, a summary history of the term and a very brief overview of existing literature, and a final and short (9 pages) discussion of some basic theory, chapter two is devoted to a discussion of the impact of Joel Coen's movie *O Brother, Where Art Thou?* on the US music market and audience, including reflections on categories like roots music, live performances of bluegrass, and the organization of large record stores. Chapter three and chapter four are grouped together in a 'double session' (Reactions to Rock) where the author elaborates on the impact of rock on country music (chapter three) and jazz (chapter four). Also chapters five and six are grouped in a 'double session' (Urban Boundaries) dealing with the jazz scene in Chicago and the work of Jeff Parker, a jazz guitarist (who also plays with the rock band Tortoise and in other independent 'mixed' projects). Finally, chapter seven (Music at American Borders) offers analyses of three recordings that in different ways challenge existing genres or are located by the author in 'spaces between genres': Ricky Martin's *The Cup of Life*, Jimmy Peters and Ring Dance Singers' *J'ai fait tout le tour du pays* (one of the recordings by John and Alan Lomax), and Flaco Jimenez's *Indita mia*.

Most of the book's content (chapters two to six) is based on the author's own experience with local scenes, musicians, producers, record store managers, critics, etc.: Holt insists on the value of this 'empirical' research, ostensibly derived from the canons of music anthropology, even if the difference between his 'ethnography' and previous accounts on genre (that he does not hesitate to describe as 'armchair research', p. 8) seems to be formal. The author suggests that such ethnographic work be more suitable for the topic (while other empirical evidence, like questionnaire-based interviews on a mass scale, does not seem to meet his requirements, cf. p. 15), but the reader remains with the doubt if some of the knowledge presented as the result of ethnography may not be considered as common sense in the musical community. So, if one scholar says that radio stations use music to target an audience for advertising other products, this might be (according to Holt) 'armchair research', but if the same very obvious piece of knowledge is presented as the result of an interview with a broadcaster (not in the 1920s, but today) then it is 'empirical', based on an ethnography. But the whole issue of what can be considered as empirical evidence in popular music studies deserves much more space than this review. However, most of the interviews and experiences reported in this book are quite valuable and interesting, and make it worth reading.

The weakest part, unfortunately, is the Introduction. One of the problems is that – as it happens quite too often in popular music studies – there is no specific reference to literature in languages other than English. Genre may have been (as the author says) out of fashion in anglophone popular music studies for a couple of decades, but in the meanwhile it has been one of the central issues of Latin American popular music studies (see Danilo Orozco González, for example). And there is more in other languages. Furthermore, the historical overview is very poor, giving no account of the birth of the usage of genre as a fundamental discursive tool for the arts in Aristotle's school and forgetting that it was a central issue again from the Renaissance as well as in music long before the nineteenth century. The only reference to genre in other arts is about cinema, with the odd observation that the concept should be more easily applied to the standardized production of movies than to music; but what about theatre or literature? What about Northrop Frye's theory, predicating the role of communities in the creation of literary genres? Most statements about musical meaning and music semiotics are frankly unacceptable, like this: 'The specificity of musical signification is one of the reasons for the strikingly limited success of semiotics in musicology compared with film and literary studies' (p. 5). Nattiez, Molino, Tagg, Stefani, and others are warned, and hundreds of students familiar with Tagg's concept of genre synecdoche should be careful. But the most striking issue that emerges in the Introduction but also in other parts of the book, is that seemingly, according to the author, whatever music becomes the mainstream ceases to be a genre (or conversely, maybe, it becomes a genre as soon as it is not the mainstream anymore). One can guess which definition of genre may prevent Tin Pan Alley (up to the Fifties, that is, until it remained the mainstream) or jazz (similarly, up to the Forties) to be a genre: one could also find reasons, even sympathize with the author, and/or wonder if such statement could be valid anywhere else in the world at any time, but the fact is that in the book this particular issue is not discussed, it is just stated. And others too: is jazz popular music? When (just in case) did it cease to be popular music? So the 'small theories and frameworks' (p. 29) put forward by the author turn out to generate big new questions. To which maybe another book with the same or a similar title shall try to answer.

Franco Fabbri

Music Reviews

J.P.E. Hartmann, *Liden Kirsten / Little Kirsten / Klein Karin, op. 44. Opera in two acts. Text by Hans Christian Andersen*, ed. Inger Sørensen and Niels Krabbe
The Hartmann Edition, IV, 1; Copenhagen: The Royal Library, 2005
lxii + 446 pp., illus., fascimiles
ISMN M-706763-08-8
DKK 1125

J.P.E. Hartmann, *Vølvens Spaadom / The Prophecy of the Sibyl / Wahrspuch der Wölwe, op. 71. Digt af den ældre Edda / Poem from the Poetic Edda / Lied der Älteren Edda, adapted by Fr. Winkel Horn*, ed. Niels Krabbe
The Hartmann Edition, V, 1; Copenhagen: The Royal Library, 2006
xxxii + 94 pp., illus., fascimiles
ISMN M-706763-09-5
DKK 562,50

Wieder hat eine der drei gewichtigen musikalischen Editionen Dänemarks – die Auswahlausgabe der Werke Johan Peter Emilius Hartmanns (1805–1900) – kurz nacheinander zwei Bände vorgelegt. Anders als bei den beiden Symphonie-Bänden geht es diesmal um Werke mit Gesang, die ganz direkt das nationale Musikverständnis (oder anders formuliert: das musikalische Selbstverständnis) Dänemarks im 19. Jahrhundert betrafen. Allerdings gehören sie unterschiedlichen Gattungen und Schaffenszeiten Hartmanns an, denn die Oper *Liden Kirsten* und die Vertonung des altnordischen Göttergedichtes *Vølvens Spaadom* für Männerchor und großes Orchester, bei der eine eindeutige Gattungsbezeichnung schwer fällt, liegen mehr als ein Vierteljahrhundert auseinander (1844/46 – 1870/72). Gemeinsam ist beiden Werken, dass sie sich im dänischen Musikleben des 19. Jahrhunderts erst allmählich, dann aber umso nachhaltiger durchsetzten.

Liden Kirsten op. 44, komponiert auf das Libretto Hans Christian Andersens, ist nach *Ravnen op. 12* (1830/32) und *Korsarerne op. 16* (1832/35) die letzte der drei vollendeten Opern Hartmanns, zu denen noch ein *Saul*-Fragment von 1864/65 kommt. Sie hat nicht nur den Rang eines 'Hauptwerkes' in Hartmanns Œuvre, sondern bildet auch einen nationalmusikalischen Markstein. Letzteres kann man ebenso von *Vølvens Spaadom* sagen – einer Komposition, die als Inbegriff von Hartmanns Kompositionen für den akademischen Gesangverein Kopenhagen – oder genauer: für die akademischen Gesangvereine von Kopenhagen und Lund – galt und zugleich dazu beitrug, dass Hartmann anlässlich der Aufführung des Werkes beim ersten nordischen Musikfest im Juni 1888, dem eigentlichen 'Durchbruch' des Werkes, als "den største Repræsentant for nordisk Musikkunst" ("größter Vertreter der nordischen Musikkunst") bezeichnet werden konnte. Noch über Hartmanns Tod hinaus wurde *Vølvens Spaadom* zumindest bis zum Gedenkkonzert zum 100. Geburtstag des Komponisten am 11. Mai 1905 besonders häufig aufgeführt (S. IX f./XV f./XXI f. im dänischen/englischen/deutschen Text). Pikanterweise geraten die beiden hier zu besprechenden Bände in puncto Popularität indirekt sogar in eine gewisse Rivalität: Da wird in Niels Krabbes Einleitung zur 2006 erschienenen Edition von *Vølvens Spaadom* ausdrücklich reklamiert, dieses Werk sei "zu Hartmanns Lebzeiten wohl das am häufigsten aufgeführte Werk des Komponisten" gewesen, wenn die Einleitung auch nur bestimmte Aufführungen zwischen 1872 und 1905 nachweist, ohne eine Gesamtzahl zu nennen (Ebd., S. IX/XV/XXII). Doch schon 2005 hatten Inger Sørensen und Niels Krabbe in ihrer Edition von *Liden Kirsten* insgesamt 130 Aufführungen der Oper "zu Hartmanns Lebzeiten" erwähnt (S. XVI/XXIX/XLI), so dass man sich als Leser automatisch fragt, ob diese Zahl von *Vølvens Spaadom* denn wirklich übertroffen wurde.

Seit dem frühen 20. Jahrhundert scheinen sich die Popularitätsgewichte weiter zugunsten der Oper verschoben zu haben. Denn für *Liden Kirsten* werden – an recht versteckter Stelle, nämlich bei der Quellenbeschreibung der Gesangs- und Orchesterstimmen im *Cricital Commentary* – insgesamt 332 Aufführungen aus den Vokal- und Orchesterstimmen des Königlichen Theaters genannt (S. 418, Quelle F). Seit 1999 liegt zudem eine neue dänische CD-Produktion von *Liden Kirsten* vor (*J.P.E. Hartmann: Liden Kirsten*. Danish National Radio Choir, Danish National Radio Symphony Orchestra, Michael Schønwandt. Copenhagen 1999, dacapo 8.224106-07). Dagegen scheint es um *Vølvens Spaadom* längere Zeit still geworden zu sein, was in der Einleitung des Bandes nur dezent angedeutet wird. Immerhin erschien 2007 eine Aufnahme (*J.P.E. Hartmann: Vølvens Spaadom, Overtures*. Lund University Male-Voice Choir, Danish National Symphony Orchestra/DR, Thomas Dausgaard. Copenhagen 2007, dacapo 8.226061).

Fällt schon der unterschiedliche äußere Umfang beider Werke unmittelbar ins Auge, so scheint die Oper auch kompositorisch letztlich das gewichtigere, vielseitigere, weniger zeitgebundene Werk zu sein. Freilich verdient *Vølvens Spaadom* ebenfalls Interesse: Mit seiner herben, manchmal massiven, manchmal gleichsam lyrisch-deklamatorischen Tonsprache, die teilweise auf dem Grat von Oper und Oratorium balanciert und harmonisch immer wieder überrascht, schlägt das Werk auf eigene Weise die Brücke zwischen Mendelssohn und Wagner und mündet im *Slutningschor* in eine harfenumrankte lyrisch-hymnische A-Dur-Apotheose; bei all dem steht das Orchester dem Männerchor zumindest gleichberechtigt gegenüber. Hört man andererseits die genannte Einspielung von *Liden Kirsten*, dann ist man beeindruckt von der Mischung aus spontan Erfundenem und Zeittypischem, aus Nationalkolorit – wie es in Dänemark in den Jahrzehnten nach der Uraufführung zunehmend empfunden, akzeptiert und gefeiert wurde – und charakteristischen Bezügen zu mitteleuropäischen Konventionen und Traditionen der Opernkomposition, etwa bei bestimmten Schreckenstopoi, Singspiel-Tonfällen oder auch Anklängen an Webers Opernidiom. Man begegnet nicht allein einem 'historisch' wichtigen Dokument, sondern einer musikalisch lebenskräftigen Partitur, die in manchen Vokal- und Tanznummern veritable 'Hits' enthält. In ihrer Verbindung von 'nordischem Ton', eigentümlichen, gegenüber *Vølvens Spaadom* freilich ganz anders eingesetzten modalen Färbungen (siehe schon Nr. 1!), teils idyllischem, teils eigentümlich blechgepanzertem Singspiel-Idiom, quellfrisch-herbsüßer Melodik, agiler Intimität und bemerkenswerter Vitalität wirkt Hartmanns Opern-Tonsprache ausgesprochen reizvoll. So kann man die Popularität von *Liden Kirsten* in Dänemark gut nachvollziehen. Dagegen war die mit vielen Hoffnungen verknüpfte Weimarer Inszenierung von 1856 trotz der Propagierung durch Franz Liszt nicht von Erfolg begleitet und verschwand bereits nach zwei Aufführungen wieder vom Spielplan. Dabei waren anlässlich der deutschen Erstaufführung eine deutschsprachige Textfassung und entsprechende Aufführungsmaterialien erstellt worden, wobei man die Namen der Hauptrollen aus teils verständlichen, teils unklaren, auch von den Herausgebern nicht näher erörterten Gründen geändert hatte (*Martha* statt *Malfred*, *Karin* statt *Kirsten*, *Hialmar* statt *Sverkel*). Entsprechend änderte sich auch der Titel der Oper: Aus *Liden Kirsten* wurde – im Deutschen nicht besonders günstig für eine Oper – *Klein Karin*. Weitere deutsche Aufführungspläne für Mannheim und Dresden zerschlugen sich bald.

Wenden wir uns den beiden neuen Editionen selbst zu: Wesentliche Charakteristika der *Hartmann-Ausgabe* wurden bereits bei der Rezension des Pilotbandes mit Hartmanns *1. Sym-*

phonie angesprochen, begrüßt, in editionsmethodischer Sicht teilweise aber auch kritisch hinterfragt.[1] In den beiden neuen Bänden hat sich konzeptionell wenig geändert: Dies gilt für die noble äußere Aufmachung und das großzügige Layout ebenso wie für die attraktiven Farbfaksimilia nach der Einleitung, die bei *Liden Kirsten* noch durch Schwarzweiß-Faksimilia dreier Textmanuskripte sowie des Erstdruckes von Andersens Libretto ergänzt werden. Unverändert ist auch das Ziel der Ausgabe, wissenschaftliche und künstlerisch-praktische Anforderungen miteinander zu verbinden. Und für die erhoffte und verdiente internationale Rezeption von Hartmanns Werken bleibt es ein praktikabler, sinnvoller Kompromiss, dass Titel, Inhaltsverzeichnis und editorische Generalbemerkungen dreisprachig (dänisch/englisch/deutsch), der *Critical Commentary* mit Abkürzungsverzeichnis, Quellenbeschreibung, Quellenbewertung, Stemma und Editionsbericht ("Editorial Emendations and Alternative Readings") dagegen ausschließlich in englischer Sprache wiedergegeben wird. Auch en détail ist die *Hartmann-Ausgabe* bestimmten editorischen Eigentümlichkeiten treu geblieben – etwa dem Verzicht auf die Kennzeichnung freier, nur per Analogie vorgenommener Ergänzungen im Notentext oder dem im Englischen unüblichen Terminus "marc." für Akzente (der leicht zu Verwechslungen mit der bei Hartmann ebenfalls verwendeten verbalen Anweisung *marc./marcato* führen kann). Wie schon bei der *1. Symphonie* werden auch in den neuen Bänden die beiden hohen Posaunenpartien stets im Tenorschlüssel notiert, obwohl Hartmann selbst, wie die entsprechenden Faksimilia zeigen, zwischen Altschlüssel-Notation in der Ouvertüre zu *Liden Kirsten* und Tenorschlüssel-Orthographie in Nr. II von *Vølvens Spaadom* unterscheidet, was vom Tonhöhenprofil der jeweiligen Partien her zweifellos sinnvoll war. (Vgl. in *Liden Kirsten* die Faksimilia auf S. LII f. mit dem Notentext auf S. 344 f. und auf S. 40 (Ausschnitte aus ursprünglicher und definitiver Fassung der Ouvertüre); in *Vølvens Spaadom* vgl. das Faksimile auf S. XXX mit S. 18 f. des Notentextes).

Viel wichtiger als solche editorischen Charakteristika ist natürlich, dass *Liden Kirsten* erstmals in einer textkritisch erarbeiteten, sorgfältig gedruckten Partitur vorliegt, nachdem zu Hartmanns Lebzeiten nur Libretto und Klavierauszug (jeweils 1846) erschienen; posthum folgte lediglich noch eine Partiturausgabe der Ouvertüre (1905). Hoffentlich weckt dieser Quantensprung der Werkpräsenz in Zukunft nicht nur in Dänemark, sondern auch international neues Interesse an dem attraktiven Werk. Ansprechend ist bereits die Einleitung des *Liden-Kirsten*-Bandes, die konzis über Entstehung, Uraufführung, weitere Aufführungsserien und die frühe Rezeption informiert und wesentliche werk- und rezeptionsgeschichtliche Dokumente zitiert. Auch weiteren prägnanten Markierungspunkten der Werk- und Rezeptionsgeschichte wird gebührende Aufmerksamkeit gewidmet, beispielsweise dem Austausch der alten Nr. 7 (*Arioso*) gegen die textlich-musikalisch neu konzipierte, erstmals am 4. März 1847 aufgeführte Kombination *Recitativ og Romance* oder den kontroversen Diskussionen über die 1869/70 vom Regisseur August Bournonville vorgenommenen Kürzungen sowie der wenig erfolgreichen deutschen Erstaufführung in Weimar. Liszts Engagement für das Werk wird durch eine kleine, im Weimarer Aufführungsmaterial gefundene, erst auf den zweiten Blick deutlicher zu erkennende Bleistiftskizze dokumentiert, die vermutlich während der Proben entstand (S. LIX; um was für ein Noten- und Text-Manuskript es sich handelt, erfährt man leider nicht). Ausgeklammert bleibt die posthume Rezeption des Werkes, über dessen mehr als 200 Aufführungen man sich gerade als nicht-dänischer Leser zumindest einen kurzen Hinweis gewünscht hätte.

Auch in anderen Fällen wäre ich als interessierter Benutzer der in jeder Beziehung gewichtigen, inhaltlich attraktiven Edition für mehr Benutzerfreundlichkeit dankbar gewesen. Denn gerade weil in beiden Editionen enorm viel philologische Mühe und ertragreiche editorische

---

1 Siehe *Danish Yearbook of Musicology*, 31 (2003), 121–29.

Arbeit steckt, sollten die Benutzer die Ergebnisse solcher Forschungsleistungen so problemlos wie möglich rezipieren können. Statt dessen waren Lektüre und Nachvollzug der editorischen Arbeit zumindest bei *Liden Kirsten* in der Praxis einigermaßen mühsam. Wer beispielsweise in dem insgesamt mehr als 500-seitigen Band die Anfänge der 12 Nummern im Notentext sucht, wird – im Gegensatz zu *Vølvens Spaadom* – nicht im Inhaltsverzeichnis fündig, sondern erst unmittelbar vor Beginn des Notentextes, das heißt nach Einleitung, Farbfaksimilia, Angabe der Orchesterbesetzung und Rollenliste. Und beim Versuch, Notentext und *Critical Commentary* aufeinander zu beziehen (was für die intensive wissenschaftliche und künstlerische Nutzung des Bandes unausweichlich ist), musste ich mir die Zahlen der Notentext-Seiten für den Anfang jeder Nummer selbst zu den entsprechenden Abschnitten des *Critical Commentary* schreiben, um schnellen Zugriff zu haben. Solche Hilfsmittel möchte man sich bei derart umfangreichen Werken und Bänden im *Critical Commentary* denn doch wünschen.

Die Sigelung der Quellen erfolgt in der *Hartmann-Ausgabe* nicht nach dem Prinzip 'sprechender' Sigel, sondern alphabetisch. Dabei sigeln beide Bände nach unterschiedlichen Gliederungsprinzipien, was zwar teilweise aus der unterschiedlichen Überlieferung der Werke und der Zugehörigkeit zu unterschiedlichen Gattungen zu erklären ist, das Memorieren der Sigel und das Nachvollziehen der editorischen Argumentation aber nicht gerade erleichtert. Auch manche Inkonsequenzen irritieren: Warum Herausgeber Krabbe in der Edition von *Vølvens Spaadom* beispielsweise die Druck- und Manuskriptquellen zu Otto Mallings Klavierreduktionen (Drucke F–H, Manuskript J) nicht zusammenfasst, bleibt unklar. Zudem wäre es angemessener gewesen, wenn er die Druckausgaben zweier ganz unterschiedlicher Typen der Klavierreduktion konsequent differenziert hätte, statt sie zu vermischen: Der zweihändige Klavierauszug nämlich enthält textierte Gesangspartien (Quelle F mit dänischem Text, Quelle H mit deutschem Text), während das von Krabbe dazwischen eingeschobene vierhändige Klavierarrangement untextiert ist (Quelle G). Ebenso ungünstig ist es, dass zwischen Hartmanns eigenhändige Skizzen- und Entwurfsmanuskripte (I: "short score, autograph, draft"; K, L: jeweils "sketches") Otto Mallings eigenhändige Niederschrift seines Klavierauszuges eingeschoben wird (J), was philologisch überhaupt keinen Sinn ergibt.

Hinzu kommen weitere Umständlichkeiten: Zwar ist es hilfreich, dass für beide Werke zwischen Notentext und *Critical Commentary* englische und deutsche Übersetzungen des Librettos bzw. Gesangstextes mitgeteilt werden. Doch es ist für die Nutzer dieser Übersetzungen in beiden Fällen recht mühsam, Bezüge zum dänischen Originaltext herzustellen, da die Texte nicht in einer Synopse erscheinen. Vielmehr folgen die Übersetzungen bei *Liden Kirsten* nach den (durchaus aufschlussreichen) Schwarzweiß-Faksimilia, die verschiedene Versionen des dänischsprachigen Librettos einschließlich des Textbuch-Erstdruckes wiedergeben. In *Vølvens Spaadom* erscheint der dänische Haupttext dagegen nur innerhalb des Notentextes, was den Vergleich mit den beiden im Anschluss an den Partiturdruck wiedergegebenen Übersetzungen zusätzlich erschwert. Hier hätte eine Synopse nach dem Notentext oder aber ein vorgeschalteter dreisprachiger Textvorspann helfen können. Zugleich fragt man sich indes, warum die Herausgeber nicht ihrer Hauptquelle (A), dem Partitur-Erstdruck von 1886, folgten. Denn dort waren die Vokalpartien mit dänischem *und* deutschem Text unterlegt, ehe 1889 auch noch eine rein deutschsprachige Partiturausgabe erschien (B).[2] Krabbes Edition beschränkt sich im Partiturdruck dagegen, aus welchen Gründen auch immer, auf den däni-

---

2 Bereits 1876 war Otto Mallings Klavierauszug – die erste Druckausgabe von *Vølvens Spaadom* überhaupt – mit dänischem Text erschienen (F); etwa 1893/94 folgte ein deutschsprachiger Klavierauszug (H); siehe *Vølvens Spaadom*, 83 f. Dagegen erfährt man als Leser nicht explizit, ob die vermutlich 1886 gedruckten Vokalstimmen (Teil von Quelle D) ein- oder zweisprachig waren (wobei Letzteres zu vermuten ist).

schen Text. Und die Frage, welche Hoffnungen Hartmann bzw. sein Verleger mit der Wiedergabe des deutschen Gesangstextes verbunden haben könnten, wird von Krabbe gar nicht erst gestellt. Dabei wäre es für den Herausgeber dieses so explizit "nordischen" Werkes vielleicht nicht unwichtig gewesen, dem Verhältnis zwischen intendierter und tatsächlicher Rezeption zumindest ansatzweise nachzugehen.

Soweit die rein immanente Lektüre erkennen lässt, scheinen beide Bände im Notentext sorgfältig redigiert zu sein. Als kleine, bei Stichproben aufgefallene Corrigenda wäre für *Liden Kirsten* zu nennen: das Fehlen eines Auflösungszeichens (S. 222, Nr. 9, T. 6, Vl. I: für c^2) und wohl auch eines Pralltriller-Zeichens (S. 245, Nr. 9, T. 191, 1. Note, Vl. solo – analog T. 187, Vl. solo, sowie analog T. 100/104, T. 152/156, jeweils Klar. 1, sofern es sich um keinen bloßen Druckfehler der neuen Edition handelt). Für den *Critical Commentary* zum *Recitativ* Nr. 2A muss es auf S. 429 beim "Comment" zu T. 23 statt "corrected to g'" gemäß dem orthographischen Kontext heißen: "corrected to g' sharp"; in der gleichen Bemerkung und im Notenbeispiel zu T. 26 ist außerdem die irrtümliche Angabe "NARREN" jeweils durch "INGEBORG" zu ersetzen, wie der Notentext auf S. 91 zeigt.

Viele der im *Critical Commentary* beider Bände begründeten editorischen Eingriffe, die zumeist aus Ergänzungen per analogiam bestehen, leuchten unmittelbar ein. Sie optimieren die optisch ansprechenden, eher grazil als gedrungen wirkenden Notentexte. Positiv sind auch die Informationen des *Critical Commentary* über ursprüngliche Lesarten zu werten, etwa zum Orchestersatz in den Takten 162–63 und 164 der Ouvertüre zu *Liden Kirsten* (S. 425 f.). Gewöhnungsbedürftig wirkt die ungewöhnlich große Schrift bei den jeweils über der Holzbläser- und der Streicherakkolade platzierten, für alle Partien verbindlichen agogischen, dynamischen, artikulatorischen oder expressiven Binnendifferenzierungen wie *poco ritenuto*, *a tempo*, *colla parte*, *dim. e smorzando* oder *con fuoco*, zumal sie der Schriftgröße der generellen Tempo- und Typusbezeichnungen (*Allegro, Maestoso, Recitativ* etc.) entspricht. Doch das mag für Dirigenten des Werkes letztlich sogar hilfreich sein.

Die Wahl der jeweiligen Hauptquelle(n) wird im *Critical Commentary* begründet. Im Falle von *Liden Kirsten* entschieden sich die Herausgeber, die Vokalpartien primär nach dem 1846 gedruckten Klavierauszug wiederzugeben und als Kollationsquelle lediglich den autographen Klavierauszug zu nutzen, nicht aber die überlieferten abschriftlichen bzw. (für den 2. Akt) autographen Partiturquellen (S. 422 f.). Die Entscheidung überzeugt nur bedingt, zumal sie nur mit der Vernichtung des Partiturautographs zum 1. Akt begründet wird, während die Geschichte und Funktion der erhaltenen Quellen kaum nachhaltig einbezogen wird. Überhaupt hätte man sich für die Editionen von *Liden Kirsten* und *Vølvens Spaadom* ein differenzierteres Vorgehen vorstellen können, ja gewünscht, wo es um die Rekonstruktion der Quellen- und Publikationsgeschichte und um die Quellenbewertung geht – auch wenn dann teilweise nur mit Hypothesen gearbeitet werden kann. Andere moderne Gesamtausgabenprojekte wagen hier mehr und gewinnen selbst dort, wo Überlieferungs- und Erkenntnislücken bleiben, mehr philologische Transparenz, die das Verständnis für den erarbeiteten Notentext fördert. In dieser Beziehung erscheinen beide Editionen oft zu deskriptiv, zu unentschieden.

In bestimmten Extremfällen fehlt es der philologischen Argumentation und den hieraus resultierenden editorischen Entscheidungen so sehr an historisch-quellenkritischem Problembewusstsein, dass man von ernsthaften Defiziten der Editionsmethodik sprechen muss. Einige Beispiele seien genannt:

1. Der von Hartmann selbst erstellte, 1846 im Druck erschienene Klavierauszug von *Liden Kirsten* (Da) wird von den Herausgebern mit Recht als wichtige musikalische Quelle bezeichnet. Denn nur in Gestalt von Klavierreduktionen lag das Werk zu Hartmanns Lebzeiten gedruckt vor: Dem Klavierauszug-Erstdruck (Da) folgte später eine revidierte Auflage (Db);

hinzu kommt eine – satztechnisch ganz eigenständige – Fassung für Klavier zu zwei Händen (Dc). Für die *Vokalpartien* der Oper wird der Klavierauszug daraufhin, wie schon erwähnt, zur Hauptquelle und lediglich mit dem Klavierauszug-Autograph (B) kollationiert. Warum aber spielen das erhaltene Partiturautograph des 2. Aktes (K) und die häufig bei Aufführungen verwendete, das heißt klanglich intensiv evaluierte Partiturkopie beider Akte (C) für die Vokalpartien nicht zumindest als Kollations- bzw. Referenzquellen eine Rolle? (Siehe S. 423 mit der Übersicht über Haupt- und Referenzquellen.) Warum sind die genannten Partiturquellen überhaupt *Hauptquellen* der *Instrumentalpartien*, nicht aber für die *Vokalpartien*? Wird hier nicht ein Fassungs- und Notationsgefüge aufgebrochen, das möglicherweise bei vielen kleinen editorischen Angleichungen hilfreiche Begründungen geliefert hätte? All das wird weder in der Einleitung noch im Rahmen der Quellenbeschreibung und Quellenbewertung des *Critical Commentary* (S. 417 ff.) hinlänglich erläutert. So bleibt unklar, ob der Klavierauszug gegenüber den erhaltenen Partiturquellen für die Vokalpartien werkgenetisch fortgeschrittenere Lesarten bietet, die einer 'Fassung letzter Hand' zuzurechnen wären. Überhaupt führt der Klavierauszug in der Einleitung des Bandes ein seltsames Schattendasein, was ein Teil des editorischen Mankos ist: Dass er – ebenso wie das Libretto – bereits 1846 im Druck erschien, erfährt man 'offiziell' erst in der Quellenbeschreibung des *Critical Commentary* (Da), ganz nebenbei freilich auch schon in der Legende zum Partiturautograph des 2. Aktes, wo man eine solche Information nicht gerade suchen würde (S. 418 und XLVI). Erwartet hätte man sie dagegen im Einleitungs-Kapitel *Musikalske Kilder/Musical Sources/Musikquellen*. Dort aber wird weder das Erscheinungsjahr des Erstdruckes (Da, 1846) noch dasjenige der revidierten späteren Auflage (Db, 1875) genannt, sondern lediglich mitgeteilt, dass das Klavierauszug-Autograph auf der Grundlage des damals noch vorhandenen Partiturautographs entstand. Zudem behaupten die Herausgeber hier und bei der Quellenbeschreibung, das Klavierauszug-Autograph (B) und eine Abschrift des Klavierauszuges (C) hätten als Stichvorlage des gedruckten Klavierauszuges gedient, da beide Quellen Eintragungen für Stecher enthielten (S. XIX/XXXI/XLIV und 418). Doch Doppel-Stichvorlagen waren in solchen Fällen nicht gerade üblich; außerdem wird nur auf zwei – in beiden Klavierauszug-Manuskripten gleichlautende – Fälle derartiger Eintragungen verwiesen, während Stichvorlagen normalerweise fortlaufende Markierungen der Seiten- und Akkoladenwechsel enthalten. Einen gewissen Widerspruch hierzu bildet schließlich das Stemma, das nur eine Beziehung zwischen dem Autograph und dem Erstdruck des Klavierauszuges herstellt (S. 423). So hätte man als Leser einen genaueren publikations-logischen Erklärungsversuch an Stelle von purer und darüber hinaus widersprüchlicher Deskription erwartet. Einmal mehr bleibt man als Leser auf sich gestellt, wenn man Quellenlage, Quellengeschichte und Quellenbewertung sowie die daraus resultierenden editorischen Entscheidungen der Herausgeber verstehen möchte.

2. Wenn man trotz der genannten Bedenken akzeptiert, dass der gedruckte Klavierauszug zur Hauptquelle einer wesentlichen Werkschicht von *Liden Kirsten* – nämlich der Vokalstimmen – wird, dann stellt sich sogleich eine andere Frage: Warum haben Sørensen und Krabbe diese für ihre Edition so eminent wichtige Quelle im Hinblick auf die metronomischen Tempoanweisungen der Oper nur halbherzig genutzt? In den Partiturmanuskripten der Oper gibt es offenbar nur für die Ouvertüre, für die Nummern 1–4 und 8 sowie für die ursprüngliche Fassung von Nr. 7 Metronomzahlen, da der Notentext der Edition nur für diese Teile entsprechende numerische Tempoanweisungen enthält. Dagegen liefert der gedruckte Klavierauszug für Nr. 6, die neue Nr. 7 sowie für Nr. 9–12 Metronomzahlen, die in Sørensens und Krabbes Edition nur im *Critical Commentary* – also relativ versteckt – mitgeteilt werden. Wollten die Herausgeber speziell in diesem Fall eine Quellen- bzw. Fassungsmischung vermeiden? Wir erfahren es nicht. Wir erfahren nicht einmal, ob die im Notentext der *Hartmann-Ausgabe*

aufgrund der Partiturquellen mitgeteilten Metronomzahlen ebenfalls im Klavierauszug zu finden sind. Zweifellos wäre es für Musiker und Musikwissenschaftler hilfreich gewesen, wenn die Neuedition von *Liden Kirsten* die doch wohl authentischen Metronomangaben des Klavierauszuges für die in den Partiturquellen unmetronomisierten Teile der Oper übernommen oder zumindest in Fußnoten unten auf den Notenseiten mitgeteilt hätte.

3. Viel problematischer sind jedoch – wie schon in Krabbes Edition der 1. Symphonie – bestimmte Analogie-Ergänzungen sowie Quellen- und Fassungsmischungen. In manchen Fällen erscheinen Eingriffe und deren Begründung so fragwürdig, ja verhängnisvoll, dass man sich fragt, was für ein philologisch-editorisches Konzept die *Hartmann-Ausgabe* überhaupt verfolgt und wie weit sie ihr Vorgehen editionsmethodisch reflektiert hat.

Zu Beginn der Ouvertüre von *Liden Kirsten* ergänzen die Herausgeber in T. 1 beim zweiten Harfenakkord ein Arpeggio "by analogy with chord 1 and as in F [= abschriftliche Gesangs- und Orchesterstimmen]" und wiederholen den Eingriff in T. 2 "by analogy with b. 1" (S. 1 und 424). Dahinter steht offenbar die Vermutung, es handle sich um eine Abbreviaturnotation, bei der das Arpeggiozeichen nur einmal notiert worden sei und für die folgenden Akkorde ergänzt werden müsse. Das wäre sicherlich bedenkenswert, zumal die Harfenstimme von Quelle F für den zweiten Akkord ebenfalls Arpeggio fordert. Doch so einfach ist die Sache nicht. Denn an anderen Stellen von *Liden Kirsten* notierte Hartmann ganz penibel vor jedem Harfenakkord, den er arpeggiert wünschte, ein eigenes Arpeggiozeichen. Das heißt: Für die erhaltenen Teile der autographen Partitur ist keine generelle Abbreviatur-Theorie zulässig (siehe Nr. 10: S. 316, T. 154, 158, vor allem aber S. 319 f., T. 173–80; Nr. 12: S. 332, T. 57–60). Außerdem geht es nicht um ein rein theoretisches oder notationspraktisch-'optisches' Lesartenproblem. Vielmehr ändert sich durch Sørensens und Krabbes Arpeggio-Ergänzungen das real erklingende Artikulationsprofil zu Beginn der Ouvertüre: Zwei gleichmäßig arpeggierte Akkorde wirken im vorgeschriebenen 3/4-Takt metrisch weniger abgestuft als die in der Hauptquelle geforderte Folge von ausdrücklich arpeggiertem erstem Akkord und nicht (oder nur geringfügig) arpeggiertem zweitem Akkord. Leider erfährt man im *Critical Commentary* nicht, ob die Quellen des Klavierauszuges in dieser Beziehung Entscheidungshilfe bieten – obwohl als Kollationsquelle für die Ouvertüre neben dem Aufführungs-Stimmensatz F auch der gedruckte Klavierauszug Da genannt wird (S. 423). Angesichts all dieser editorischen Unklarheiten halte ich die Eingriffe in T. 1–2 vorläufig für problematisch und ihre Begründung für oberflächlich. Hinzu kommt, dass der Eingriff eine Dominowirkung hat: Denn wenn die Harfenakkorde vor dem Beginn des durchführungsartigen Mittelteils der Ouvertüre in T. 137–40 modifiziert wiederkehren, werden alle Arpeggios ergänzt, wobei die Begründung des *Critical Commentary* lautet: "by analogy with bb. 1–2". So bewegen sich die Herausgeber auf zunehmend unsicherem editorischem Boden.

Zwei weitere Eingriffe erscheinen mir – gemessen am heutigen Stand der Editionsmethodik und in Anbetracht weithin standardisierter Publikationsverfahren des späteren 19. Jahrhunderts – nicht nur problematisch, sondern konzeptionell fatal:

In Nr. II von *Vølvens Spaadom* forderte der Partitur-Erstdruck (A), der mit Recht die Hauptquelle der Edition bildet, dass das 1. Ventilhorn in T. 35–38^1 die Partie der 1. Violinen klanglich verstärkt, die mit markanter Motivik die repetitive Deklamation des Chores überlagert. Krabbe aber eliminiert die Hornpartie im Notentext seiner Edition, gibt sie im *Critical Commentary* per Notenbeispiel als Lesart der Hauptquelle wieder und begründet den Eingriff mit dem Argument: "omitted by analogy with bb. 87–90 and as in C, E" (S. 21 f. und 88). Tatsächlich sind die Takte 87–90, auf die er verweist, Bestandteil eines musikalischen (aber nicht textlichen) Wiederholungsabschnittes, der satztechnisch-instrumentatorisch erheblich modifiziert ist. Warum soll die Hornpartie von diesen Modifikationen ausgenommen werden? So erscheint mir Krabbes Eingriff in mehrfacher Hinsicht verfehlt. Wenn die "Filiation" für Hauptquelle A ausdrücklich konstatiert: "A reveals a number of revisions and completions compared with C" (S. 85), dürfte das doch nichts anderes bedeuten, als dass solche "revisions and completions" als Bestandteile des definitiven Notentextes – oder anders formuliert: als 'Fassung letzter Hand' – gelten müssen, die von Hartmann initiiert und autorisiert wurden. (Auszunehmen wären nur solche Fälle, in denen nachweislich oder vermutlich fehlerhafte Lesarten in den Druck gelangten, die aufgrund der genannten Manuskriptquellen korrigiert werden könnten). Das heißt: Musikalisch schlüssige Abweichungen der 1886 gedruckten Partitur (A) von Hartmanns 1872 abgeschlossenem Partiturautograph (C) und vom abschriftlichen Stimmensatz (E) müssen zunächst einmal als Resultate von Hartmanns Revision vor oder bei der Drucklegung gelten. So ist im hier diskutierten Fall nicht einzusehen, warum diese editorische Prämisse nicht auch für die im Druck gegenüber den Manuskriptquellen hinzugefügte Ventilhorn-Stimme gelten sollte. (Bedauerlicherweise teilt Krabbes Kommentar nicht mit, ob die betreffenden Takte in der gedruckten Hornstimme D dem Partiturdruck A entsprechen, was wohl vermutet werden darf). Welches editorische Konzept hinter dem verhängnisvollen Eingriff steht, der leider auch in die oben genannte neue Einspielung von *Vølvens Spaadom* gelangte – die entsprechende Stelle findet sich in Track 2, ca. 0'53"–0'58" –, bleibt unklar: Der zitierte editorische Kommentar Krabbes könnte suggerieren, dass für ihn an dieser Stelle die in Hartmanns eigener Handschrift im Partiturautograph C sichtbaren und von den Stimmenabschriften E bestätigten Pausentakte die einzig legitimen Belege für Hartmanns kompositorischen Willen sind, so dass er dem (frühen) Autograph mehr traut als der (späteren) Druckausgabe. Aber ist das nicht zu kurz und unhistorisch gedacht? Anders gefragt: Was sollte bei einer *adäquaten* editorischen Entscheidung bedacht werden? Nach Krabbes Rekonstruktion der Quellengeschichte diente die autographe Partiturreinschrift C nicht als Stichvorlage, obwohl sie Eintragungen für den Stich enthält, die jedoch nicht mit dem Seitenumbruch des Partitur-Erstdruckes A übereinstimmen. Stattdessen benutzte Hartmann eine (verschollene) Partiturabschrift (X) des akademischen Gesangvereins (S. XIII f./XIX f./XXVI; im Text der Einleitung wird das Sigel der verschollenen Partiturabschrift (X) nicht genannt, sondern lediglich in "Filiation" und "Stemma" des *Critical Commentary*, S. 85). Wenn man also bei der Mitwirkung des 1. Ventilhorns in den genannten Takten weder von einem 'Irrtum' sprechen kann noch eine arglistige Fälschung des Kopisten oder des Notenstechers unterstellen will – was angesichts der professionellen Drucklegungs-Verfahren des späteren 19. Jahrhunderts und angesichts von Hartmanns damaliger künstlerischer Position eine ziemlich naive Vorstellung wäre –, dann kann die Lesart des Erstdruckes nur auf einen Eingriff des Komponisten selbst zurückgehen. Hartmann muss also entweder in der verschollenen Partiturabschrift (X) oder spätestens beim Korrekturlesen des gestochenen Notentextes eine Änderung vorgenommen haben, die das 1. Ventilhorn zur Verstärkung der 1. Violinen heranzieht. Dadurch erhöhte er die satztechnisch-instrumentatorische Komplexität der Stelle: Anders als später in T. 87 ff., wo das Horn zunächst pausiert und dann zusammen mit den hohen Holzbläsern die halbtaktige kanonische Imitation der Bassstimmen übernimmt, hat die Hornpartie nach Lesart des Partitur-Erstdruckes in T. 35 ff. eine andere Funktion, die durch den andersartigen Orchestersatz geprägt und bedingt ist: Hier wechselt das Horn als 'Scharnier-Instrument' die klanglichen Rollen, indem es vom Gleichklang mit den 1. Violinen (T. 35–38¹) ab T. 38² in die Kanonstimmen springt. Hartmann muss bei den Aufführungen vor der Drucklegung irgendwann den Wunsch nach einer solchen Variante empfunden und diese spätestens beim Korrekturlesen der gestochenen Partitur, vielleicht aber auch schon vorher, schriftlich fixiert haben. Genau diesen kompositorischen Arbeitsschritt macht Herausgeber Krabbe aus unerfindlichen Gründen wieder zunichte.

In zahlreichen anderen Fällen verfährt Krabbes historisch-kritische Edition von *Vølvens Spaadom*, wie man gerechterweise hinzufügen muss, durchaus adäquat – etwa wenn im *Slut-*

ningschor (Nr. V) für T. 44–46 die Version von Partiturautograph C und die hiervon ihrerseits abweichende Lesart der abschriftlichen Orchesterstimmen E im *Critical Commentary* als frühere Lesarten per Notenbeispiel dokumentiert werden, während der Notentext selbst die Lesart des Partitur-Erstdruckes A wiedergibt (S. 93 und 72 f.). Gerade dieser Fall belegt aber auch, dass das Werk zwischen autographer Reinschrift und Partiturdruck an bestimmten Stellen mehrere 'Fassungen' durchlief. Darüber wird in Krabbes Edition insgesamt zu wenig reflektiert.

Nicht nachvollziehbar und möglicherweise durch ein überholtes 'Urtext'-Verständnis geprägt ist auch ein weiterer problematischer Eingriff in den Schlusstakten von *Vølvens Spaadom*: Im *Slutningschor* (Nr. V) eliminiert Krabbe in den Takten 62–65^{I} die Lesart des Partitur-Erstdruckes (C), bei der die Schlusswendung solistisch vorbereitet und chorisch bekräftigt wird. Statt dessen gibt er die quasi-doppelchörige Fassung mit Überlappung von solistischem und chorischem Einsatz wieder, wie sie in sämtlichen anderen Quellen – angefangen bei den Skizzen bis hin zum 1876 publizierten Klavierauszug Otto Mallings – zu finden ist. Auch diesmal vermisst man eine generelle oder spezielle Reflexion über das Zustandekommen der gedruckten Lesart. Und auch hier macht Krabbe – so meine Vermutung – fatalerweise genau das rückgängig, was Hartmann spätestens bei der Drucklegung der Partitur gegenüber den früheren Manuskript- und Druckquellen änderte. Leider folgt die erwähnte neue Einspielung auch in diesem Fall Krabbes Edition statt Hartmanns satztechnisch einfacherer, klanglich klarerer Druckfassung (Track 5, ca. 4'26"–4'42"). Das bedeutet: Auch hier wird die von Hartmann mit Erscheinen des Partitur-Erstdruckes autorisierte, *definitive* Lesart ('Fassung letzter Hand') durch ein werkgenetisch früheres Stadium ersetzt.

Leider erreicht die deutsche Übersetzung – anders als bei der *1. Symphonie* – in beiden Bänden das Niveau der englischen Übersetzung nicht. Oft wird so wörtlich aus dem Dänischen übertragen, dass man als Leser nicht genau weiß, was gemeint ist, und sich an die weit bessere englische Übersetzung oder ans dänische Original halten muss. Auch die Redaktion beider Übersetzungen, vor allem aber des deutschen Textes, ist teilweise unzureichend: In *Vølvens Spaadom* ist die Wiedergabe des deutschen Gesangstextes alles andere als fehlerfrei (S. 81), und schon im Inhaltsverzeichnis mutiert H.C. Andersens zweiter Vorname zu "Chrisitan". Die deutsche Übersetzung von *Vølvens Spaadom* schreibt sich auf dem Titelblatt und in der Textübersetzung gemäß der dänisch-deutschen Partitur-Erstausgabe *Wahrspruch der Wölwe*, während sie in der deutschen Einleitung stets als *Wahrspruch der Wölve* erscheint. Die sorglose Redaktion der Übersetzungen kann bis zu inhaltlichen Irritationen führen. So mutiert in der Edition von *Liden Kirsten* das im Dänischen korrekt als X bezeichnete Quellensigel des verschollenen Autographs zum 1. Akt im englischen und deutschen Text teilweise zu XX, bis im *Critical Commentary* nur noch das falsche Sigel XX übrig bleibt (vgl. S. XVIII f.: X; S. XXX f.: zweimal X, einmal XX; S. XLIII f.: einmal X, zweimal XX; S. 417 (im Zusammenhang mit Quelle A) und S. 423 (Stemma): jeweils XX). Als Leser glaubt man zunächst natürlich, man habe es mit zwei Quellen zu tun.

Trotz der Einwände, die hier gegen Handhabbarkeit und Editionsmethodik der beiden neuen Bände vorgebracht wurden, ist und bleibt die Hartmann-Auswahlausgabe ein wichtiges, ernsthaftes Projekt. Sie gilt Werken, die unbestreitbar ihren Platz in der Musikgeschichte Dänemarks und Europas haben und die auch im Musikleben eine Rolle spielen oder spielen sollten. Man möchte diesem Projekt dreierlei dringend wünschen. Erstens: eine verlässliche und kontinuierliche finanzielle, organisatorische und personelle Planungssicherheit, die im Generalvorwort der Bände zwei verhängnisvolle Sätze künftig überflüssig macht, nämlich: "Die Ausgabe folgt keinem von Beginn an festgelegten Editionsplan. Das Erscheinen der Bände richtet sich vielmehr nach den jeweils vorhandenen Ressourcen." (S. VIII). Zweitens: eine sorgfältigere redaktionelle Betreuung, die angesichts der dreisprachig-internationalen

Präsentation der *Hartmann-Ausgabe* unverzichtbar ist. Drittens: eine revidierte Editions-methodik. Deren Konzept sollten die Herausgeber in der Auseinandersetzung mit anderen aktuellen historisch-kritischen Musiker-Gesamtausgaben evaluieren und revidieren und dabei der Rekonstruktion von Entstehungs- und Publikationsprozessen größere Aufmerk-samkeit widmen. Sonst sind neue Bände der *Hartmann-Ausgabe* teilweise schon veraltet, wenn sie erscheinen.

Michael Struck

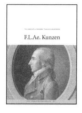

F.L.Ae. Kunzen, *Gesammelte Klavierwerke / Samlede klaverværker*
ed. Gorm Busk and Heinrich W. Schwab
Capella hafniensis editions, series K, 1
Copenhagen: The Royal Library, 2004
xviii + 101 pp.
ISNM M-706785-04-2
DKK 250

Capella Hafniensis Editions were established in 2000 with the aim of publishing music, prima-rily vocal, from the Renaissance to the present day, and from an area described (liberally) as 'the Baltic Sea area'. For early vocal music this is a very valuable process; the sources are often scattered, and almost certainly in separate part-books. There will be questions of obsolete clefs and notation which would baffle a modern singer, as there might well be for *ficta*, underlay, spelling, bar-lines, proportional tempi and many other *arcana*. All these have to be solved and transliterated by a modern editor into a full-score format.

This volume of keyboard music by Kunzen junior, the only instrumental music so far issued in this project, does not on the whole present these problems. With the exception of the occasional C-clef, the notation and layout of late eighteenth-century keyboard music sources are almost immediately accessible to a modern player; while there may be the odd quirk of calligraphy in a manuscript, or moments of careless engraving in a printed text, the music is basically as we would expect to read it today. So, if we are to reissue such music for the contemporary performer, the question becomes 'to what extent can we improve on the original in presentation without compromising musicological exactness?'.

Some series editors have decided that little improvement is possible or practical and settled for a facsimile product, such as 'The London Pianoforte School', a 20-volume facsimile series issued by Garland and edited ('overseen' is probably the better verb) by Nicholas Temperley, the same publisher's collection of C.P.E. Bach keyboard music, controlled by Darrell Berg or the Scarlatti 'Parma MS' sonatas supervised by Kenneth Gilbert. With such a policy, the music is presented 'as was', maybe with accompanying comments to alert the modern user to any changes of usage that might confuse them ('pp' meaning 'più piano' rather than 'pianissimo', for example) or practices of the time which have since altered (until well into the nineteenth century a Minuetto *da capo* was to be played *with* both its repeats, for instance, unless speci-fied to the contrary).

Overlooking the enormous problems faced by a Denkmäler-style edition which covers more than five centuries (will any single homogenised editorial policy be possible over such a range? – I rather think not), one is forced to ask what re-editing and re-engraving can offer in any individual case. The answers can be legibility, uniformity, accuracy, convenience (format, page-turns, etc.) plus the contextual and performing help given in commentary and critical apparatus (here both in German and Danish). In most of these categories the new edition scores well; elegant to look at and spacious in layout – sometimes to the detriment of page-turns (all Menuetts and Trios involve two turns).

With Kunzen's keyboard music there are no source comparisons; almost all 17 pieces included here come from single printed sources: 11 from the 1798 and 1799 *Musikalsk Nyeaars-gave* volumes ('Frauenzimmer' collections of single pieces), the effective version of the G major symphony 'für das Clavier eingerichtet' and a Scherzando from Kunzen's *Zerstreute Compositionen* published in 1789, and a slightly gauche single-movement Divertimento (the earliest composition) from Rellstab's *Melodie und Harmonie*. Only the stormy Sonata in C♯ minor (unusually in four movements) comes from a manuscript source, once part of Weyse's collection; its first Menuett was printed in the *Musikalisches Wochenblatt* for February 1792, but no textual comparisons are made here. Two pieces from the 1789 collection (a *Marsch* and an *Allegro*) are not mentioned here, nor the two dances and a march found in *Polyhymnia* (1806). Maybe as arrangements they did not qualify, but since the symphony is included, the question lingers. Most of the pieces would be effective on the early fortepiano, all of them would have been played on the clavichord (given their ubiquity in Danish households).[1]

Three facsimiles (two music pages, one title-page) give the user a chance to compare original with new – and provoke a few questions concerning 'modernisation':

Kunzen's dashes (*Strich*) have been adapted to dots (*Punkt*); the *Neue Mozart Ausgabe* (a useful model for this period) uses both signs, and Henle caught up in the 1990s. It is probably no longer necessary to make the conversion, and certainly a pity that dashes on the minims in the *Sinfonie*, bar 2, have been removed; since we find them on semibreves in the finale of the 'Jupiter' Symphony, they are probably meaningful here too.

Doubled dynamics have been eliminated (usually with no loss of information), but a deal of articulation has been added 'by analogy'; taking the first 30 bars of the Sonata and comparing them with the facsimile, we find six added slurs, and several which have been extended. The editors apparently felt that many original slurs in all sources were 'under-stated' (starting too late, ending too soon); thus in the first page of the *Sinfonie* Kunzen's [♪] is extended to [♪] in all but one case and the (admittedly ambiguous) slurring of four semiquavers in the *Sonata* is 'corrected' to cover five notes [♪] . In the *Sinfonia* first movement several dynamics have been tacitly suppressed (including quite a useful *f* in bar 23), and beaming is modernised (but not in the *Sonata*) where: [♪] , one of the 18th century's means of suggesting phrasing, becomes [♪] . These changes would matter less if we were aware of them as being editorial – the player can then decide – but the commentary is silent, and conventions such as dotted slurs or square brackets are not used. However, in the *Variations on a theme from 'Vinhøsten'*, where the expected repeat marks are mysteriously (but uniformly) missing in the source, they are sensibly suggested here, together with the necessary upbeats, all identified as editorial.

None of Kunzen's ornaments need (or get) explanation, but it might interest the player to know that in his introduction to *Weisen und Lyrische Gesänge* (1788) the composer stated that he wanted his songs sung as written, without any of the fashionable additions of trills and embellishments; possibly he expected the same for his keyboard music, and it is certainly worth a comment. The making of such an edition offers a chance not to reinforce existing (and sometimes erroneous) expectations but to lead the way and educate the performer.

Christopher Hogwood

---

1 See Christopher Hogwood, 'The Copenhagen Connection: Resources for clavichord players in 18th-century Denmark', *Fund og Forskning*, 46 (2007), 105–41.

Bibliography 2007

The bibliography is primarily based on questionnaires. It has a dual purpose: to register on the one hand the scholarly work of Danish musicologists, and on the other the publications of music researchers from abroad dealing with Danish music. It includes only titles published in the year with which the bibliography is concerned, as well as addenda to the bibliography for the preceeding year. As a rule the following types of work are not included: unprinted university theses, newspaper articles, reviews, CD booklets and encyclopaedia entries.

I. BIBLIOGRAPHICAL PUBLICATIONS

Christensen, Mogens, 'Skrevet af, om og med Orla Vinther', in Mogens Christensen (ed.), *At skabe interesse… Festskrift for Orla Vinther* (Esbjerg: VMK forlag, 2007), 241–48.

Jensen, Anne Ørbæk, 'Bibliography 2006', *Danish Yearbook of Musicology*, 34 (2006), 102–18.

Portell, Patricio, *Répertoire de musique imprimée, 1670–1780, pour la flûte à bec, le flageolet et le galoubet* (Courlay: Éditions Fuzeau classique, 2007), 228 pp.

II. YEARBOOKS, CONFERENCE REPORTS, FESTSCHRIFTEN, ANTHOLOGIES ETC.

Christensen, Mogens (ed.), *At skabe interesse… Festskrift for Orla Vinther* (Esbjerg: VMK forlag, 2007), 248 pp.

Danish Yearbook of Musicology, 34 (2006), ed. Michael Fjeldsøe and Thomas Holme Hansen (Copenhagen: Danish Musicological Society/DanMusik, 2007), 123 pp.

Dansk Kirkesangs Årsskrift, 2006, ed. Stefan Lamhauge Hansen, Michael Hemmingsen, Peter Thyssen, and Peter Weincke (København: Samfundet Dansk Kirkesang, 2006), 112 pp.

Graversen, Harry, Peter E. Nissen, and Claus Røllum-Larsen (eds.), *Efterklange af romantikken i dansk orgelmusik* (København: Det Danske Orgelselskab, 2007), 120 pp.

Meddelelser fra Musikmuseet – Musikhistorisk Museum & Carl Claudius' Samling, 10 (2005–6), ed. Lisbet Torp (København: Musikmuseet – Musikhistorisk Museum og Carl Claudius' Samling, 2007), 79 pp.

Nordisk musikkpedagogisk forskning – Årbok. Nordic Research in Music Education – Yearbook, 9 (2007), ed. Frede V. Nielsen, Sven-Erik Holgersen, and Siw Graabræk Nielsen (Oslo: Nordisk Netværk for Musikpædagogisk Forskning/Norges Musikkhøgskole, 2007), 251 pp.

Psyke & Logos, 28/1 (2007/1), *Tema: Musik og psykologi*, ed. Lars Ole Bonde (Dansk Psykologisk Forlag, 2007), 640 pp.

III. MUSICAL HISTORY
GENERAL

Glahn, Henrik, *Supplement til 'Salmemelodien i dansk tradition 1569–1973'. Registrant vedrørende melodisamlinger til 'Den Danske Salmebog 2002' samt rettelser til 'Salmemelodien i dansk tradition 1569–1973'*, ed. Inge Bønnerup (København: Anis, 2007), 31 pp.

Gravesen, Finn, *Hansen. Wilhelm Hansen Musikforlag 1857-2007* (København: Edition Wilhelm Hansen, 2007), 343 pp.

Hvidt, Eva, 'Køn og kor – mandssang og kvindestemmer i europæisk kortradition', in Henrik Palsmar (ed.), *På elverskud. Strejftog i dansk kormusik. Festskrift, DR Radiokoret 75 år* (København: DR, 2007), 86–98.

Palsmar, Henrik, 'Hønen og ægget – om forholdet mellem kormusik og professionel korsang', in Henrik Palsmar (ed.), *På elverskud. Strejftog i dansk kormusik. Festskrift, DR Radiokoret 75 år* (København: DR, 2007), 8–25.

Before *c.* 1600

Christoffersen, Peter Woetmann, 'Alexander Agricola's Vocal Style – "bizarre" and "surly", or the Flower of the Singer's Art?', in Nicole Schwindt (ed.), *Alexander Agricola. Musik zwischen Vokalität und Instrumentalismus* (Trossinger Jahrbuch für Renaissancemusik, 6 (2006); Kassel: Bärenreiter, 2007), 59–79.

Christoffersen, Peter Woetmann, 'The Music Sections of Amiens, BM 162: Copyists, Purpose, Corbie, Confréries and the Role of Antoine de Caulaincourt', paper presented at the Colloque International *In Seculum Amiens. Les manuscrits musicaux d'Amiens au Moyen Âge, November 22–24, 2007.* Online publication: http://www.staff.hum.ku.dk/woetmann/Amiens%20conf/Amiens2007Conf.html.

Kongsted, Ole, 'Herlufsholm-Samlingen. R 121–125 og danskerne i Italien omkring 1600', in John T. Lauridsen and Olaf Olsen (eds.), *Umisteligt. Festskrift til Erland Kolding Nielsen* (København: Det Kongelige Bibliotek, 2007), 101–18.

Troelsgård, Christian, 'Simple Psalmody in Byzantine Chant', in László Dobszay (ed.), *Cantus Planus. Papers Read at the 12th Meeting of the IMS Study Group, Lillafüred/Hungary 2004, August 23–28* (Budapest: Institute for Musicology of the Hungarian Academy of Sciences, 2006), 83–92.

Troelsgård, Christian, 'Stylistic Variation in the Old Sticherarion', in Grigorios Stathis (ed.), *Theory and Practice in Greek Church Music. Second International Congress of Byzantine Musicology, Athens 15–19 October 2003* (Athens: Institute for Byzantine Musicoloy, 2006), 225–32.

C. 1600 till *c.* 1910

Bergsagel, John, 'An English Composer and Danish Authors in the Year 1899', *The Delius Society Journal,* 142 (Autumn 2007), 44–54.

Brown, A. Peter, *The Symphonic Repertoire, 3/A The European Symphony from ca. 1800 to ca. 1930: Germany and the Nordic Countries, Section Two* (Bloomington: Indiana University Press, 2007), 1168 pp.

Dam-Jensen, Elsemarie, ' "Grüss Gott mit hellem Klang!" Aspekter af Tønders musikliv i 1800- og 1900-tallet', *Sønderjysk månedsskrift,* 2007/5, 163–71.

Dam-Jensen, Elsemarie, 'Kirkemusik og stadsmusik i Tønder', *Sønderjysk månedsskrift,* 2007/1, 3–11.

Dam-Jensen, Elsemarie, 'Når musikken spiller … Flere glimt af musiklivet i Tønder i det 20. århundrede', *Sønderjysk månedsskrift,* 2007/8, 283–92.

Giver, Kristian, 'Liszt, Rafael, Michelangelo og de "skjulte forbindelser" ', in Mogens Christensen (ed.), *At skabe interesse… Festskrift for Orla Vinther* (Esbjerg: VMK forlag, 2007), 73–102.

Hansen, Jørgen, 'Johan Adam Krygell. Organist og orgelkomponist', in Harry Graversen, Peter E. Nissen, and Claus Røllum-Larsen (eds.), *Efterklange af romantikken i dansk orgelmusik* (København: Det Danske Orgelselskab, 2007), 93–119.

Hansen, Jørgen Ernst, 'Melodierne til "Gud Helligånd, vor trøstermand" og "Påske vi holde" ', *Dansk Kirkesangs Årsskrift,* 2006, 91–98.

Havsteen, Sven Rune, 'Musikalsk renæssance og praxis pietatis i den lutherske tradition', *Fønix,* 31/1 (May 2007), 40–48.

Havsteen, Sven Rune, 'Quied commisisti, o dulcissime puer? En musikalsk meditation over korsbegivenheden', in Tine Reeh and Anna Vind (eds.), *Reformationer. Universitet – Kirkehistorie – Luther. Festskrift til Steffen Kjeldgaard-Pedersen 28. april 2006* (København: C.A. Reitzel, 2006), 129–40.

Holman, Peter, 'Buxtehude on CD: a tercentenary survey', *Early Music,* 35/3 (Aug. 2007), 385–96.

Jensen, Lisbeth Ahlgren, *Det kvindelige spillerum. Fem kvindelige komponister i Danmark i 1800-tallet* (København: Multivers, 2007), 250 pp.

Jullander, Sverker, 'Bibliska bilder. Om Otto Mallings orgelmusik', in Harry Graversen, Peter E. Nissen, and Claus Røllum-Larsen (eds.), *Efterklange af romantikken i dansk orgelmusik* (København: Det Danske Orgelselskab, 2007), 47–70.

Koudal, Jens Henrik, *Grev Rabens dagbog. Hverdagsliv i et adeligt miljø i 1700-tallet* (Folke-mindesamlingens kulturstudier, 10; Odense: Syddansk Universitetsforlag, 2007), 318 pp.

Krabbe, Niels, 'Panofkas stambog', *Magasin fra Det Kongelige Bibliotek*, 20/3 (Sept. 2007), 37–40.

Kuhn, Hans, 'Das Überleben barocker Kirchenlieder in Skandinavien im 20. Jahrhundert', in Walter Baumgartner (ed.), *Ostsee-Barock. Texte und Kultur* (Nordische Geschichte, 4; Münster und Berlin: Lit, 2006), 183–98.

Kuhn, Hans, 'Paul Gerhardt, ein adaptierter Klassiker des Kirchenlieds. Beobachtungen zur modernen Editionspraxis', *Lied und populäre Kultur/ Song and Popular Culture. Jahrbuch des Deutschen Volksliedarchivs*, 52 (2007), 83–95.

Kuhn, Hans, 'Paul Gerhardts Passions- und Auferstehungslieder in den Gesangbüchern. Beobachtungen aus literarischer Sicht', *Musik und Gottesdienst*, 61/3 (2007), 98–101.

Nebelong, Henrik (ed.), *Richard Wagner: Den flyvende hollænder. Tysk og dansk tekst med indledning og kommentarer* (København: Vandkunsten, 2007), 60 pp.

Nebelong, Henrik (ed.), *Richard Wagner: Lohengrin. Tysk og dansk tekst med indledning og kommentarer* (København: Vandkunsten, 2007), 91 pp.

Nebelong, Henrik (ed.), *Richard Wagner: Tristan og Isolde. Tysk og dansk tekst med indledning og kommentarer samt tekst og oversættelse af Mathilde Wesendonk: Fünf Gedichte für Frauenstimme* (København: Vandkunsten, 2007), 109 pp.

Nissen, Peter E., 'Franz Liszt and the Birth of Modern Musical Institutions. The reception of Franz Liszt in Danish musical life, 1839–1928', *Danish Yearbook of Musicology*, 34 (2006), 47–63.

Nissen, Peter E., 'Gustav Helsted ved orglet. Aspekter til forståelse af orgelmusikken i Danmark omkring år 1900', in Harry Graversen, Peter E. Nissen, and Claus Røllum-Larsen (eds.), *Efterklange af romantikken i dansk orgelmusik* (København: Det Danske Orgelselskab, 2007), 71–91.

Nissen, Peter E., 'Med sang til byens folk. KFUM's sangkor i København i begyndelsen af det 20. århundrede', *Folk og Kultur*, 2007, 101–17.

Nissen, Peter E., 'Musik, ungdomsliv og sjæles frelse. Musik og tro i Københavns KFUM omkring år 1900', *Kirkehistoriske Samlinger*, 2007, 205–55.

Parly, Nila, 'Visions of the Ring', *The Wagner Journal*, 1/3 (Nov. 2007), 57–63.

Parly, Nila, 'Wagner – mit Weib und Seele', *Grane*, 2 (Oct. 2006), 51–57.

Pedersen, Thomas Viggo, 'Melodierne til "Nåden, hun er af kongeblod" og "Fyldt af glæde over livets under"', *Dansk Kirkesangs Årsskrift*, 2006, 102–6.

Røllum-Larsen, Claus, 'En hidtil upåagtet kongelige nodesamling', in John T. Lauridsen and Olaf Olsen (eds.), *Umisteligt. Festskrift til Erland Kolding Nielsen* (København: Det Kongelige Bibliotek, 2007), 321–34.

Røllum-Larsen, Claus, 'Gottfred Matthison-Hansens orgelforedrag i Trinitatis Kirke 1882–1902: En repertoireundersøgelse', in Harry Graversen, Peter E. Nissen, and Claus Røllum-Larsen (eds.), *Efterklange af romantikken i dansk orgelmusik* (København: Det Danske Orgelselskab, 2007), 7–45.

Schneider, Matthias, 'Choralfantasie und italienische Canzona in der Orgelmusik von Dietrich Buxtehude', in Nils Grinde et al. (eds.), *La livets kilde rinne. Festskrift til Ove Kristian Sundberg på 75-årsdagen 22. juni 2007* (Oslo: Norsk Musikkforlag, 2007), 119–32.

Schwab, Heinrich W., 'Carl Maria von Webers Konzertaufenthalt in Kopenhagen (1820)', *Weber-Studien*, 8 (2007), 317–42.

Schwab, Heinrich W., 'Creatio in musica – "Creation" in Music. On the New Manner of Composing in the Years around 1800', in Sven Rune Havsteen, Nils Holger Petersen, Heinrich W. Schwab, and Eyolf Østrem (eds.), *Creations. Medieval Rituals, the Arts, and the Concept of Creation* (Ritus et Artes: Traditions and Transformations, 2; Turnhout: Brepols, 2007), 139–63.

Snyder, Kerala J., *Dietrich Buxtehude. Organist in Lübeck* (Eastman Studies in Music, 44; Rochester: University of Rochester Press, 2007), 554 pp.

Teuber, Jan, 'Dansk romantisk kormusik', in Henrik Palsmar (ed.), *På elverskud. Strejftog i dansk kormusik. Festskrift, DR Radiokoret 75 år* (København: DR, 2007), 26–35.

Vorre, Ida-Marie, 'To gange fødselsdag – to gange violin', *Fynske Minder*, 2006, 67–75.

Webber, Geoffrey, 'Modes and tones in Buxtehude's organ works', *Early Music*, 35/3 (Aug. 2007), 355–69.

Wollny, Peter, 'From Lübeck to Sweden: thoughts and observations on the Buxtehude sources in the Düben collection', *Early Music*, 35/3 (Aug. 2007), 371–83.

Yearsley, David Gaynor, 'In Buxtehude's footsteps', *Early Music*, 35/3 (Aug. 2007), 339–53.

Østrem, Eyolf, 'Finnes det en musikalsk renessanse?', *Fønix*, 31/1 (May 2007), 49–59.

AFTER *c*. 1910

Andersen, Mogens, 'På sporet af en studiekreds', in Mogens Christensen (ed.), *At skabe interesse… Festskrift for Orla Vinther* (Esbjerg: VMK forlag, 2007), 151–56.

Balslev, Povl Christian, 'Fornyelsen af den folkelige sang – Om Thorvald Aagaard og Laub', *Fønix*, 31/2 (Dec. 2007), 126–40.

Bergsagel, John, 'Henrik Glahn 29.5.1919 – 16.8.2006', *Danish Yearbook of Musicology*, 34 (2006), 65–66.

Beyer, Anders, 'Manden med den magiske musik. Interview med den amerikanske komponist George Crumb', *Dansk Musik Tidsskrift*, 82/2 (Oct.–Nov. 2007), 44–49.

Beyer, Anders, 'Vi vil bygge den bedste af alle verdener. DMT på besøg hos DR Radio-UnderholdningsOrkestret i DR Byen', *Dansk Musik Tidsskrift*, 82/1 (Aug.–Sept. 2007), 4–8.

Brøndsholm, Annie, *Kvinder med takt og toner* (Ballerup: Skytten, 2007), 227 pp.

Fabricius-Bjerre, Bent, *Tanker ved tangenterne* (Albertslund: Schultz, 2006), 256 pp.

Fjeldsøe, Michael, 'Aufstieg und Fall der Stadt Mahagonny in Copenhagen, 1933/34: An Early Debate about Performing Style', *Kurt Weill Newsletter*, 25/1 (Spring 2007), 4–8.

Frederiksen, Steen, *M.K. Čiurlionis. Maler af musik og komponist af billedkunst* (Holte and Aalborg: Gl. Holtegaard and Nordjyllands Kunstmuseum, 2007), 119 pp.

Friis, Henrik, 'Brændende kilder – interview med komponisten Hanne Ørvad', in Henrik Palsmar (ed.), *På elverskud. Strejftog i dansk kormusik. Festskrift, DR Radiokoret 75 år* (København: DR, 2007), 66–75.

Gravesen, Finn, 'Fra pirattrykker til internationalt musikforlag. Edition Wilhelm Hansen fylder 150 år', *Dansk Musik Tidsskrift*, 82/2 (Oct.–Nov. 2007), 64–69.

Gronow, Pekka and Björn Englund, 'Inventing recorded music. The recorded repertoire in Scandinavia 1899–1925', *Popular Music*, 26/2 (May 2007), 281–304.

Groth, Sanne Krogh, 'Ett ting i världen' [Intervju med tonsättaren Juliana Hodkinson], *Nutida musik*, 50/2 (2007), 36–41.

Groth, Sanne Krogh, 'Sound art as a distinct practice', *Nutida musik*, 49/4–50/1 (2006/2007), 48–52.

Groth, Sanne Krogh, 'To musikkulturer – én institution. Om det svenske elektronmusikstudie EMS' tilblivelse', *Dansk Musik Tidsskrift*, 81/6 (June 2007), 196–200.

Hannibal, Sine Tofte, 'Kan man høre lyden? Et portræt af lydkunstneren Martin Stig Andersen', *Dansk Musik Tidsskrift*, 81/5 (May 2007), 170–74.

Hannibal, Sine Tofte, 'Musik med en fjeder fra en truck, fire trækasser, en taiwanesisk stege-pande og en tom whiskyflaske, Glenfiddich – og den trekantede. Et portræt af multi-per-cussionisten Mathias Reumert', *Dansk Musik Tidsskrift*, 82/1 (Aug.–Sept. 2007), 20–24.

Hansen, Stefan Lamhauge, 'Stemthed – Synspunkter på musik og gudstjeneste hos Søren Ulrik Thomsen og Laub', *Fønix* 31/2 (Dec. 2007), 73–80.

Hillier, Paul, *John Cage and the music of always. 79 mesostics re and not re John Cage* (Copen-hagen: Theatre of Voices Edition, 2007), upag.

Holdt, Claus, *Herbert von Karajan. Karriere i en krisetid 1929–1945. En del-biografi* (Eget forlag, 2007), 99 pp.

Jensen, Eva Maria, 'Polsk musik i dag', *Musikhøst*, 2007, 16–21.

Jensen, Jørgen I., 'Fra Carl Nielsen til Per Nørgård – undervejs med Radiokoret', in Henrik Palsmar (ed.), *På elverskud. Strejftog i dansk kormusik. Festskrift, DR Radiokoret 75 år* (Køben-havn: DR, 2007), 36–55.

Jensen, Jørgen I., 'Så er det tid til de laubske melodier', *Fønix*, 31/2 (Dec. 2007), 116–25.

Krabbe, Niels, 'A Survey of the Written Reception of Carl Nielsen 1931–2006', *Notes*, 64/1 (Sept. 2007), 43–56.

Krabbe, Niels, 'Carsten E. Hatting 15.5.1930 – 30.5.2006', *Danish Yearbook of Musicology*, 34 (2006), 67–68.

Laut, Jane, 'Spørgsmål til Laub', *Fønix*, 31/2 (Dec. 2007), 81–90.

Martens, Marie, 'Kunstmaler Niels Vagn Jensens operasamling', *Meddelelser fra Musikmuseet*, 10 (2005–6), 65–72.

Mortensen, Jørgen, 'Sibelius' 7. symfoni og den ældre lytter', in Mogens Christensen (ed.), *At skabe interesse… Festskrift for Orla Vinther* (Esbjerg: VMK forlag, 2007), 39–58.

Munk, Ivar, 'Fremtidens radiokor – refleksioner over Radiokorets og Vokalensemblets udvik-ling', in Henrik Palsmar (ed.), *På elverskud. Strejftog i dansk kormusik. Festskrift, DR Radio-koret 75 år* (København: DR, 2007), 122–29.

Munk, Jørgen, 'Orla og Den danske Sang', in Mogens Christensen (ed.), *At skabe interesse… Festskrift for Orla Vinther* (Esbjerg: VMK forlag, 2007), 229–36.

Nielsen, Bendt Viinholt, 'Rued Langgaards kormusik – i Radiokorets spejl', in Henrik Palsmar (ed.), *På elverskud. Strejftog i dansk kormusik. Festskrift, DR Radiokoret 75 år* (København: DR, 2007), 56–65.

Petersen, Kirsten Flensborg, '"Danmark, i tusind år" – sangens tekst, tilblivelse og reception', in John T. Lauridsen and Olaf Olsen (eds.), *Umisteligt. Festskrift til Erland Kolding Nielsen* (København: Det Kongelige Bibliotek, 2007), 283–91.

Petersen, Petur Birgir, *Den færøske komponist Waagstein set i lyset af romantikken* (Rungsted Kyst: Wier & Petersen, 2007), 116 pp.

Poulsen, Anya Mathilde, *Feminint forstærket. Syv samtaler med kvindelige musikere* (København: DR, 2007), 191 pp.

Rasmussen, Karl Aage, *Svjatoslav Richter, pianist* (København: Gyldendal, 2007), 401 pp.

Rasmussen, Per Erland, *Acoustical canvases. The music of Poul Ruders – up to and including The handmaid's tale* (Snekkersten: Dmt publishing, 2007), 439 pp.

Stefania, Serafin, 'Computer generation and manipulation of sounds', in Nick Collins and Julio d'Escrivan (eds.), *The Cambridge Companion to Electronic Music* (Cambridge: Cam-bridge University Press, 2007), 203–17.

Sørensen, Bent, 'Kormusik og klenodier på kassettebånd', in Henrik Palsmar (ed.), *På elverskud. Strejftog i dansk kormusik. Festskrift, DR Radiokoret 75 år* (København: DR, 2007), 76–85.

Teglbjærg, Hans Peter Stubbe, 'Fanfare for en 40 årig!', *Dansk Musik Tidsskrift*, 81/6 (June 2007), 202–9.

Thomsen, Niels, 'Den store stil', *Fønix*, 31/2 (Dec. 2007), 91–103.

Thyssen, Peter, 'Alternative salmemelodier – et dansk fænomen', *Dansk Kirkesangs Årsskrift*, 2006, 87–90.

Thyssen, Peter, 'Thomas Laubs musikforståelse', *Fønix*, 31/2 (Dec. 2007), 104–15.

IV. SYSTEMATIC MUSICOLOGY

MUSICOLOGY

Fjeldsøe, Michael, 'Samfundsnyttige åndsarbejdere', *Musikvidenskaben mellem synlighed og faglig legitimitet*, Symposium arrangeret af Dansk Selskab for Musikforskning 21.4.2007 i København. Online publication, http://www.hum.au.dk/musik/dsfm/dsfm_m/Symp2007/Fjeldsoe.doc (2007), 6 pp.

Fjeldsøe, Michael, 'Will Musicology Survive?', *Danish Yearbook of Musicology*, 34 (2006), 9–11.

Graakjær, Nicolai Jørgensgaard, 'Musikvidenskabelig interesse og interesse om musikvidenskaben – eksemplificeret ved reklamemusik', *Musikvidenskaben mellem synlighed og faglig legitimitet*, Symposium arrangeret af Dansk Selskab for Musikforskning 21.4.2007 i København. Online publication, http://www.hum.au.dk/musik/dsfm/dsfm_m/Symp2007/Nicolai.doc (2007), 8 pp.

Holt, Fabian, 'Om musik', in Olav Harsløf and Søren Kjørup (eds.), *Om... Festkompendium til Niels Erik Wille: Om performance-design, sprog og visuel kultur* (Roskilde: Institut for kommunikation, virksomhed og informationsteknologier, Roskilde Universitetscenter, 2007), 144–50.

THEORY AND ANALYSIS

Bonde, Lars Ole, 'Musikalske skabelsesmyter. Udkast til en kultur- og bevidsthedshistorisk undersøgelse af sammenhængen mellem syntax og semantik i udvalgte værker fra 4 musikhistoriske perioder', in Mogens Christensen (ed.), *At skabe interesse... Festskrift for Orla Vinther* (Esbjerg: VMK forlag, 2007), 27–38.

Busk, Gorm, *Den klassiske musiks former. Kontrast og variation* (København: Nyt Nordisk Forlag Arnold Busck, 2007), 166 pp.

Harsløf, Olav, 'Om puls', in Olav Harsløf and Søren Kjørup (eds.), *Om... Festkompendium til Niels Erik Wille: Om performance-design, sprog og visuel kultur* (Roskilde: Institut for kommunikation, virksomhed og informationsteknologier, Roskilde Universitetscenter, 2007), 191–95.

Hodkinson, Juliana, *Presenting absence. Constitutive Silences in Music and Sound Art Since the 1950s*, Ph.D. thesis (København: Institut for Kunst- og Kulturvidenskab, Københavns Universitet, 2007), 214 + 12 pp.

Jensen, Jesper Højvang, Dan P.W. Ellis, Mads Græsbøll Christensen, and Søren Holdt Jensen, 'A Chroma-based Tempo-insensitive Distance Measure for Cover Song Identification', Online publication: http://vbn.aau.dk/fbspretrieve/12795160/jensen07mirex.pdf (2007), 4 pp.

Jensen, Jesper Højvang, Mads Græsbøll Christensen, and Søren Holdt Jensen, 'A Framework for Analysis of Music Similarity Measures'. Online publication: http://vbn.aau.dk/fbspretrieve/12795037/jensen07eusipco.pdf (2007), 4 pp.

Jensen, Jesper Højvang, Mads Græsbøll Christensen, Manohar Murthi, and Søren Holdt Jensen, 'Evaluation of MFCC Estimation Techniques for Music Similarity', Online publication: http://vbn.aau.dk/fbspretrieve/5757792/jensen06mfcc.pdf (2006), 5 pp.

Jensen, Kristoffer, 'Multiple Scale Music Segmentation Using Rhythm, Timbre, and Harmony', *EURASIP Journal on Advances in Signal Processing* (2007), Article ID 73205 (doi:10.1155/2007/73205), 11 pp.

Leino, Sakari, Elvira Brattico, Mari Tervaniemi, and Peter Vuust, 'Representation of harmony rules in the human brain. Further evidence from event-related potentials', *Brain Research*, 1142 (Apr. 2007), 169–77.

Mølle, Thorkil, 'Kontrapunkt – mellem kompleksitet og kaos', in Mogens Christensen (ed.), *At skabe interesse… Festskrift for Orla Vinther* (Esbjerg: VMK forlag, 2007), 103–14.

Nielsen, Per Drud, 'Ludus, expressio og indices', in Mogens Christensen (ed.), *At skabe interesse… Festskrift for Orla Vinther* (Esbjerg: VMK forlag, 2007), 115–28.

Nielsen, Steen Kaargaard, 'Wife Murder as Child's Game – analytical reflections on Eminem's performative self-dramatization', *Danish Yearbook of Musicology*, 34 (2006), 31–46.

Parly, Nila, *Absolut sang. Klang, køn og kvinderoller i Wagners værk* (København: Multivers, 2007), 368 pp.

Vuust, Peter, Andreas Roepstorff, Mikkel Wallentin, Kim Mouridsen, and Leif Østergaard, 'It don't mean a thing … Keeping the rhythm during polyrhythmic tension, activates language areas (BA47)', *Neuroimage*, 31/2 (June 2006), 832–41.

AESTHETICS AND PHILOSOPHY

Ahrendt, Peter, *Music Genre Classification Systems. A Computational Approach*, Ph.D. thesis (*IMM-PHD*-2006-164), (Kongens Lyngby: Informatics and Mathematical Modelling, Technical University of Denmark, 2006), xiv + 162 pp. Also online at: http://www2.imm.dtu.dk/pubdb/views/edoc_download.php/4438/pdf/imm4438.pdf.

Bevers, Ton, 'Cultural Education and The Canon', *Musikbladet*, 2007/1, 51–60.

Bonde, Lars Ole, 'Skabelsesmyter i musikken', in Mogens Christensen (ed.), *At skabe interesse… Festskrift for Orla Vinther* (Esbjerg: VMK forlag, 2007), 27–38.

Breinbjerg, Morten, 'Musikkens interfaces', in Søren Pold (ed.), *Interface. Digital kunst & kultur* (Århus: Aarhus Universitetsforlag, 2007), 137–69. Also online at: (Center for Digital Æstetik-forskning, Skriftserie, 11; Århus: Center for Digital Æstetik-forskning, 2006), http://imv.au.dk/~cua/center/indholdssider/nyhedsarkiv/Dokumenter/arbejdspapirer/11_Breinbjerg_net.pdf, 43 pp.

Christensen, Erik, 'Musikpsykologiens fremtid og fortid', *Psyke & Logos*, 28/1 (2007), 597–601.

Deckert, Hans Erik, *Musik & menneske. Artikler og essays* (Skanderborg: Musik og menneske, 2006), 174 pp.

Have, Iben, 'Baggrundsmusik og baggrundsfølelser – underlægningsmusik i audiovisuelle medier', *Psyke & Logos*, 28/1 (2007), 228–47.

Iversen, Marie Kølbæk, 'Lyden af smedejernssøjler på Broadway', *Dansk Musik Tidsskrift*, 81/5 (May 2007), 160–65.

Jensen, Klaus Bruhn, 'Sounding the media. An interdisciplinary review and research agenda for digital sound studies', *Nordicom review*, 27/2 (2006), 7–33.

Jensen, Kristoffer, 'Aspects of the Multiple Musical Gestures', in *Computer Music Modeling and Retrieval. Proceedings of the CMMR* (Pisa: CNR, 2006), 267–76.

Johansen, Stine Liv and Nicolai Jørgensgaard Graakjær, 'The sound of children's television – or why it makes sense to watch television facing away from the screen', *p.o.v.*, 23 (Mar. 2007), 41–65. Also online at: http://pov.imv.au.dk/Issue_23/POV_23cnt.html.

Jørgensen, Kristine, 'On transdiegetic sounds in computer games', *Northern Lights*, 5 (2007), 105–18.

Jørgensen, Kristine, *What are those grunts and growls over there? Computer game audio and player action*. Ph.D. thesis (København: Det Humanistiske Fakultet, Københavns Universitet, 2007), 204 pp.

Knakkergaard, Martin, 'Klingende tidsrum. Om vilkår for opnåelse af indsigt i forhold mellem musik og tid', *Psyke & Logos*, 28/1 (2007), 138–59.

Krabbe, Niels, 'Den danske musikkanon – generelle overvejelser og bemærkninger til udvalgte værker', in John T. Lauridsen and Olaf Olsen (eds.), *Umisteligt. Festskrift til Erland Kolding Nielsen* (København: Det Kongelige Bibliotek, 2007), 695–718.

Kühl, Carl Erik, 'Den størknede dialektik', in Mogens Christensen (ed.), *At skabe interesse… Festskrift for Orla Vinther* (Esbjerg: VMK forlag, 2007), 59–72.

Kühl, Ole, 'A Semiotic Approach to Jazz Improvisation', *Journal of Music and Meaning*, 4 (Winter 2007), section 4.1. Online publication: http://www.musicandmeaning.net/issues/ showArticle.php?artID=4.4.

Kühl, Ole, 'A Top-Down Approach to Musical Meaning'. Online publication: http:// www.hum.au.dk/semiotics/docs2/pdf/kuehl_ole/musical_meaning.pdf (2006), 4 pp.

Kühl, Ole, *Musical Semantics* (European Semiotics/Sémiotique Européenne, 7; Bern etc.: Peter Lang, 2007), 261 pp.

Kühl, Ole, 'The Semiotic Gesture'. Online publication: http://www.hum.au.dk/semiotics/ docs2/pdf/kuehl_ole/semiotic_gesture.pdf (2006), 4 pp.

Lundberg, Pia, 'Blindhedens akustiske horisonter. Om auditive kundskaber og en akustisk virkelighed', *Antropologi*, 54 (2006–7), 21–44.

Malmberg, Fredrik, 'Korsang – folkebevægelse som kunstform', in Henrik Palsmar (ed.), *På elverskud. Strejftog i dansk kormusik. Festskrift, DR Radiokoret 75 år* (København: DR, 2007), 100–7.

Meinertsen, Per, *Lydens rolle – Notater om lyd og musik til film* (København: Den danske filmskole, 2006), 184 pp.

Meng, Anders, *Temporal Feature Integration for Music Organisation*, Ph.D. thesis (*IMM-PHD-2006-165*), (Kongens Lyngby: Informatics and Mathematical Modelling, Technical University of Denmark, 2006), xii + 192 pp. Also online at: http://www2.imm.dtu.dk/pubdb/ views/edoc_download.php/4502/pdf/imm4502.pdf.

Michelsen, Morten, 'Writing Local Histories within Transnational Frameworks', *Danish Yearbook of Musicology*, 34 (2006), 13–29.

Nielbo, Frederik Laigaard, 'Site-specifik kunst i det postmoderne rum', *Dansk Musik Tidsskrift*, 81/5 (May 2007), 166–69.

Nielsen, Frede V., 'Musik og bevidsthed: Et fænomenologisk perspektiv', *Psyke & Logos*, 28/1 (2007), 61–85.

Nielsen, Klaus, 'Mimesis og musik', *Psyke & Logos*, 28/1 (2007), 160–78.

Olsen, Ole Andkjær and Bo Møhl, 'Musik og psykologi – set fra sidelinien', *Psyke & Logos*, 28/1 (2007), 5–9.

Sangild, Torben, 'Klik, tik, bip, sssss, fffff. Glitch-musik og æstetiseringen af det teknologiske lydmiljø', in Ulrik Bisgaard and Carsten Friberg (eds.), *Det æstetiskes aktualitet* (København: Multivers, 2006), 157–68.

Schmidt, Ulrik, *Minimalismens æstetik* (København: Museum Tusculanum, 2007), 322 pp.

Storm, Sanne, 'Den menneskelige stemme – psykologi og psykodynamisk stemmeterapi', *Psyke & Logos*, 28/1 (2007), 447–77.

Søndergaard, Morten, 'Lyden af et transdisciplinært felt', *Dansk Musik Tidsskrift*, 81/4 (Mar. 2007), 120–24.

Sørensen, Bent, 'Musik, medier og kultur: Musik som historisk og kulturel tekst', *Cultural studies essays in Danish*. Online publication: http://www.hum.aau.dk/~i12bent/Texts/ MusiksomKulturelTekst.doc (2006), 8 pp.

Sørensen, Helge Baun, 'At synge i kor – et musikalsk fænomen nøgternt og kreativt betragtet', in Henrik Palsmar (ed.), *På elverskud. Strejftog i dansk kormusik. Festskrift, DR Radiokoret 75 år* (København: DR, 2007), 108–21.

Sørensen, Niels Ulrik, 'Musikalske markeringer', *Ungdomsforskning*, 5/3 (Sept. 2006), 13–17.

Sørensen, Søren Møller, 'Med romantikken i bakspejlet. Tobias Nordlind-föreläsning, Växjö 7. juni 2006', *Svensk tidskrift för musikforskning*, 89 (2007), 11–29.

Sørensen, Søren Møller, 'Sound without Properties? German 19th-Century Discourses on the Parametrical Hierarchy', *Paragrana. Internationale Zeitschrift für Historische Anthropologie*, 16/2 (2007), 44–55.

Thyssen, Peter, 'Gudstjeneste, æstetik og musik', *Dansk Kirkesangs Årsskrift*, 2006, 57–66.

Vuust, Peter, 'Musikkens sprog', *Psyke & Logos*, 28/1 (2007), 186–209.

Werner, Sven Erik, *Skrålys. Musik – politik – musik. Udvalgte artikler*, ed. Niels Krabbe (København: Edition Samfundet and Det Kongelige Bibliotek, 2007), 243 pp.

Ylander, Lars Henrik, 'Æstetiske erfaringer og den moderne unge musikforbruger', in Ulrik Bisgaard and Carsten Friberg (eds.), *Det æstetiskes aktualitet* (København: Multivers, 2006), 169–81.

PEDAGOGY AND MUSIC THERAPY

Bang, Claus, 'En drøm gik i opfyldelse', in Hanne Mette Ridder (ed.), *Musikterapiuddannelsen 25 år. Festskrift* (Aalborg: Institut for Kommunikation. Aalborg Universitet, 2007), 12–16.

Beck, Bolette Daniels, 'Traume og mestring – receptiv musikterapi i ungdomspsykiatrisk ambulatorium', *Psyke & Logos*, 28/1 (2007), 499–524.

Bergstrøm-Nielsen, Carl, 'Åbne kompositioner og frit improviseret musik', *Musikbladet*, 2007/1, 32–45.

Bertelsen, Olav W., Morten Breinberg, and Søren Pold, 'Instrumentness for creativity mediation, materiality & metonymy', in *Creativity and Cognition. Proceedings of the 6th ACM SIGCHI conference on Creativity & Cognition* (Washington, D.C.: ACM, 2007), 233–42. Online publication: http://portal.acm.org/citation.cfm?id=1254992&dl=&coll=GUIDE.

Bonde, Lars Ole, 'Dansk musikterapis historie – i korte træk og årstal', in Hanne Mette Ridder (ed.), *Musikterapiuddannelsen 25 år. Festskrift* (Aalborg: Institut for Kommunikation. Aalborg Universitet, 2007), 6–11.

Bonde, Lars Ole, 'Imagery, Metaphor and Perceived Outcome in Six Cancer Survivor's BMGIM Therapy', in Anthony Meadows (ed.), *Qualitative Inquiries in Music Therapy*, 3 (Gilsum: Barcelona Publishers, 2007), 132–64.

Bonde, Lars Ole, 'Introduktion til musikpsykologi og musikterapi', *Psyke & Logos*, 28/1 (2007), 26–60.

Bonde, Lars Ole, 'Kreative Methodenintegration in der musiktherapeutischen Forschung: Reflexionen über Methodenwahl und Methodenprobleme im Forschungsprojekt "Rezeptive Musiktherapie mit Krebspatientinnen in der Rehabilitationsphase"', *Musiktherapeutische Umschau*, 28/2 (2007), 93–109.

Bonde, Lars Ole, 'Music as Co-Therapist. Investigations and reflections on the relationship between music and imagery in The Bonny Method of Guided Imagery and Music', in Isabelle Frohne-Hagemann (ed.), *Receptive Music Therapy. Theory and Practice* (Wiesbaden: Ludwig Reichert, 2007), 43–74.

Bonde, Lars Ole, 'Music as Metaphor and Analogy', *Nordic Journal of Music Therapy*, 16/1 (2007), 60–81.

Bonde, Lars Ole, 'Music, Metaphor, and Narrative in a Music Therapy Context, Meaningful Interaction in a Local Context', in Rut Wallius (ed.), *Nordic Sound. Proceedings from the 5th Nordic Music Therapy Conference*. Online publication: www.musikterapi.se (2006), 10 pp.

Bonde, Lars Ole, 'Music Therapy in Denmark', *Voices – A World Forum for Music Therapy* (Jan. 2007). Online publication: http://www.voices.no/country/monthdenmark_january2007.html.

Bonde, Lars Ole, 'Musik og psykologi = Musikpsykologi', *Psyke & Logos*, 28/1 (2007), 10–25.

Bonde, Lars Ole, 'Steps in Researching the Music in Therapy', in Tony Wigram and Thomas Wosch (eds.), *Microanalysis. Methods, Techniques and Applications for Clinicians, Researchers, Educators and Students* (London: Jessica Kingsley, 2007), 273–84.

Breinbjerg, Morten, Ole Caprani, Rasmus Lunding, and Line Kramhøft, 'An Acousmatic Composition Environment', in *New Interfaces For Musical Expression. Proceedings of the 2006 Conference on New Interfaces for Musical Expression* (Paris: IRCAM, 2006), 334–37. Online publication: http://portal.acm.org/citation.cfm?id=1142297.

Christensen, Mogens, 'Når knopperne grønnes...', in Mogens Christensen (ed.), *At skabe interesse… Festskrift for Orla Vinther* (Esbjerg: VMK forlag, 2007), 195–208.

Christensen, Mogens, *Ugler i Musen. Om viden, tænkning og refleksion på musikkonservatoriet – et forsøg på at lægge et uglæg* (PUFF, 1–07; Esbjerg: Vestjysk Musikkonservatorium, 2007). Online publication, http://www.vextra.dk/Log/USERFILES/Ugler_i_musen_samlet.pdf, 25 pp.

Darnley-Smith, Rachel and Helen M. Patey, *Musikterapi*, oversat og bearbejdet af Hanne Mette Ochsner Ridder and Lars Ole Bonde (Virum: Dansk Psykologisk Forlag, 2007), 264 pp.

Enevold, Margrete and Inge Marstal (ed.), *Børnekor. En antologi* (Herning: Dansk Sang, 2007), 109 pp.

Essendrop, Thomas, *Teknologistøttet musikundervisning* (Herning: Dansk Sang, 2007), 131 pp.

Fink-Jensen, Kirsten and Sven-Erik Holgersen, 'Evidensbegrebet – i (musik)pædagogisk forskning', *Nordisk musikkpedagogisk forskning. Årbok*, 9 (2007), 213–22.

Fink-Jensen, Kirsten, 'Attunement and Bodily Dialogues in Music Education', *Philosophy of Music Education Review*, 15/1 (Spring 2007), 53–68.

Fink-Jensen, Kirsten, 'Hvorfor vælge Ricoeur frem for Gadamer? Svar på kommentar fra Finn Thorbjørn Hansen til min artikel "Hermeneutiske perspektiver på musikalsk samhandling" i NNMpF's årbog 8, 2006', *Nordisk musikkpedagogisk forskning. Årbok*, 9 (2007), 231–34.

Fink-Jensen, Kirsten, 'Kontakt og intersubjektivitet i musikalske samhandlinger med specielle børn. Et fænomenologisk perspektiv', *Psyke & Logos*, 28/1 (2007), 288–309.

Green, Anders Christian, 'To Know it is to Love it? A Psychological Discussion of the Mere Exposure and Satiation Effects in Music Listening', *Psyke & Logos*, 28/1 (2007), 210–27.

Grocke, Denise and Tony Wigram, *Receptive Methods in Music Therapy. Techniques and Clinical Applications for Music Therapy Clinicians, Educators and Students* (London: Jessica Kingsley, 2006), 288 pp.

Hannibal, Niels Jørgen, 'Relevansen af nyere psykodynamisk teori for det klinisk musikterapeutiske arbejde med psykiatriske patienter med personlighedsforstyrrelser', *Psyke & Logos*, 28/1 (2007), 385–407.

Hansen, Finn Thorbjørn, 'Hermeneutik er ikke videnskab, men kunsten at skabe og være i et undringsfællesskab', *Nordisk musikkpedagogisk forskning. Årbok*, 9 (2007), 223–30.

Holck, Ulla, 'Ethnographic descriptive approach to video microanalysis', in Tony Wigram and Thomas Wosch (eds.), *Microanalysis. Methods, Techniques and Applications for Clinicians, Researchers, Educators and Students* (London: Jessica Kingsley, 2007), 29–40.

Holck, Ulla, 'Meaningful Interaction in a Local Context. Music Therapy with Children having Severe Functional Limitations including Autism', in Rut Wallius (ed.), *Nordic Sound. Proceedings from the 5th Nordic Music Therapy Conference*. Online publication: www.musikterapi.se (2006), 12 pp.

Holck, Ulla, 'Musikterapi i lyset af musikalske træk i tidlige dialoger', *Psyke & Logos*, 28/1 (2007), 408–26.

Holgersen, Sven-Erik, 'Den synlige og den usynlige krop' and 'Kropslighed i musikalske udtryk', in Mia Herskind (ed.), *Kropslighed og læring i daginstitutioner* (Værløse: Billesø & Baltzer, 2007), 10–24, 191–204.

Holgersen, Sven-Erik, 'Kan Daniel Sterns kernebegreber bidrage til en fænomenologisk orienteret musikpsykologi?', *Psyke & Logos*, 28/1 (2007), 86–102.

Holgersen, Sven-Erik, 'Musical intersubjectivity in music teaching and learning. In search of a theoretical framework for Micro Pedagogy', in Louie Suthers (ed.), *Touched By Musical Discovery; Disciplinary And Cultural Perspectives* (Macquarie: Institute of Early Childhood, 2006).

Holgersen, Sven-Erik, 'Musical Meaning in Childhood. A Western European Perspective', in Liora Bresler (ed.), *International Handbook of Research in Arts Education*, 16 (Dordrecht: Kluwer Academic Publishers, 2007), 895–97.

Holgersen, Sven-Erik, 'Musikpædagogiske oplevelser og eftertanker', in Mogens Christensen (ed.), *At skabe interesse... Festskrift for Orla Vinther* (Esbjerg: VMK forlag, 2007), 139–46.

Holten, Nina, 'Dansk Forbund for Musikterapi 1969 til 2007', *Dansk musikterapi*, 4/1 (2007), 3–11.

Hummelgaard, Ole, 'Musik – hvorfor musik', in Pernille Bjarnhof Storm (ed.), *Udtryk, musik og drama for pædagoger* (København: Frydenlund 2007), 83–103.

Jacobsen, Stine and Tony Wigram, 'Music Therapy for the Assessment of Parental Competencies for Children in need of Care', *Nordic Journal of Music Therapy*, 15/2 (2007), 129–43.

Kühl, Carl-Erik, *Lytning og Begreb. En pædagogisk manual i elementær auditiv analyse* (PUFF, 3–07; Esbjerg: Vestjysk Musikkonservatorium, 2007). Online publication, http://www.vextra.dk/Log/USERFILES/lytning_og_begreb_samlet.pdf, 31 pp.

Larsen, Annette Møller, 'Det udviklede sig til en sang', *Ungdomsforskning*, 5/3 (Sept. 2006), 35–38.

Lind, Tore Tvarnø, 'Urkraft naturel på cd. Om naturbegrebet og naturlyde i healingmusik', *Psyke & Logos*, 28/1 (2007), 248–70.

Lindvang, Charlotte, 'Bevidsthed, erkendelse og kreativitet – om egenterapi på Musikterapiuddannelsen, set i lyset af kybernetisk psykologi', *Psyke & Logos*, 28/1 (2007), 548–73.

Lyhne, Erik, 'Kunsten at sætte spor', in Mogens Christensen (ed.), *At skabe interesse... Festskrift for Orla Vinther* (Esbjerg: VMK forlag, 2007), 159–66.

Miller, Helen Odell, *The Practice of Music Therapy for Adults with Mental Health Problems. The Relationship between Diagnosis and Clinical Method*. Ph.D. thesis (Aalborg: Institut for Kommunikation, Aalborg Universitet, 2006), 440 pp.

Moe, Torben, 'Receptiv musikterapi med misbrugspatienter – et pilotprojekt', *Psyke & Logos*, 28/1 (2007), 478–98.

Nielsen, Frede V., 'Forskning og læreruddannelse på musikkonservatorierne set fra en musikpædagogisk vinkel', in Mogens Christensen (ed.), *At skabe interesse... Festskrift for Orla Vinther* (Esbjerg: VMK forlag, 2007), 177–93.

Nielsen, Frede V., 'Music (and arts) education from the point of view of Didaktik and Bildung', in Liora Bresler (ed.), *International Handbook of Research in Arts Education* I-II (Dordrecht: Springer, 2007), 265–85.

Oberborbeck, Ingrid and Bodil Ørum, *Det legende musikalske samvær med små børn* (Odense: Det Fynske Musikkonservatorium, 2007), 117 pp.

Pade, Steen, 'De kunstneriske uddannelser i systemteoretisk perspektiv', *Nordisk musikkpedagogisk forskning. Årbok*, 9 (2007), 37–60.

Pedersen, Inge Nygaard, '25 år i modvind og medvind, susende storme og strålende solskin', in Hanne Mette Ridder (ed.), *Musikterapiuddannelsen 25 år. Festskrift* (Aalborg: Institut for Kommunikation. Aalborg Universitet, 2007), 26–39.

Pedersen, Inge Nygaard, *Counter-Transference in Music Therapy. A Phenomenological Study on Counter-Transference used as a Clinical Concept by Music Therapists Working with Musical Improvisation in Adult Psychiatry*. Ph.D. thesis (Aalborg: Institut for Kommunikation, Aalborg Universitet, 2006), 390 pp.

Pedersen, Inge Nygaard, 'Gegenübertragung in der aktiven Musiktherapie mit Patienten der Erwachsenenpsychiatrie', *Musiktherapeutishe Umschau*, 28/2 (2007), 140–52.

Pedersen, Inge Nygaard, 'Ich fühle mich, als wäre mein Körper eingeschnürt – nur im Verlassen des Körpers ist etwas Freiheit', in Susanne Metzner (ed.), *Nachhall. Musiktherapeutische Fallstudien* (Giesen: Psychosozialverlag, 2007), 211–46.

Pedersen, Inge Nygaard, 'Musikterapeutens disciplinerede subjektivitet', *Psyke & Logos*, 28/1 (2007), 358–84.

Pedersen, Inge Nygaard, 'Pioner serien: Inge Nygaard Pedersen', *Dansk Musikterapi*, 4/2 (2007), 15–28.

Pedersen, Peder Kaj, 'Musikterapeutiske forskningsstrategier. Profane replikker fra sidelinien', in Hanne Mette Ridder (ed.), *Musikterapiuddannelsen 25 år. Festskrift* (Aalborg: Institut for Kommunikation. Aalborg Universitet, 2007), 81–83.

Pio, Frederik, 'Om det uhørte. Bidrag til musikalitets-dannelsens fænomenologi', *Nordisk musikkpedagogisk forskning. Årbok*, 9 (2007), 121–52.

Pio, Frederik, 'The heritage of the musicality discourse. A genealogy of the medical concept amusia', *Zeitschrift für Kritische Musikpädagogik* (2007), 39–53. Online publication: http://www.zfkm.org/.

Ridder, Hanne Mette Ochsner, 'En integrativ terapeutisk anvendelse af sang med udgangspunkt i neuropsykologiske, psykofysiologiske og psykodynamiske teorier', *Psyke & Logos*, 28/1 (2007), 427–46.

Ridder, Hanne Mette Ochsner, 'Microanalysis on selected video clips with focus on communicative response in music therapy', in Tony Wigram and Thomas Wosch (eds.), *Microanalysis. Methods, Techniques and Applications for Clinicians, Researchers, Educators and Students* (London: Jessica Kingsley, 2007), 54–66.

Scheiby, Benedikte B., '"Svaneægget der blev til et guldæg" frit efter H.C. Andersen', in Hanne Mette Ridder (ed.), *Musikterapiuddannelsen 25 år. Festskrift* (Aalborg: Institut for Kommunikation. Aalborg Universitet, 2007), 40–46.

Schou, Karin, 'Musikmedicin og musikterapi i medicin', *Psyke & Logos*, 28/1 (2007), 525–47.

Skou, Ole, 'Det modne band – hvad samles de om?', *Nordisk musikkpedagogisk forskning. Årbok*, 9 (2007), 243–46.

Søgaard, Fredrik, *Lyden af Viking. Et musikformidlingsprojekt på en virksomhed* (PUFF, 2–07; Esbjerg: Vestjysk Musikkonservatorium, 2007). Online publication, http://www.vextra.dk/Log/USERFILES/Lyden_af_viking_samlet.pdf, 11 pp.

Theilgaard, Alice, 'Musik og hjerneforskning', *Psyke & Logos*, 28/1 (2007), 179–85.

Ugorskij, Andreas, 'Helhedssansning i musikpædagogikken', in Pernille Bjarnhof Storm (ed.), *Udtryk, musik og drama for pædagoger* (København: Frydenlund 2007), 105–29.

Wigram, Tony, '"An Englishman in Denmark" – What have I learned from Dansk Musikterapi?' and 'Doctoral Research School in Music Therapy, Aalborg University', in Hanne Mette Ridder (ed.), *Musikterapiuddannelsen 25 år. Festskrift* (Aalborg: Institut for Kommunikation. Aalborg Universitet, 2007), 47–50 and 73–78.

Wigram, Tony and Thomas Wosch (eds.), *Microanalysis. Methods, Techniques and Applications for Clinicians, Researchers, Educators and Students* (London: Jessica Kingsley, 2007), 328 pp.

Wigram, Tony, Christian Gold, Tor Olav Heldal, and Trond Dahle, 'Music Therapy for People with Schizophrenia or other Psychoses. A Systematic Review and Meta Analysis', *British Journal of Music Therapy*, 20/2 (2006), 100–8.

Wigram, Tony, *Improvisation. Methods and Techniques for Music Therapy Clinicians, Educators and Students* (Seoul: Hakjisa, 2006), 290 pp.

Wigram, Tony, Martin Voracek and Christian Gold, 'Effectiveness of Music Therapy for Children and Adolescent with Psychopathology. A quasi-experimental design', *Psychotherapy Research*, 17/3 (2007), 292–300.

Wigram, Tony, Martin Voracek, and Christian Gold, 'Predictors of Change in Music Therapy with Children and Adolescents. The Role of Therapeutic Techniques', *Psychology and Psychotherapy. Theory research and practice*, 80 (2007), 577–89.

Wigram, Tony, 'Microanalysis in Music Therapy. Introduction and Theoretical Basis', 'Analysis of Notated Music Examples Selected from Improvisation of Psychotic Patients' (with Jos de Backer), 'Event Based Analysis of Improvisation Using the Improvisation Assessment Profiles (IAP's)' and 'Microanalysis in Music Therapy. A Comparison of Different Models and Methods and Their Application in Clinical Practice, Research and Teaching Music Therapy', in Tony Wigram and Thomas Wosch (eds.), *Microanalysis. Methods, Techniques and Applications for Clinicians, Researchers, Educators and Students* (London: Jessica Kingsley, 2007), 13–28, 120–33, 211–27 and 298–316.

Wigram, Tony, 'Music Therapy Assessment: Psychological assessment without words', *Psyke & Logos*, 28/1 (2007), 333–57.

Willert, Søren, ' "Verdens bedste universitetsstudium ..." – musikterapistudiet som universitetspædagogisk lærestykke', in Hanne Mette Ridder (ed.), *Musikterapiuddannelsen 25 år. Festskrift* (Aalborg: Institut for Kommunikation. Aalborg Universitet, 2007), 51–58.

RESEARCH ON INSTRUMENTS AND PERFORMANCE PRACTICE

Bergstrøm, Ture, 'På sporet af Peter Heises klaver', *Meddelelser fra Musikmuseet*, 10 (2005–6), 57–64.

Brock-Nannestad, George, 'The Sound Recording As a Source To Performance', in Maria Emanuela Marinelli and Anna Grazia Petaccia (eds.), *Musicus Discologus. Musiche e scritti per l'80mo anno di Carlo Marinelli* (Pisa: Edizioni ETS, 2007), 203–21.

Bryndorf, Bine, 'Salmesang og orgelklang. Orgelledsagelse af menighedssang – historisk og aktuelt', *Dansk Kirkesangs Årsskrift*, 2006, 67–86.

Carstens, Lars, 'Det nye orgel i Bjæverskov Kirke', *Orglet*, 2007/1, 23–26.

Christiansen, Toke Lund, *Fløjtespil i Danmark indtil år 1800* (København: Langkilde & Høst, 2007), 264 pp.

Hansen, Søren Gleerup, 'Carsten Lund-orglet i Brahetrolleborg Kirke', *Orglet*, 2007/2, 24–28.

Hogwood, Christopher, 'The Copenhagen Connection: Resources for clavichord players in 18th-century Denmark', *Fund og Forskning*, 46 (2007), 105–41.

Kjersgaard, Mads, 'Nyt om "Buxtehude-orglet" i Torrlösa', *Orglet*, 2007/2, 4–17.

Larsen, Peter Ettrup, *Mød dirigenten. Hvad er det egentlig, han laver?* (Rørvig: Ettrup-Art, 2007), xi + 291 pp.

Mikkelsen, Sven-Ingvart, 'Marcussen & Søn-orglet i Frederiksborg Slotskirke', *Orglet*, 2007/1, 18–22.

Møller, Per Rasmus, 'Visit the Olsen-organ of Vivild', *Orglet*, 2007/2, 29–37.

Nørfelt, Henrik Fibiger, 'Helsingør Sct. Mariæ Kirkes orgel', *Orglet*, 2007/2, 18–23.

Nørfelt, Henrik Fibiger, 'Over 40 år i dansk orgelbygning – en samtale med orgelbygger Richard Thomsen', *Orglet*, 2007/1, 4–15.

Olesen, Ole, 'Autodidakternes epoke', *Meddelelser fra Musikmuseet*, 10 (2005–6), 43–56.

Stormlund, Anton, *Kino orglet – musikkens mageløse multi-instrument* (Vejle: Anton Stormlund, 2007), 88 pp.

Westman, Bror, 'Vind, mennesker, lyd', *Antropologi*, 54 (2006–7), 11–20.

Popular music

Borre, Thomas, *Nephew: familie inc.* (København: Gaffa, 2007), 160 pp.

Christensen, Jeppe Krogsgaard, *En nat bliver det sommer. Ind i en ny dansk sangskrivning* (København: Informations Forlag, 2006), 205 pp.

Dvinge, Anne Christine, *Between history and hearsay. Imagining jazz at the turn of the 21st century*. Ph.D. thesis (København: Department for English, Germanic & Romance Studies, University of Copenhagen, 2007), xi + 252 pp.

Eigtved, Michael, 'Religious Imagery in Popular Music Theatre – the Cases of *Carousel* and *Evita*', *Nordic Theatre Studies*, 19 (2007), 111–17.

Fahnøe, Preben, 'Niels-Henning Ørsted Pedersen. An interview', *Bass world. The magazine of the International Society of Bassists*, 30/2 (2007), 11–18.

Haarder, Jon Helt, 'Praleri som underholdning ved øldrikning. Identitetsdesign i dansk rap', *Kritik*, 40/184 (2007), 48–53.

Hartvigson, Niels Henrik, 'Subjektivitet, lyrik, performance og showstoppers. Musicalnummerets logik', *Kosmorama*, 238 (Winter 2006), 155–66.

Holt, Fabian, 'Across The Atlantic. Acculturation and Hybridization in Jazz and The African Diaspora', *Jazzforschung/Jazz Research*, 38 (2006), 11–23.

Holt, Fabian, *Genre in Popular Music* (Chicago: University of Chicago Press, 2007), xiv + 221 pp.

Holt, Fabian, 'Music at American Borders. A Decentered Genre Study', *Columbia Colloquium Paper* (2007). Online publication: http://www.ruc.dk/upload/application/pdf/f51d6748/Columbia-colloquium.pdf, 9 pp.

Holt, Fabian, 'Populärmusik und Jazzmodernismus nach Elvis', in W. Knauer (ed.), *Verrat!!! … oder Chance? Der Jazz und sein gespaltenes Verhältnis zur Popularmusik* (Darmstädter Beiträge zur Jazzforschung; Hofheim: Wolke Verlag, 2006), 61–73.

Høyer, Ole Izard and Anders H.U. Nielsen, *Da den moderne jazz kom til Danmark* (Aalborg: Aalborg Universitetsforlag, 2007), 157 pp.

Jørgensen, Karsten, *Paul McCartney – mennesket, myten og musikken. En biografi* (København: Haase, 2007), 440 pp.

Kramshøj, Erik, *Kramshøjs rockhistorie* (København: DR, 2007), 191 pp.

Lindberg, Ulf, Gestur Gudmundsson, Morten Michelsen, and Hans Weisenthaunet, 'Critical Negotiations. Rock Criticism in the Nordic Countries', *Popular Music History*, 1/3 (2006), 241–62.

Larsen, Charlotte Rørdam and Ansa Lønstrup, 'Det rytmiske Norden. Fra politik til policy', *Nordisk Kulturpolitisk Tidsskrift*, 2 (2006), 134–66.

Malmberg, Kjell and Olle Lundin, *The Who in Denmark & Norway & Finland* (Uppsala, Squeeze Books, 2006), 127 pp.

Martinov, Niels, *C.V. Jørgensen. En biografi om den danske rockpoet* (København: People's Press, 2007), 254 pp.

Matthiessen, Ole, *Trommernes rejse – Historien om den rytmiske musik* (København: Husets Forlag, 2006), 556 pp.

Michaëlis, Bo Tao, '*Gotta Dance*! Busby Berkeley og den episke og integrerede fimmusical', *Kosmorama*, 238 (Winter 2006), 167–74.

Smith-Sivertsen, Henrik, *Kylling med soft ice og pølser – Populærmusikalske versioneringspraksisser i forbindelse med danske versioner af udenlandske sange i perioden 1945–2007*. Ph.D. thesis (København: Institut for Kunst- og Kulturvidenskab, Afdeling for Musikvidenskab, Det Humanistiske Fakultet, Københavns Universitet, 2007), 207 pp.

Svendsen, Emil, 'Det satans oprør. Om ondskab og oprør i heavy metal og hos Jean Baudrillard', *Kulturo*, 13/25 (2007), 58–64.

Sørensen, Dorte Hygum, *Rock. Fra rhythm'n blues til mash up* (København: Politiken, 2007), 311 pp.

Toft-Nielsen, Frank, *Otto Brandenburg – spor af en baggårdspuma* (København: Gaffa, 2006), 396 pp.

Turéll, Dan, *Charlie Parker i Istedgade. Tekster om jazz*, ed. Lars Movin (København: Bebop, 2006), 324 pp.

Tuxen, Henrik, *Gaffas kulturkanon. 12 milepæle i dansk rock* (København: Gaffa, 2007), 124 pp.

Wickström, David-Emil, 'Heute Bundes, Gestern Warschau. Gedanken über Trends der St. Petersburger Populärmusik, *Norient* (2007). Online publication: http://www.norient.com/ html/show_article.php?ID=106.

Østlund, Bo, *Etta Cameron. Hun gav smerten vinger* (København: People's Press, 2007), 351 pp.

Sociology

Adrian, Rasmus, 'Fra elfenbens- til kontroltårn – nye kompetencer til dansk musikliv', *Dansk Musik Tidsskrift*, 81/4 (Mar. 2007), 126–30.

Bærenholdt, Jørgen Ole and Michael Haldrup, 'Mobile networks and place making in cultural tourism – Staging viking ships and rock music in Roskilde', *European Urban and Regional Studies*, 13/3 (July 2006), 209–24.

Graakjær, Nicolai Jørgensgaard, 'Butiksmusik. Om købssituationens påduttede ledsagemusik', in Christian Jantzen and Tove A. Rasmussen, *Forbrugssituationer. Perspektiver på oplevelser* (Aalborg: Aalborg Universitetsforlag, 2007), 283–314.

Hanke, Peter, 'Lederskab og performance. Musik i Center for Kunst og Lederskab – af en praktikers dagbog', in Steen Nepper Larsen, Alexander Carnera, and Martin Fuglsang (eds.), *Filosofiske stemmer. Festskrift til Ole Fogh Kirkeby på 60-årsdagen d. 9. februar 2007* (Frederiksberg: Samfundslitteratur, 2007), 349–66.

Harsløf, Olav, 'Musik for misbrugere', *Antropologi*, 54 (2006–7), 87–98.

Holt, Fabian, 'Kreuzberg Activists. Musical Performance as Social Vehicle', *Popular Music and Society*, 30/4 (2007), 469–92.

Korpe, Marie (ed.), *All that is Banned is Desire. Conference on Freedom of Expression in Music, Beirut 2005* (Copenhagen: Freemuse, 2006), 54 pp. Online publication: http://www.freemuse.org/ sw13988.asp.

Korpe, Marie (ed.), *Music Will Not Be Silenced – 3rd Freemuse World Conference on Music & Censorship, Istanbul 25–26. November 2006* (*Report* 8), (Copenhagen: Freemuse, 2007), 75 pp. Online publication: http://www.freemuse.org/sw21038.asp.

Korpe, Marie, Ole Reitov, and Martin Cloonan, 'Music Censorship from Plato to the Present', in Steven Brown and Ulrik Volgsten (eds.), *Music and Manipulation. On the Social Uses and Social Control of Music* (Oxford and New York: Berghahn, 2006), 239–63.

Lesle, Lutz, 'Holger Danske auf Kussraub im Morgenland. Der dänische Kulturkanon-Export-modell für Deutschland?', *Das Orchester*, 54/7–8 (July–Aug. 2006), 26–31.

Monrad, Anders, 'Fjernt fra virkeligheden', *Dansk Musik Tidsskrift*, 82/1 (Aug.-Sept. 2007), 16–19.

Pedersen, Linda Kaul and Julie Smed Jensen, *KorVid. Korlivets aktuelle vilkår i Danmark* (Herning, Videncenter for Unge Stemmer, 2007), 212 pp.

Reitov, Ole, 'Music Censorship – The Clash within Civilisations', *Music and Identity*, Edvard Grieg 2007 September Festival, 13.–14.9.2007 in Bergen. Online publication: http://www.grieg07.com/ index.php?page=75&show=199, (2007).

Sernhede, Ove, 'Hvorfor er unge så optaget af musik?', *Ungdomsforskning*, 5/3 (Sept. 2006), 9–12.

Wang, Peter, 'Musik: Kultur eller underholdning?', in Mogens Christensen (ed.), *At skabe interesse ... Festskrift for Orla Vinther* (Esbjerg: VMK forlag, 2007), 167–76.

ETHNOMUSICOLOGY

Andersen, Mette Lund, 'Rockmusik og lovsang. To vestjyske musikfestivaler med kulturhistoriske rødder', *Folk og kultur*, 2006, 43–60.

Horvei, Reidun, 'Kvar er folkesongen i Danmark?', *Årbok for norsk folkemusikk*, 15 (2006), 17–28.

Kirkegaard, Annemette, 'African Islamic Pop – What kind of musical identity?', *Music and Identity*, Edvard Grieg 2007 September Festival, 13.–14.9.2007 in Bergen. Online publication: http://www.grieg07.com/index.php?news=741&history=search, (2007).

Kirkegaard, Annemette, 'East African Taarab as a Mediator of the Diversity and Vitality of a Musical Tradition within Islamic Culture', *Conference Proceedings Music in the World of Islam, Assilah, Morocco 8–13 august 2007*. Online publication: http://www.mcm.asso.fr/site02/music-w-islam/articles/Kirkegaard-2007.pdf (2007), 9 pp.

Kjærholm, Lars, 'Gekkoens lyd, mantraer og klassisk musik i Indien', *Antropologi*, 54 (2006–7), 99–115.

Koudal, Jens Henrik, 'Nationalsange – kongehymner, revolutionsmarcher eller folkesange?', in Palle Ove Christiansen and Jens Henrik Koudal (eds.), *Det ombejlede folk. Nation, følelse og social bevægelse* (København: C.A. Reitzel, 2007), 97–125.

Lind, Tore Tvarnø, 'Meaning, Power and Exotism in Medicinal Music. A Case Study of Musicure in Denmark', *Ethnomusicology Forum*, 16/2 (2007), 209–42.

Reitov, Ole, 'Sufimusik – føde for sjælen', *Carsten Niebuhr Biblioteket*, 13 (2007), 20–28.

DANCE RESEARCH

Lybech, Arne, *Tak for dansen. Et faktuelt, litterært og personligt tilbageblik på Aalborgs nu lukkede danserestauranter* (Aalborg: Lindtofte, 2006), 55 pp.

Urup, Henning, *Dans i Danmark. Danseformer ca. 1600-1950* (København: Museum Tusculanum, 2007), 417 pp.

PHILOLOGY

Foltmann, Niels Bo and Lisbeth Ahlgren Jensen, 'Det Kongelige Bibliotek som udgiver af den musikalske kulturarv – belyst ved udgivelsen af Carl Nielsens musik', in John T. Lauridsen and Olaf Olsen (eds.), *Umisteligt. Festskrift til Erland Kolding Nielsen* (København: Det Kongelige Bibliotek, 2007), 571–88.

Krolick, Bettye, *Ny international regelbog i braille musiknotation* (København: Dansk Blindesamfund, 2006), xiv + 301 pp.

ICONOGRAPHY

Hellers, Bo G., 'Musik vid Karl V:s festliga intåg med Christian II i Bryssel 1521. Nytolkning av en flamländsk tapet', *Dokumenterat*, 38 (Apr. 2007), 31–41.

Müller, Mette, 'Kattemusik', *Meddelelser fra Musikmuseet*, 10 (2005–6), 32–42.

V. CRITICAL EDITIONS

Clausen, Marianne (ed.), *Andlig Vísuløg í Føroyum upptikin 1902–2002/Spiritual Songs in the Faroes. Melodies Recorded 1902–2002* (Hoyvik: Stiðin, 2006), 542 pp.

Fanger, Eva-Brit (ed.), *Heinrich Panofka. Ein musikalisches Stammbuch (Königliche Bibliothek Kopenhagen)* (Tutzing: Schneider, 2007), 2 vols., 103 + 168 pp.

Fellow, John (ed., introduction and notes), *Carl Nielsen Brevudgaven, vol. 3: 1906–1910* (København: Multivers, 2007), 589 pp. Online indexes: http://www.multivers.dk/carl.

Gade, Niels W., *Symphony No. 5 Op. 25/Symphonie Nr. 5 Op. 25*, ed. Niels Bo Foltmann (Niels W. Gade Works/Werke, I/5; København: Foundation for the Publication of the Works of Niels W. Gade/Stiftung zur Herausgabe der Werke Niels W. Gades, 2007), xxviii + 215 pp.

Nielsen, Carl, *Incidental Music 1/Skuespilmusik 1*, ed. Niels Bo Foltmann, Lisbeth Ahlgren Jensen and Kirsten Flensborg Petersen (Carl Nielsen Værker I/6; Copenhagen: The Carl Nielsen Edition, The Royal Library/Edition Wilhelm Hansen, 2007), lxxiv + 337 pp.

Nielsen, Carl, *Incidental Music II/Skuespilmusik 2*, ed. Elly Bruunshuus Petersen and Kirsten Flensborg Petersen (Carl Nielsen Værker I/9; Copenhagen: The Carl Nielsen Edition, The Royal Library/Edition Wilhelm Hansen, 2007), lxxviii + 343 pp.

Nielsen, Carl, *Music for Holger Drachmann's Sir Oluf he rides –. A Danish Summer-Night's Drama in four Acts and a Prelude/Musik til Holger Drachmann's Hr. Oluf han rider – . Den danske sommernats drama i fire akter og et forspil*, ed. Peter Hauge (Carl Nielsen Værker I/7; Copenhagen: The Carl Nielsen Edition, The Royal Library/Edition Wilhelm Hansen, 2007), xxxiii + 255 pp.

Schulz, Johann Abraham Peter, *Lieder im Volkston*, ed. Walther Dürr und Stefanie Steiner unter Mitarbeit von Michael Kohlhäufl (*Das Erbe Deutscher Musik*, 105 (*Frühromantik*, 4); München: Henle Verlag, 2006), xxxvi + 224 pp.

Weyse, C.E.F., *Sange med klaver 1–2*, ed. Sten Høgel (København: Edition Samfundet, 2007), 153 + 135 pp.

Publications received

PERIODICALS, YEARBOOKS ETC.

Meddelelser fra Dansk Dansehistorisk arkiv, 25 (2006), ed. Henning Urup, 36 pp., illus., ISSN 0107-685x.

Meddelelser fra Dansk Dansehistorisk arkiv, 26 (2007), ed. Henning Urup, 47 pp., illus., ISSN 0107-685x.

Meddelelser fra Musikmuseet – Musikhistorisk Museum & Carl Claudius' Samling, 10 (2005–6), ed. Lisbet Torp, 79 pp., illus., ISSN 0900-2111.

Mitteilungen der Paul Sacher Stiftung, 20 (Mar. 2007), 60 pp., illus., ISSN 1015-0536.

Hans-Hinrich Thedens (ed.): *Musikk og dans som virkelighet og forestilling* (Norsk Folke-musikklag. Skrift nr. 20) (2006), 156 pp., illus., music exx., ISSN 0800-3734.

Psyke & Logos, 28/1 (2007), *Tema: Musik og psykologi*, ed. Lars Ole Bonde (Dansk Psykologisk Forlag, 2007), 640 pp., illus., ISSN 0107-1211, ISBN 978-87-7706-457-9.

Svensk tidskrift för musikforskning. Swedish Journal of Musicology, 89 (2007), ed. Anders Carlsson (Göteborg: Svenska samfundet för musikforskning, 2006), 176 pp., illus., music exx., ISSN 0081-9816.

BOOKS

39th Baltic Musicology Conference. The 20th Century and the Phenomenon of Personality in Music. 9–11 October, 2006, Riga. Selected Papers, ed. Laila Ozaliņa and Imants Mežaraups (Riga: Latvijas Komponistu savienība and Musica Baltica, 2007), 180 pp., illus., music exx., ISBN 978-9984-588-38-4.

Ahrend, Peter, *Music Genre Classification Systems – A Computational Approach*, Ph.D. thesis (Lyngby: Informatics and Mathematical Modelling, Technical University of Denmark, 2006), 162 pp., internet publication: http://www2.imm.dtu.dk/pubdb/views/edoc_download.php/4438/pdf/imm4438.pdf.

Busk, Gorm, *Den klassiske musiks former. Kontrast og variation* (København: Nyt Nordisk Forlag Arnold Busck, 2007), 166 pp., illus., music exx., ISBN 978-87-17-03946-9.

Christiansen, Palle Ove and Jens Henrik Koudal (eds.), *Det ombejlede folk. Nation, følelse og social bevægelse* (Folkemindesamlingens kulturstudier, 12; Copenhagen: C.A. Reitzel, 2007), 166 pp., illus., isbn 978-87-7876-509-3/87-7876-509-9.

Cook, Nicolas, *The Schenker Project. Culture, Race, and Music Theory in Fin-de-siècle Vienna* (Oxford: Oxford University Press, 2007), 355 pp., illus., ISBN 978-0-19-517056-6.

Fellow, John (ed.), *Carl Nielsen Brevudgaven*, vol. 3: *1906–1910* (Copenhagen: Multivers, 2007), 589 pp., illus., ISBN 978-87-7919-225-8.

Gjerdingen, Robert O., *Music in the Galant Style* (New York: Oxford University Press, 2007), 514 pp., illus., music exx., ISBN 978-0-19-531371-0.

Glahn, Henrik, *Supplement til Salmemelodien i dansk tradition 1569–1973. Registrant vedrørende melodisamlinger til 'Den danske Salmebog 2002' samt rettelser til 'Salmebogen i dansk tradition 1569–1973'*, ed. Inge Bønnerup (København: Forlaget Anis, 2007), 31 pp., ISBN 978-87-7457-466-0.

Graversen, Harry R., Peter E. Nissen, and Claus Røllum-Larsen, *Efterklange af romantikken i dansk orgelmusik. Tre komponister og en repertoireundersøgelse* (Det Danske Orgelselskabs Skriftserie, 1; Jelling: Det Danske Orgelselskab, 2007), 120 pp., illus., music exx., ISBN 978-87-88238-10-5.

Holt, Fabian, *Genre in Popular Music* (Chicago and London: Chicago University Press, 2007), 221 pp., illus., music exx., isbn 0-226-35037-1/978-0-226-35037-0 (cloth), 0-226-35039-8/978-0-226-35039-4 (paper).

Jensen, Lisbeth Ahlgren, *Det kvindelige spillerum – fem kvindelige komponister i Danmark i 1800-tallet* (København: Multivers, 2007), 250 pp., ISBN 978-87-7919-192-3.

Knust, Martin, *Sprachvertonung und Gestik in den Werken Richard Wagners. Einflüsse zeitgenössischer Rezitations- und Deklamationspraxis* (Greifswalder Beiträge zur Musikwissenschaft, 16; Berlin: Frank & Timme, 2007), 524 pp., illus., music exx., ISBN 978-3-86596-114-3.

Koudal, Jens Henrik, *Grev Rabens dagbog. Hverdagsliv i et adeligt miljø i 1700-tallet* (Folkemindesamlingens kulturstudier, 10; University of Southern Denmark Studies in History and Social Sciences, 330; Odense: Syddansk Universitetsforlag, 2007), 318 pp., illus., ISBN-10: 87-7674-173-7, ISBN-13: 978-87-7674-173-0.

Kühl, Ole, *Musical Semantics* (European Semiotics: Language, Cognition, and Culture, 7; Bern etc: Peter Lang, 2007), 261 pp., illus., music exx., ISSN 1423-5587, ISBN 978-3-03911-282-1.

Meng, Anders, *Temporal Feature Integration for Music Organisation*, Ph.D. thesis (Lyngby: Informatics and Mathematical Modelling, Technical University of Denmark, 2006), 192 pp., internet publication: http://www2.imm.dtu.dk/pubdb/views/edoc_download.php/4502/pdf/imm4502.pdf.

Nyqvist, Niklas, *Från bondson till folkmusikikon. Otto Andersson och formandet av 'finlandssvensk folkmusik'* (Åbo: Åbo Akademi University Press, 2007), 310 pp., illus., music exx., ISBN 978-951-765-374-9, ISBN 978-951-765-375-6 (digital).

Rosengren, Henrik, *'Judarnas Wagner'. Moses Pergament och den kulturella identifikationens dilemma omkring 1920–1950* (Lund: Sekel, 2007), 382 pp., illus., ISBN 978-91-85767-01-4.

Stigar, Petter: *Lær å lytte* (Bergen: Fakbokforlaget, 2007), 344 pp., music exx., incl. 1 CD, ISBN 978-82-450-0329-1.

Urup, Henning, *Dans i Danmark. Danseformerne ca. 1600 til 1950* (Copenhagen: Museum Tusculanum, 2007), 417 pp., illus., ISBN 978-87-635-0580-2.

MUSIC EDITIONS

Bertholusius, Vincentius, *Sacrarum cantionum (1601)*, ed. Ole Kongsted (Capella hafniensis editions, series A, 6; Copenhagen: The Royal Library, 2005), xxx + 90 pp., ISNM M-706785-05-9.

del Mel, Rinaldo, *Liber primus motettorum (1581)*, ed. Ole Kongsted (Capella hafniensis editions, series B, 1; Copenhagen: The Royal Library, 2005), xxiii + 96 pp., ISNM M-706785-03-5.

Kunzen, F.L.Ae., *Gesammelte Klavierwerke/Samlede klaverværker*, ed. Gorm Busk and Heinrich W. Schwab (Capella hafniensis editions, series K, 1; Copenhagen: The Royal Library, 2004), xviii + 101 pp., ISNM M-706785-04-2.

Stockmann, Bartholomaeus, *Lejlighedsværker/Gelegenheitswerke/Occational Works*, ed. Ole Kongsted (Capella hafniensis editions, series A, 3; Copenhagen: The Royal Library, 2004), xxvii + 62 pp., ISNM M-706785-02-8.

Tollius, Jan, *Opera omnia I. Liber primus motectorum quinque vocum (1591)*, ed. Ole Kongsted (Capella hafniensis editions, series A, 4; Copenhagen: The Royal Library, 2005), xxxi + 102 pp., ISNM M-706785-07-3.

Tollius, Jan, *Opera omnia II. Motectorum quinque vocum liber secundus (1591)*, ed. Ole Kongsted (Capella hafniensis editions, series A, 5; Copenhagen: The Royal Library, 2005), xxiii + 112 pp., ISNM M-706785-08-0.

Tollius, Jan, *Opera omnia III. Moduli trium vocum (1597)*, ed. Ole Kongsted (Capella hafniensis editions, series A, 7; Copenhagen: The Royal Library, 2005), xxiii + 44 pp., ISNM M-706785-09-7.

COMPACT DISCS
MC Tia, *Super Fresh Remix Mixtape.*

WEBSITES
www.10klassikere.systime.dk, ed. Jørgen Mortensen, VMK – Konservatoriet for musik og formidling, systime.dk 2007 (betalingssite, undervisningsmateriale vedr. 10 værker).

Contributors to this issue

ANDREA F. BOHLMAN, Ph.D. fellow, MMus, Music Department, Music Building, North Yard, Harward University, Cambridge, MA-02138, USA, abohlman@fas.harvard.edu

PHILIP V. BOHLMAN, FBA, Mary Werkman Distinguished Service Professor of the Humanities and of Music, Ph.D., Music Department, University of Chicago, 1010 E. 50th Street, Chicago, IL-60637, USA, boh6@uchicago.edu

BENGT EDLUND, professor, Institutionen för konst- och musikvetenskap, Lund University, box 117, SE-22100 Lund, bengt.edlund@musvet.lu.se

FRANCO FABBRI, Chair, IASPM – Italian branch, University of Turin, Dipartimento di discipline delle arti, musica e spettacolo, Via Sant'Ottavio, 20, Turin, Italy, franco.fabbri@unito.it

MICHAEL FJELDSØE, associate professor, Ph.D., Section of Musicology, Department of Arts and Cultural Studies, University of Copenhagen, Klerkegade 2, DK-1308 Copenhagen K, fjeldsoe@hum.ku.dk

NIELS BO FOLTMANN, senior researcher, mag.art., The Carl Nielsen Edition, The Royal Library, Postbox 2149, DK-1016 Copenhagen K, nbf@kb.dk

MIKAEL GARNÆS, organist, cand.mag., Gothersgade 107, 1.tv., DK-1123 Copenhagen K, mikael.garnaes@get2net.dk

AXEL TEICH GEERTINGER, Ph.D. fellow, Section of Musicology, Department of Arts and Cultural Studies, University of Copenhagen, Klerkegade 2, DK-1308 Copenhagen K, atg@hum.ku.dk

SANNE KROGH GROTH, Ph.D. fellow, Section of Musicology, Department of Arts and Cultural Studies, University of Copenhagen, Klerkegade 2, DK-1308 Copenhagen K, groth@hum.ku.dk

NICOLAI JØRGENSGAARD GRAAKJÆR, lecturer, Section Psychology, Department of Communication and Psychology, Aalborg University, Kroghstræde 3, DK-9220 Aalborg Ø, nicolaig@hum.aau.dk

FINN EGELAND HANSEN, professor emeritus, dr.phil., Klokkervej 14, DK-8210 Aarhus V, feh@hum.aau.dk

THOMAS HOLME HANSEN, associate professor, Ph.D., Department of Musicology, Institute of Aesthetic Studies, University of Aarhus, Langelandsgade 139, DK-8000 Aarhus C, musthh@hum.au.dk

IBEN HAVE, assistant professor, Ph.D., Institute of Information and Media Studies, University of Aarhus, IT Park, Helsingforsgade 14, DK-8200 Aarhus N, musih@hum.au.dk

CHRISTOPHER HOGWOOD, CBE: Honorary Professor of Music, Cambridge University, 10 Brookside, Cambridge CB2 1JE, U.K., chogwood@compuserve.com

ANNE ØRBÆK JENSEN, research librarian, cand.mag., Department of Music and Theatre, The Royal Library, Postbox 2149, DK-1016 Copenhagen K, aoj@kb.dk

LISBETH AHLGREN JENSEN, senior researcher, mag.art., The Carl Nielsen Edition, The Royal Library, Postbox 2149, DK-1016 Copenhagen K, laj@kb.dk

MADS KROGH, postdoc. fellow, Ph.D., Department of Musicology, Institute of Aesthetic Studies, University of Aarhus, Langelandsgade 139, DK-8000 Aarhus C, musmk@hum.au.dk

CHARLOTTE RØRDAM LARSEN, associate professor, Department of Musicology, Institute of Aesthetic Studies, University of Aarhus, Langelandsgade 139, DK-8000 Aarhus C, muscrl@hum.au.dk

KATHARINE LEISKA, Ph.D. fellow, fil mag, Musikwissenschaftliches Institut der Christian-Albrechts-Universität zu Kiel, Wilhelm-Seelig-Platz 1, D-24118 Kiel, katharine@leiska.de

TORE TVARNØ LIND, assistant professor, Ph.D., Section of Musicology, Department of Arts and Cultural Studies, University of Copenhagen, Klerkegade 2, DK-1308 Copenhagen K, ttlind@hum.ku.dk

ANSA LØNSTRUP, associate professor, Department of Aesthetics and Culture – Interdisciplinary Aesthetic Studies, Institute of Aesthetic Studies, University of Aarhus, Langelandsgade 139, DK-8000 Aarhus C, aekal@hum.au.dk

RENÉ MICHAELSEN, wissenschaftlicher Assistent, MA, Department of Musicology, University of Cologne, Albertus Magnus Platz, D-50923 Cologne, rene.michaelsen@uni-koeln.de

BJARKE MOE, Ph.D. fellow, Section of Musicology, Department of Arts and Cultural Studies, University of Copenhagen, Klerkegade 2, DK-1308 Copenhagen K, bjarkemo@hum.ku.dk

STEEN KAARGAARD NIELSEN, associate professor, Ph.D., Department of Musicology, Institute of Aesthetic Studies, University of Aarhus, Langelandsgade 139, DK-8000 Aarhus C, musskn@hum.au.dk

SVEND HVIDTFELT NIELSEN, lecturer, cand.mag., Section of Musicology, Department of Arts and Cultural Studies, University of Copenhagen, Klerkegade 2, DK-1308 Copenhagen K, svendhvidtfelt@get2net.dk

PETER E. NISSEN, research librarian, mag.art., University Library of Southern Denmark, Islandsgade 2, DK-5000 Odense C, peternissen@bib.sdu.dk

HENRIK PALSMAR, organist, cand.phil., Strindbergsvej 73, DK-2500 Valby, hpalsmar@tiscali.dk

MICHAEL STRUCK, Dr., wissenschaftlicher Mitarbeiter und Mitglied der Editionsleitung, Johannes Brahms Gesamtausgabe, Forschungsstelle, Musikwissenschaftliches Institut der Universität Kiel, Olshausenstr. 40, D-24098 Kiel, brahmsausgabe@email.uni-kiel.de

DAVID-EMIL WICKSTRÖM, Ph.D. fellow, cand.phil., Section of Musicology, Department of Arts and Cultural Studies, University of Copenhagen, Klerkegade 2, DK-1308 Copenhagen K, davidw@hum.ku.dk

Guidelines for authors

Danish Yearbook of Musicology is a peer-reviewed journal published by the Danish Musicological Society featuring contributions related to Danish music and musical research in the widest sense. The yearbook accepts articles in English, German, and Danish. All articles will be subjected to peer reviewing by the Editorial Board, the composition of which is 'dynamic' and may vary from year to year depending on the number and character of articles submitted. The submission of an article is taken to imply that it has not previously been published and has not been submitted for publication elsewhere. Proposals for articles, reviews and reports are welcomed, and submissions should be sent by e-mail to the editors, preferably in the form of an attached MS Word document, as well as a printout sent to the editorial office (see the colophon). All contributors are asked to state their name, academic position and degree, address and e-mail.

Articles consisting of more than 45,000 keystrokes including notes and spaces are not normally accepted. Musical examples and illustrations are to be provided by the author. Extensive musical examples and illustrations may only be included by prior agreement. Contributors are responsible for obtaining permission to reproduce any material in which they do not own copyright for use in print and electronic media, and for ensuring that the appropriate acknowledgements are included in their manuscripts. The full texts of articles published in *Danish Yearbook of Musicology* will be made available in electronic form.

In principle notes and references follow British practice as indicated in the *Oxford Style Manual*, with use of the Author–title system in the event of repeated citations. In texts written in English, British quotation practice is to be used. Contributors from North America, though, may use North American spellings. In texts written in Danish the latest edition of *Retskrivningsordbogen* is to be used. The most recent issue of the Yearbook should be consulted for style, bibliographical citation practice, and general approach.

The deadline for proposals or contributions for Vol. 36 (2008) is 1 October 2008.

Danish Musicological Society

Danish Musicological Society was founded 1954. The society aims at addressing issues of musicological interest, that is, results that may be based on scholarly research as well as the conditions of musicological research. It holds meetings, arranges symposiums and conferences, as well as being a publisher of books, music, and the *Danish Yearbook of Musicology*. The society is member of the International Musicological Society.

Membership including a subscription to *Danish Yearbook of Musicology* can be obtained by anyone interested in supporting the aims of the Society. The fee is DKK 250 for individual members, DKK 100 for students and DKK 300 for couples. Application for membership and letters to the society should be mailed to Thomas Holme Hansen, musthh@hum.au.dk or Morten Michelsen, momich@hum.ku.dk, or sent to Danish Musicological Society, c/o Section of Musicology, University of Copenhagen, Klerkegade 2, DK–1308 Copenhagen K. Further information is available at www.musikforskning.dk.

PUBLICATIONS OF DANISH MUSICOLOGICAL SOCIETY

Dansk Årbog for Musikforskning, 1–30 (1961–2002).
Danish Yearbook of Musicology, 31– (2003 ff.).
Dania Sonans. Kilder til Musikkens Historie i Danmark:
 I *Værker af Mogens Pederson*, ed. Knud Jeppesen (København, 1933).
 II *Madrigaler fra Christian IV's tid* [Nielsen, Aagesen, Brachrogge], ed. Jens Peter Jacobsen (Egtved: Musikhøjskolens Forlag, 1966).
 III *Madrigaler fra Christian IV's tid* [Pederson, Borchgrevinck, Gistou], ed. Jens Peter Jacobsen (Egtved: Musikhøjskolens Forlag, 1967).
 IV *Musik fra Christian III's tid. Udvalgte satser fra det danske hofkapels stemmebøger (1541)*, part 1, ed. Henrik Glahn (Egtved: Edition Egtved, 1978).
 V *Musik fra Christian III's tid. Udvalgte satser fra det danske hofkapels stemmebøger (1541)*, part 2 and 3, ed. Henrik Glahn (Egtved: Edition Egtved, 1986).
 VI J.E. Hartmann, *Fiskerne*, ed. Johannes Mulvad (Egtved: Edition Egtved, 1993).
 VII J.E. Hartmann, *Balders Død*, ed. Johannes Mulvad (Egtved: Edition Egtved, 1980).
 VIII C.E.F. Weyse, *Samlede Værker for Klaver 1–3*, ed. Gorm Busk (København: Engstrøm & Sødring, 1997).
 IX C.E.F. Weyse, *Symfonier.* Vol. 1: *Symfoni nr. 1 & 2*; Vol. 2: *Symfoni nr. 3 & 4*; Vol. 3: *Symfoni nr. 5 (1796 & 1838)*; Vol. 4: *Symfoni nr. 6 & 7*, ed. Carsten E. Hatting (København: Engstrøm & Sødring, 1998, 2000, 2002, 2003).
Report of the Eleventh Congress, Copenhagen 1972, ed. Henrik Glahn, Søren Sørensen and Peter Ryom – in cooperation with International Musicological Society (Copenhagen: Edition Wilhelm Hansen, 1974).
20 Italienske Madrigaler fra Melchior Borckgrevinck »Giardino Novo I–II«, København 1605/06, ed. Henrik Glahn et al. (Egtved: Edition Egtved, 1983).
Die Sinfonie KV 16a »del Sgr. Mozart«. Bericht über das Symposium in Odense anlässlich der Erstaufführung des wiedergefundenen Werkes Dezember 1984, ed. Jens Peter Larsen and Kamma Wedin (Odense: Odense Universitetsforlag, 1987).
Heinrich Schütz und die Musik in Dänemark zur Zeit Christians IV. Bericht über die wissenschaftliche Konferenz in Kopenhagen 10.-14. November 1985, ed. Anne Ørbæk Jensen and Ole Kongsted (København: Engstrøm & Sødring, 1989).
13th Nordic Musicological Congress – Aarhus 2000, Papers and Abstracts, ed. Thomas Holme Hansen (Studies & Publications from the Department of Musicology, University of Aarhus, 7; Århus: Aarhus University, 2002).